D0844649

# The Great Wheel:
# the world monetary system

# The Great Wheel: the world monetary system A REINTERPRETATION

## Sidney E. Rolfe
## James Burtle

**McGraw-Hill Book Company**

New York • St. Louis • San Francisco • Düsseldorf • Mexico • Montreal
Panama • Paris • São Paulo • Tokyo • Toronto

Library
I.U.P.
Indiana, Pa.
332.45 R644g
C.1

Copyright © 1973 by Quadrangle/The New York Times Book Co.
All rights reserved, including the right to reproduce this book or
portions thereof in any form. For information, address Quadran-
gle/The New York Times Book Co., 10 East 53 Street, New York,
N.Y., 10022. Manufactured in the United States of America. Published simultaneously in Canada by Fitzhenry & Whiteside, Ltd.,
Toronto.

Library of Congress Catalog Card Number: 73-79929


Design by Jared Pratt
Production by Planned Production


0-07-053562-0


Reprinted by arrangement with Quadrangle/The New York Times
Book Company
First McGraw-Hill Paperback Edition, 1975.


1 2 3 4 5 6 7 8 9 MU MU 7 9 8 7 6 5

# Contents

# List of Charts

# List of tables

# Introduction to the Paperback Edition

n this paperback edition a few ideas should be added on two subjects: inflation and oil. The authors have been criticized for inadequate attention to inflation, while the monetary consequences of the oil shortage became important after October 1973, when the original edition of this book was at the printer.

With respect to inflation, we have argued that its control is largely a domestic economic problem. Governments, and governments alone, determine the rate of increase and consequently the total of the money supply, with some leads and lags. Goods increase "naturally" at the rate of about 3½% to 4% per year in the United States, reflecting productivity gains. But the money supply—including both money and credit, which are tantamount to the aggregate demand for goods and services—can be increased (or decreased) at any rate governments choose. If the money supply increases at about the same 4%, prices would be stable; if more, the result is inevitably inflation; if less (as in the Depression) deflation, falling prices and unemployment. To be sure, inflation can be and was transmitted internationally through the fixed exchange rate system, a point to which this introductory note will return.

A few numbers will illustrate the relation between the money supply and inflation, and its international transmission. The problem originated in the

United States from 1964 on, the period we have termed Disintegration (Chapter 8). In this period the combined cost of the Vietnam War and the Great Society programs were not offset by appropriately increased tax revenues. Deficit spending made up the difference between federal revenues and expenditures, and the Federal Reserve System increased the money supply to provide banks and other lenders the funds necessary to buy government bonds and other IOUs. From 1965 to 1974, the U.S. federal budget deficit totalled over $102 billion. As a consequence of these deficits and validation through increased money supply, in the five-year Johnson era, through 1968, the money supply increased no less than 47%, from $259 billion to $382 billion. In the same period the supply of goods increased just about 22%, i.e., the 4% productivity increase compounded over five years. The discrepancy is obvious and the result was inflation. Nor did the Nixon Administration do any better. In the five years from 1969 through 1973 the money supply increased 49%, from $382 billion to $571 billion, more than double the same 22% gain in the output of goods. Taking the Vietnam decade as a whole, from 1964 through 1973 the U.S. money supply more than doubled, increasing 120%, while productivity increased the supply of goods at best only by some 50%.

Step two in the Great Inflation was the transmission of the American inflation to the rest of the developed world through the international monetary system because of firm adherence to the fixed exchange rate system prior to 1973.

Dollars cascaded out of the United States, first, as a result of the negative trade balance and, second, because of speculative withdrawals against an imminent devaluation, procedures detailed in Chapter 9. The foreign recipients in the surplus countries sold their dollars to their central banks in exchange for local currency. The central banks received the dollars as residual holders, and gave back to their own domestic banks an equivalent value, either in their own currency or in credit. And this increased the money supply in the various countries, reflecting the inflow of dollars. For the decade 1964 to 1973 the money supply of the ten leading industrial nations more than doubled. Output in this decade again increased by only about 50%. The gap between increased aggregate demand and supply had to be closed by inflation, that is, by rising prices, and the cost of living rose by over 50% in the ten countries in the decade.

Had floating exchange rates been in effect in this period the inflation would not have been transmitted from the United States. To be sure, the dollar would have fallen in value because of the American inflation, and the inability of Americans to sell goods abroad, and after the dollar devaluation the trade balance would have been restored as it was in fact after February 1973 when floating rates came into effect. It may be significant that since floating rates began In 1973 the international transmission of inflation seems to have abated. Thus in the ten industrial nations cited, the annual rate of change of the money supply for each six-month period from June 1971 through 1973, was 10.8%, 16.2%, 13.6%, 10.2%, but only 6.8% in the latter half of 1973.

Of course, the surplus nations complained about the inflow of dollars. But they could have done something more constructive. They could have revalued their currencies, or permitted the dollar to devalue *unilaterally,* a course American officials had advocated in 1970-71 to no avail. Either adjustment would have permitted the United States to pay its way in world trade. But much as the surplus nations professed to fear inflation, they obviously preferred export surpluses more and, behind the facade of the belief in fixed exchange rates, made no adjustments at all, until "benign neglect" forced an adjustment, as detailed in Chapters 8 and 9.

The authors' view of inflation as a function primarily of money supply increase is popularly called "demand pull" inflation. Newspaper readers will ask what of "cost push" (wage increase) inflation? And what of sharply rising food, grain and commodity prices in 1973? In reply, cost push is, in our view, a response to rising prices as workers (i.e., unions) try, understandably, to catch up. The initiative, however, lies with money supply management, i.e., government deficits and creation of money supply. As for rising grain and commodity prices, and the anchovies that swam the wrong way, these elements are important but have been at most marginal contributors (or, in the case of oil price increases, very late comers). Had there been no endemic inflation these increases might have raised prices as a whole 1% or 2%, although more than that for specific goods such as wheat, beef, gasoline, etc. Putting it differently these price increases converted, say, a 10% inflation to perhaps a 12% inflation. These shortages would have been much less important if the rapid increase in money supply all over the world had not resulted in simultaneous booms in all industrial countries so that there was unprecedented demand pressure on supplies of almost all raw materials. Under these conditions the world is especially sensitive to any chance shortages, or to cartel actions as in the case of the oil producers.

If commodity price increases in 1973 may be considered the straw that broke the camel's already overloaded back, the question is not which straw, but why so much load? The fact that the commodity shortages were not central to the inflation but rather peripheral to it is underscored by the fact that in 1974 many wholesale commodity prices dropped sharply with little overall impact on the cost of living. Wheat, for example, fell from over $6.10 to just over $4.62 a bushel; beef from 48¢ per pound to 37¢; copper, soy beans and others did the same. None of these commodity drops, however, succeeded in abating the inflation to any significant extent. In fact, since the money supply could not be rolled back, nothing could abate the rise in prices needed to equilibrate the supply of goods with the demand for them (the money supply). Only in future, if the money supply is more rationally contained, can price rises—the manifestation of inflation—be abated.

Floating exchange rates were established in early 1973, endorsed by most international business, and recognized as the best (or only) available *modus operandi* by mid 1974, when even the IMFs Committee of Twenty mercifully quit trying to reform the system back to fixed rates. (See Chapter 10 for an early espousal of this decision.) Nevertheless, disquietude about floating rates has continued. One criticism worthy of reply suggests floating rates exacerbate inflation by introducing a ratchet-price rise effect on goods, both domestic and exported. Thus a nation which has devalued but which imports extensively to live, e.g., the United Kingdom, must raise its prices to reflect higher costs of food or raw materials. By the same token, a nation which revalues (e.g., Germany) gets imports more cheaply: but German exports which ought in consequence to be cheaper, in fact fail to reflect these lower costs because of insensitive market prices. There is thus an asymmetrical tendency for prices to rise when in fact rises and falls in devaluing and revaluing nations should offset each other. Thus floating rates are blamed to some extent for inflation. In reply, it seems quite wrong to blame floating rates for the market insensitivities of revaluing countries; and even if this ratchet-like effect is inevitable, it is a relatively small price to pay to be rid of the far greater difficulties of all types, including the international transmission of inflation, caused by fixed exchange rates.

With respect to oil, the facts are simple if stark. In October 1973 the cartel of oil producing nations (Organization of Petroleum Exporting Countries, or OPEC) in a quantum leap quadrupled the price of oil. This "trillion-dollar ripoff" was enforced by a boycott of oil shipments, ostensibly related to the 1973 Arab-Israeli war, although the boycott in fact outlived that war and probably had nothing to do with it. In consequence a vast, revolutionary shift of international monetary power is unfolding before our eyes. In 1974 alone, the OPEC countries will have increased dollar and other foreign exchange reserves by some $60 billion: by 1980 the estimates run to at least $200 to $250 billion—astronomic figures—paid over by the non-oil producing, consuming nations who must now go into deficit to support the huge new surplus of the oil-producing nations.

In terms of the balance of payments, this is a special problem. No devaluations of the oil-consuming or revaluations of the oil-producing nations' currencies can equilibrate this transfer. Some of the OPEC nations are developing rapidly (Algeria, Iran, Venezuela, and a few others) and will spend their wealth for goods or arms in the developed world. But enormous oil and eventually monetary reserves are held by nations which cannot develop industrially in the forseeable future (e.g., Kuwait, Saudi Arabia, Libya). These must use their new riches largely for investment: but where, how, and with what consequences?

Scenarios—courses of action whose consequences flow from a series of steps, interruptible at any point—rather than forecasts are relevant to anticipate the future. The optimistic scenario is less frightening than early apocalyptic visions predicted: countless writers had assured us that no system can exist with such imbalances. But the optimistic scenario is that the new-rich oil nations will deposit their new wealth in the Eurodollar banks or directly in domestic banks or invest in some nations paying heavily for oil. While it is vexing to have to pay first a quadruple price for oil, and then interest payments on this money as well, to do so is neither impossible nor unfeasible. The interest payments are heavy but bearable: the debt itself, in this scenario, could be "rolled over" and would probably never be amortized.

But the scenario can become more pessimistic quickly. First, if the Arabs do not find what they deem good investment outlets, they have the option of keeping the oil in the ground, the equivalent of keeping money in a mattress.

Second, there is the question of risk. A major problem arises because not all of the consuming nations are equally strong, or creditworthy from the Arabs' point of view. Thus, the oil-rich producers may have no hesitancy in investing their money, at long or short term, in the United States or Germany, or maybe even Britain which has historic ties and some special guarantees, especially for Kuwait. But Italy is a bad risk, and France, Japan and others may become increasingly so. From whom can these "bad risk" nations borrow to offset their oil deficit? The real danger lies in the less-developed countries (LDCs). Desperately hit by the new cost of oil, their balance of payments increasingly in deficit, developing nations will receive little if any Arab investments directly to offset the drain. Moreover, the LDCs have borrowed extensively from the Eurodollar markets. If they default, the chain reaction of bank losses will reverberate through the banking systems of the United States, Germany, Japan, the United Kingdom and other nations, which own the Eurodollar banks and should—they are morally but not legally obligated—make good the losses of the Eurodollar banks from such defaults. The Eurodollar problem is potentially even more dangerous: Eurobanks borrow short and lend long. If the Arabs deposit in them at the outset, but then decide abruptly to withdraw substantial deposits, the Eurodollar loss could cause a chain reaction. And since there are neither reserve requirements, rules, nor lenders of last resort for the Eurodollar banks (other than their "morally obligated" owners in New York, Frankfurt, etc.) it would be very hard to stop a run on these banks. Should a run start and widespread bank failures threaten, the central banks will be forced to choose whether to intervene to save the banks, but at a cost of increasing money supply, a cost to be borne by all citizens because it can be inflationary.

Numerous attempts to persuade the rich nations, including now the Arabs, to rechannel funds to the LDCs and the poorer developed countries will take place into the mid-1970s. Most of this persuasion has been entrusted to International Monetary Fund or World Bank officials, with mediocre results through 1974.

The recycling of Arab riches must be only a first order and very interim "solution." The real solution to this problem lies in the development of alternative sources of energy to oil. The United States uniquely has the power to do so, as it sits on coal deposits which are four times as great in stored energy as all the oil in the Mid-East. But "sits" is the operative word. For the United States has lacked policies or incentives or even ideas to get that coal out and used. This despite the fact that coal can be used now, and eventually rendered environmentally acceptable by gasification or other metamorphoses at a better (cheaper) price than imported oil. And if the United States tripled its coal output, it would eliminate virtually all of its oil imports—a path both technologically and economically feasible. International oil prices for the rest of the world would crumble with U.S. demand withdrawn (or withdrawing) and the whole problem would disappear as rapidly as it appeared.

The U.S. government and particularly Secretary Kissinger have undertaken vigorous diplomatic offensives to persuade the oil-producers, and particularly the Arabs, to reduce oil prices and to persuade the oil-consuming nations, particularly in Europe, to work together for conservation, oil sharing and price reduction—a type of counter-cartel. Through 1974 neither diplomatic effort has succeeded primarily because there was no economic force behind the diplomatic rhetoric. Had the Americans used their coal as an alternative energy supply, then a real threat to the oil producers and a real hope to the oil users would have been operative. The task at hand, a year after the cartel quadrupled prices, is still to use the coal alternative effectively, and hence give meaning to the American diplomatic initiatives.

In the end, energy creation and storage without oil, coal or other hydrocarbons is the real answer. It is perhaps characteristic of the sloth of the mid-1970s that atomic fusion or solar energy to create, or hydrogen or flywheels to store, energy are called "exotic" solutions, when properly funded research and development, and incentives to bring new technology to the markets, would transform exotic to imminent.

James L. Burtle
Sidney E. Rolfe

# Introduction

his book is about the international monetary system, the "Great Wheel," as Adam Smith called it, that organizes monetary trade and investment relations among countries. As long as the wheel is turning effortlessly, the goods of the world can flow profitably, enriching and gratifying men and nations in the process. Like a well-ordered inheritance, it works quietly in the background, making possible the fuller economic life.

But when the wheel stops or goes awry, the consequences can be serious, even disastrous. As every newspaper reader knows, the world's money system is, or has recently been, in crisis. The relationship among currencies is in flux. World money is afloat, the familiar buoys and landmarks lost. In 1969, the dollar would buy over 4 German marks; by mid-1973, about 2½—a change of some 40 percent. What will tomorrow bring? Unless fixed and firm relations are restored, under clear rules of behavior, will there not be new upheavals? Are those people right who flee paper money of insecure value to buy gold at more than $120 an ounce, nearly treble its "official" price? Whatever happened to the international monetary rules, formulated at Bretton Woods and known by that name, that guided the postwar world to peace and prosperity? The United States and its dollar were the center of the system, and yet American action suspended the system. Can it be restored? Should it?

Legitimate questions all, but unfortunately not susceptible to simple answers. An old adage has it that if one does not know where he is going, any road will take him there. More than in most fields, attitudes toward world money are conditioned by historic experience (or, more accurately, what some people believe to have happened in the past); by sentiments, largely political and psychological in origin; and by a rhetoric that manages to argue in its own terms without ever making explicit its unconsciously held vision of power or of economic purpose. Lord Keynes once remarked, while reading some United States Treasury officialese on a dimly lit train to Oxford, that "this language is back-hinged, involuted, from North America and not English; it must be Cherokee."

These considerations define the purpose of the book. It is meant to impart a sense of historical perspective to the flow of forms of the Great Wheel of international monetary organization, and to extract from that perspective what is central and what is peripheral to its effective operation. Accordingly, it is organized on a time axis. Part I examines the world "Before World War II." The period of the Bretton Woods system, from 1944 through its abandonment in 1971 to mid-1973, and the proposals for reform are discussed in Part II. Such deceptively simple questions as why we have floating exchange rates and why they are likely to persist are examined. Part III indicates how a corporate treasurer, an international money manager, or an intelligent layman can cope with, and even predict the course of, floating rates in the future.

Two chapters in Part II do not, strictly speaking, fit into the time sequence, but rather are designed to add depth to the perceptions or motives by which men are guided. Accordingly Chapter 11 deals with the Eurodollar markets, that is, the financial flows, particularly of short-term money, which have grown up side by side with the "real" flows of goods and services among countries. The financial flows are now enormous, and indeed the cascade of short-term money flowing among nations has served to precipitate those changes and fluctuations in the exchange rates for which the movements of real time competitive devaluations, trade wars, depression, beggar-my-neighbor policies, and ultimately World War II." The allusion to the association between floating rates and competitive devaluations is usually vague with respect to time. In Part I we will try to pinpoint just what this association was in fact, with some surprising results—it appears that the interwar years were not at all periods of competitive devaluation. If that term has any meaning at all, it must mean (1) that a country will devalue its currency by a greater amount than its trading partners in order (2) to increase its export surplus, and possibly its reserves as well. Yet the analysis of the interwar period reveals that this kind of competitive devaluation never really happened, or at worst happened with respect to one or two currencies of small countries, which could hardly have shaken the system.

One reason for which this analysis of the interwar years may differ from the conventional is that we have excluded developing countries and restricted our inquiry to those 11 major trading nations now known as the Group of Ten. In part the idea that the interwar years were characterized by competitive devaluations might reflect the tendency of the recorders, notably the League of Nations, to lump developed and developing countries in their statistical details and to issue reports that said "Belgium and Bolivia" did thus or so. With no disrespect to the developing nations, the focus on the important trading nations of the developed world gives a different picture of the interwar years. What it shows is that nations attempted to reestablish a fixed and high value for their currencies rather than to devalue competitively. Thus England, for example, returned to a fixed- and high-value pound in 1925. It did so in order to restore the capital value of assets held by the wealthy, in those days mostly in the form of bonds. It did so further in order that the pound should become the center of the gold exchange system agreed upon at the Genoa Conference of 1922 and that English banking should thereby gain advantages in international operations. These moves were thoroughly excoriated by Lord Keynes in *The Economic Consequences of Mr. Churchill*. The overvalued pound created depression and unemployment within England; to compensate, increasing trade barriers were erected. As pounds piled up in the reserves of foreign central banks, the British gold supply, meant to back them, proved inadequate, and the British abandoned convertibility in 1931, just as the Americans did in 1971. The pound was left to float to find its new, market-determined level of exchange rates. The French-led bloc did not, as the theory of competitive devaluation would suggest, then devalue even more than the British. On the contrary, the French organized a continental "gold bloc" and raised the value of the franc in order to protect and even try to restore capital asset values to their wealthy. The French and their associates experienced a similar sequence of events: unemployment, increasing trade barriers, political unrest, the eventual triumph of the Popular Front in 1936, and the abandonment of the overvalued franc.

It would seem that modern scholars have applied their own value systems and ideas to the interwar years. They have assumed that devaluations happened in the modern manner, in order to increase exports and employment. Had they seen the world through the eyes of the leaders of the time, they would have realized that full employment was a lower priority to those leaders than was the preservation of asset values for the rich, which could be attained only by reestablishing overvalued currencies. The evidence further shows that floating exchange rate periods led to expansion rather than contraction.

Coming into the postwar period, economists turned their skills to the more sophisticated problems of demand management and various types of economic planning. They accepted a false view of history. Indeed, the discipline of economic history became less significant as an intellectual pursuit. Consequently the theory of economic management was built on a superstructure of faulty historical foundation. A reexamination of the interwar history would have provided a more solid foundation.

After World War II there was a widespread and uncompromising belief that fixed exchange rates were required to avoid the pitfalls of the interwar years. While the rules of Bretton Woods allowed for exchange rate flexibility, practices in the Bretton Woods period militated strongly against it, a prohibition enforced at least until 1968 by the United States and by the officialdom of the International Monetary Fund (IMF), whose task it was to carry out the Bretton Woods rules.

We have divided the Bretton Woods period into three parts. The first, beneficial disequilibrium, ran from the outset until 1958. In this period the United States insisted on violent depreciations of other currencies. The German and Japanese currencies, for example, were depreciated more than 90%; the French and Italian, between 60% and 70%; the British, 30.5% by 1949. In consequence of these depreciations, the United States went into deficit by 1950 and has stayed there, with minor exceptions, ever since. The deficits created the rising supply of dollars which in turn resulted in the miraculous growth of the economies of the deficit nations. Yet under the conditions that existed at the close of the war, the Bretton Woods system was probably the best possible. It gave to the world a perception of stability, with the United States as its center, motivating the will to work and to export that accounts for the rise of the fallen nations. The asymmetry of the initial years of Bretton Woods is underscored by the fact that prior to 1958 most nations, apart from the United States, worked in a straitjacket of restrictions on the convertibility of their currencies. In 1958 currency convertibility was restored; one currency could freely be traded for any other. And it became evident almost immediately that the nations which had sought so hard to earn dollars for their reserves, which had lived in the shadow of a "dollar shortage" many believed to be perpetual —that these nations in fact had an excess of dollars.

We have used the term "revelation" to characterize the period from 1958 to 1965, during which it became apparent that the dollar shortage had in fact become a dollar glut. Yet this seven-year period is the only time Bretton Woods can be said to have worked, albeit with a panoply of ever hardening American controls. An enormous conversion of dollars owned by foreigners to gold took place, and it became evident that the system was in trouble. It may be argued that the overvaluation of the dollar became apparent in this period. The Kennedy administration, which had to cope with the problem, concluded after study that the long-term trend of rising costs in Europe would restore the American trade surplus, overcome the deficit, and eventually restore the strength of the dollar. As a "temporary" measure the administration imposed controls on investment abroad. Perhaps the Kennedy prognosis might have been correct had not the period of "disintegration" commenced about

1965. That disintegration, which coincides roughly with the Johnson administration, was also the period of enormous American inflation because of the simultaneous expenditures for Vietnam and for internal welfare policies, against which appropriate taxes were not levied. In this period, too, the forced devaluation of sterling, which the United States fought bitterly to prevent, further shook confidence in the dollar.

With the coming of the Nixon administration, the decision was reached that the devaluation of the dollar, though essential, was impossible to engineer by international agreement. While the Europeans and Japanese complained bitterly about the excess of dollars in the world, they resisted the proposals for unilateral American devaluation that would have staunched the flow. Consequently the Nixon administration adopted the policy of "benign neglect," designed eventually to force a devaluation of the dollar by permitting the admittedly excess supply of dollars to continue to go abroad with little intervention. Foreign central banks "bought" the inrush of dollars, rather than allow their currencies to float up, and thereby reduce their capacities to export. Finally, in 1971, the United States abandoned the convertibility of dollars into gold and ended the central feature of the Bretton Woods system. At the same time it imposed a 10-percent import surcharge, which it traded in exchange for a reshuffling of exchange rates and the desired dollar devaluation.

The first reshuffling came in the form of the Smithsonian Agreement in December 1971, in which fixed but new exchange rates were established. Since it is almost impossible arbitrarily to fix the correct exchange rates, this pattern collapsed again in February 1973, when a further dollar devaluation took place and some other revaluations replaced the Smithsonian pattern. From March 1973, most major currencies floated.

In the conventional view, pursuant to the Smithsonian Agreement, "reform" of the world monetary system is in order. Yet it must be apparent that a good deal of that reform has already taken place by the enforced dollar devaluation. Despite the fears that devaluation would restrict trade and create another depression, world trade has not been adversely affected by the reappearance of floating, or at least more flexible, exchange rates.

The dollar devaluation that could not be brought about by agreement was forced on the world by the huge movements of short-term capital, by "speculating" against the dollar. In the conditions that prevailed from 1971 to 1973, these speculations have proved correct—and profitable. Ironically, the Eurodollar market itself, the source of much of this speculation, is the consequence of American exchange controls and restrictions, instituted under the Kennedy administration and reinforced under its successor. The "dollar overhang," nearly $100 billion in foreign hands, is a major barrier to reform of the system. Most nations have erected capital controls designed to prevent further dollar inflow. The United States announcement that most of its capital controls would be lifted in 1974 promises, however, to diminish both the question of the dollar overhang and the need for capital controls, and to shrink the Eurodollar market abroad, the creature of American controls.

With dollar devaluation it is likely that basic equilibrium will have been restored to the world's currencies. The American balance of payments is improving and the dollar promises again to become a strong currency, although more reshufflings may be in order before that is achieved. Nevertheless, whether by reform or by a continuation of the present system, there will be more flexible exchange rates in the future than there have been in the past. The system of rigidly fixed exchange rates is unlikely to be reestablished.

To the managers of international money this state of affairs requires new levels of managerial expertise. "Insurance" against movements of currencies, which can wipe out all of the profits earned in production and distribution, can be bought through the forward markets. Devaluations or revaluations can be anticipated by understanding the criteria which indicate that these devaluations or revaluations are in order.

While forecasting exchange rate changes is still more of an art than a science, money managers can use some of the leading indicators that have been developed for this purpose. For example, the decline in reserves below a certain number of months' imports is usually a portent of devaluation to come; the seepage of reserves into the money supply, threatening inflation, is symptomatic of revaluation to come. Obviously these rules of thumb should be supplemented by in-depth analyses of the nation's balance of payments. And money managers must be aware that while economic criteria are the *necessary* condition for changes in the exchange rate, political decisions are the *sufficient* condition to bring them about. Thus it is also necessary to understand the political decision-making process with respect to exchange rate changes.

For the mathematically minded, an econometric model is appended.

# Before
# World War II

# 1.
# The
# Money
# Machine

 t is axiomatic that men seek certainty; paradoxically, the more uncertain the world seems, the greater the quest for unchanging landmarks. This quest is true in the financial world, as well as in politics, religion, or personal life. As the dollar has ceased to be the unvarying currency of the postwar world, many have turned to gold instead. In Europe and the Mid-East, where in many countries gold may be freely bought and sold, the demand for the metal has driven its price to historic heights, over $120 per ounce, nearly treble the official price (ie., the price at which the central banks nations can trade gold among themselves in settlement of deficits and surpluses). New laws in Japan and even in the United States would permit the average man to own gold, promising new demands.

In the expanding ranks of "gold bugs," illusions about gold have spread as well. It has been imbued, in the popular mythology, with the aura of an eternal verity, always used, always valuable. And many, encouraged by some dubious scholarship, now look back to the golden age, which they imagine to have lasted from the beginning of recorded history to recent days, as a period of economic growth, stability, fixed exchange rates, and general well-being.

Nothing could be further from the truth. Wide-

3

spread adherence to the gold standard, far from extending to time immemorial, lasted only 35 years, from 1879 to 1914.

In ancient Rome, copper was the standard coinage, although gold and silver coins also circulated. In the Middle Ages, there appear to have been cycles in which either gold or silver coins were used more frequently, though neither coinage seems ever to have disappeared entirely. In the tenth century silver appears to have been the most frequent coinage, but by the fourteenth and fifteenth centuries there was a switch to gold florins and ducats, originally from Italy. England, usually credited with inventing the gold standard, almost never used gold coins until 1344, during the reign of Edward III. In the sixteenth century the inflow of silver from the New World (in greater quantity than the inflow of gold) led to widespread silver coinage.

Because of a process known as Gresham's law, there was a tendency for one type of coin to become dominant when governments were willing to exchange silver for gold, or gold for silver, according to a specific standard. Under these conditions either the gold or silver coin could be expected to circulate less. If, for example, the free bullion market gave more silver for gold than the government standard for coinage at the government mint, the natural tendency would be to melt down gold coins and sell them for silver on the free market. On the other hand, if the free bullion market gave more gold for silver than the government mint, the tendency would be for gold to be coined while silver coins would be melted down for bullion to sell in the free market. How in practice did Gresham's law work? The "bad" money, that containing the metal less favored in the free market compared with the government standard, drove out the "good" money, that containing the metal more favored in the free market. Gresham's law was for centuries a bête noire to governments issuing bimetallic currencies, because as the market ratio between them would change, one currency would tend to move out of circulation. Often this would mean the inconvenience to commerce that either low-denomination coins (usually silver) or high-denomination coins (usually gold) would not circulate, or, even more damaging to commerce, there might be a "currency reversal" in which one currency would supplant another currency.

To overcome the difficulty of maintaining both low-value and high-value coins in circulation, England began a series of experiments in the seventeenth century that was to replace bimetallism with the gold standard about 150 years later. In 1663 England issued a gold coin called the guinea (from the region in West Africa where gold was mined), for which no equivalent silver value was given. As a result the so-called double standard, which had tended to force one or the other coinage out of circulation, was replaced by the "parallel standard," in which every commodity was priced in gold and also in silver. The parallel standard was an obvious nuisance to trade, and in 1717 England reverted to the double standard. As can be seen from Table 1, in the period between 1721 and 1760 the official British ratio of exchange of silver for gold at 15.20 was higher than the market level, i.e., silver could be exchanged for more gold in the free market. Thus gold was brought to the mint for coinage and silver tended to move out of circulation. In the 1761–1780 period, the rapid increase in gold output in Brazil tended to depress further the market silver/gold ratio, as indicated in Table 1, and thus assure the continuance of gold as the main circulating medium. In the 1781–1800 period, however, the market ratio at which silver exchanged for gold climbed to an average of 15.09 and threatened to move above the official 15.20 ratio. This would have resulted in a coinage reversal, pushing gold out of circulation and bringing silver back into circulation. Table 1 also indicates the main causes of the 1781–1800 rise in the silver/gold market exchange ratio; average annual silver production was up from 533,145 kg. in 1741–1760 to 879,060 in 1781–1800, while gold production declined from 24,610 kg. in 1741–1760 to 17,790 kg. in 1781–1800. The main reason for the rise in silver production was the unprecedented increase by about 250,000 kg. in average annual Mexican silver output between the 1741–1760 period and that of 1781–1800. For gold production, on the other hand, the decline was due to the exhaustion of the Brazilian mines.

In 1798, mainly to prevent a currency reversal in which silver coins would have pushed gold coins out of circulation, England stopped the coinage of silver altogether, except for token money that had a higher official value than its silver content. After interruptions

**Table 1**

Production and prices of gold and silver: 1531–1920

| Date | Average annual gold production (kg.) | Average annual silver production (kg.) | No. of ounces of silver exchanged for 1 oz. of gold |
|------|------|------|------|
| 1531–1580 | 6,840 | 299,500 | 11.50 |
| 1581–1600 | 7,380 | 418,900 | 11.80 |
| 1601–1620 | 8,520 | 422,900 | 12.25 |
| 1621–1640 | 8,300 | 393,600 | 14.00 |
| 1641–1660 | 8,770 | 366,300 | 14.50 |
| 1661–1680 | 9,260 | 337,000 | 15.00 |
| 1681–1700 | 10,765 | 341,900 | 15.00 |
| 1701–1720 | 12,820 | 355,600 | 15.21 |
| 1721–1740 | 19,080 | 431,200 | 15.08 |
| 1741–1760 | 24,610 | 533,145 | 14.75 |
| 1761–1780 | 20,705 | 652,740 | 14.72 |
| 1781–1800 | 17,790 | 879,060 | 15.09 |
| 1801–1810 | 17,778 | 894,150 | 15.61 |
| 1811–1820 | 11,445 | 540,770 | 15.51 |
| 1821–1830 | 14,216 | 460,560 | 15.80 |
| 1831–1840 | 20,289 | 596,450 | 15.75 |
| 1841–1850 | 54,579 | 780,415 | 15.83 |
| 1851–1855 | 199,388 | 886,115 | 15.41 |
| 1856–1860 | 201,750 | 904,990 | 15.30 |
| 1861–1865 | 185,057 | 1,101,150 | 15.40 |
| 1866–1870 | 195,026 | 1,339,085 | 15.55 |
| 1871–1875 | 173,904 | 1,969,425 | 15.97 |
| 1876–1880 | 172,414 | 2,450,252 | 17.81 |
| 1881–1885 | 154,959 | 2,808,400 | 18.63 |
| 1886–1890 | 169,869 | 3,387,532 | 21.16 |
| 1891–1895 | 245,170 | 4,901,333 | 26.32 |
| 1896–1900 | 387,257 | 5,154,551 | 33.54 |
| 1901–1905 | 485,434 | 5,226,121 | 36.20 |
| 1906–1910 | 652,302 | 6,135,348 | 35.68 |
| 1911–1920 | 647,936 | 5,906,681 | 29.63 |

Source: Karl Helfferich, *Money* (New York: Adelphi, 1927).

during the Napoleonic wars, England in 1816 adopted the policy of free coinage of gold—any amount of gold brought to the mint would be coined into gold sovereigns worth 20 shillings. Shillings were silver pieces, but their actual silver content was less than their stated value so that the problem of coins going out of circulation was overcome.

Thus 1798 can be set as the year of the inception of the gold standard in England, though it did not become fully operative until 1823 when convertibility of gold to notes was established. Rather than a great design, the gold standard was set up as an ad hoc move to prevent a currency reversal from gold to silver. The dominance of gold in British monetary circulation throughout most of the eighteenth century had been maintained via Gresham's law by the rapid growth of production in the Brazilian gold mines. Thus the silver/gold exchange ratio in the free market was kept below the official ratio, and silver tended to move out of circulation. But, as the Brazilian mines became exhausted, a currency reversal threatened.

The main innovation of the 1798 gold standard was not so much the free coinage of gold coins. It was rather the creation of silver token money: the issuance of silver coins containing less silver than their stated value. But this could, in principle, have been the other way round—with a silver standard and gold token money.

During the Napoleonic wars, England wanted to protect its gold supply. It stopped minting gold coins and issued paper money of the same legal value as the gold coins that were no longer issued. But, in fact, holders of metal coins demanded and received a premium over paper money. After 1823, however, paper money became redeemable for gold, the premium of coins over paper money disappeared, and the gold standard in England for paper money as well as for coins was fully established.

While Britain had adopted the gold standard, most of Europe remained on bimetallic standards. Since most official standards tended to overstate the value of silver, it remained in circulation while gold was forced out of circulation. The bimetallic, silver-circulating system might have continued indefinitely except for two developments in the 1850s and 1860s.

First, there was a rapid increase of gold production in California and Australia. Table 1 shows that world average gold production, which had stagnated at less than 20,000 kg. per year between 1781 and 1800, jumped to 201,750 kg. from 1856–1860. Secondly, India absorbed all of world silver production as its currency—which was silver—expanded in 1856–1865 mainly because of expenditures there for railroad building, the costs of putting down the so-called mutiny of 1857, and supplying cotton to England during the American Civil War.

Thus the gold discoveries and the exodus of silver to India tended to force up the market price of silver in Europe and, via Gresham's law, to push it out of circulation. As England had done in 1798, European countries issued token money to preserve silver coinage for smaller transactions.

Whether or not the German states would have enough gold reserves to apply the gold standard was doubtful. However in 1871, with the payment in gold of a large part of the Franco-Prussian War indemnity, Germany too adopted the gold standard. Free (not token money) silver coinage was discontinued in the United States in 1873. Other countries followed, and by 1879 most of the world was on the gold standard.

But even before the gold standard was generally accepted, the stage had been set for it to fight for its life. Between the 1866–1870 period and that of 1881–1885, average annual gold production, because of exhaustion of the California mines, declined from 195,026 kg. to 154,959 kg., while average annual silver production increased from 1,339,085 kg. to 2,808,400 kg. (as shown in Table 1). Without a gold standard these developments would have led to a coinage reversal.

In the period beginning about 1880, the world limped along without enough gold. When one major country absorbed large amounts of gold, another lost it and, in line with the gold standard rules discussed later, reduced its money supply, income, and output. The world gold shortage was a major factor in the United States depression of 1882–1885 and in the United States period of stagnation, 1891–1897. In both cases there was an outflow of gold from the United States mainly to England. Milton Friedman and Anna J. Schwartz in their monumental *Monetary History of the United States, 1867–1960* view the slack situation in the United States in 1891–1897 as similar, in some respects, to the post–World War II experience in the United Kingdom: Both countries were trying to hold to an unrealistic exchange rate.

The gold standard was especially challenged in the United States. Restated in modern monetarist terms, William Jennings Bryan's argument, "You shall not crucify mankind on a cross of gold," meant that economic growth was threatened by a stagnant money supply dependent on a slow-growing gold supply. Bryan wanted a vast increase in the quantity of money, and its most convenient source was in the monetization of the rising U.S. silver output. Bryan lost the 1896 election to McKinley, but his aim of a soaring money supply was achieved because of the chance discovery of vast gold supplies in South Africa, as well as Colorado and Alaska, and improved, lower-cost methods of mining gold. Between the 1891–1895 period and that of 1906–1910, average annual gold production more than doubled from 245,170 kg. to 652,302 kg. Thus, until the 1914–1918 war, the gold standard was firmly enthroned.

It would be difficult, however, to exaggerate the role of contingencies in the acceptance of the gold standard. Key events, without which its development might have been aborted, were the exhaustion of the gold mines in Brazil, the discovery of gold in California and Australia, the so-called Indian Mutiny of 1857, the French indemnity payment to Germany in 1871, and finally the development of gold mines in South Africa.

The discovery of gold after 1890 led, with some delayed reaction, to a surge in world monetary gold supplies. As a result, gold losses and balance of payments stringency were less of a drag on economic progress in the 1900–1914 period. Because gold was no longer a stone around the neck of the world economy, it was almost universally credited with being an engine of economic progress that had almost lifelike qualities. Discipline, constancy, stability, and immutability were its attributes.

It seemed that no panegyric was too extreme. Kipling in "Puck of Pook's Hill" rhapsodized:

... the earth's gold moves with the seasons, and the crops, and the winds; circling and looping and rising and sinking like a river, a wonderful underground river. (p. 290)

The gold standard and its workings, real and imagined, are worth a close look. Although the gold standard did not become generally adopted until 1879, paradoxically its principles were discovered by the Scottish philosopher David Hume in the eighteenth century, long before there was a gold standard. It was uncertain in the late 1700s whether gold or silver would become the dominant medium of international exchange, a point noted earlier. So Hume used the vague word "specie," meaning either gold or silver, to develop the now standard theory of the "specie flow mechanism."

The value of each currency was fixed in ounces of gold (or silver), but exchange rates between currencies—for example British pounds per dollar—showed temporary variations. When exchange rates diverged enough to cover a margin for transportation and insurance —the well-known gold points—traders could buy gold in one country and sell it at a profit in another.

According to the gold standard theory, such an inflow of gold would, in a series of sequential steps which follow, bring down again the exchange rate that had gone up. In sequence, as gold entered a country, if—and this is a shaky "if"—the gold standard rules were followed, there would be a corresponding increase of new circulating money, either gold or paper convertible into gold. This was the function of gold as cover for the money supply. As the money supply increased, prices in the gold-receiving country would rise. At higher prices relative to the rest of the world, the exports of the gold-receiving country would be less competitive. As its exports declined (and imports increased), there would be a decline in demand for its currency. The exchange rate between currencies would return to near where it was in the first place, and there would be no further incentive for shipping gold. Indeed, the process might well reverse.

The same line of argument could be applied, somewhat more broadly, to show that under the gold standard system all international payments would be nearly in balance. Any imbalance would mean a rise or fall in demand for a particular currency. For example, if France had a good wine year, Britain would buy more wine; and if everything else stayed the same, there would be a rise in demand for French francs. The increase in demand for the French franc would, like rising demand for anything else, tend to raise the price, i.e., its exchange rate in terms of pounds. If the French franc rate went above the gold point, it would set off, as discussed, an inflow of gold into France. If France followed gold cover rules and raised its money supply, its prices would rise, its exports would decline, and its imports would rise until international payments were readjusted, and again in balance. Similar but opposite adjustment would simultaneously be occurring in Great Britain.

The weakest links of the gold standard mechanism were (1) the sometime failure of governments to issue currency in line with the amount of their gold holdings—hence failure to follow the gold standard's "rules of the game," and (2) government action to cut the tie between currency increases (decreases) and price increases (decreases), often called the "quantity theory of money."

Governments were often irrational in their desire to accumulate gold; far from acting to stop the gold inflow, they sometimes allowed it to become bigger by "sterilization" policies, i.e., by bond issues, taxation, or other methods that avoided an addition to the money supply by preventing the issue of additional currency as the gold came in. On a more logical basis than the so-called mercantilist urge to accumulate gold were the premonitions, though not fully developed intellectually until later, that inflation from money issue following the gold inflow would be harmful and that an outflow of gold and decline in the money supply would adversely affect output and employment. Fortunately in the 1900–1914 heyday of the gold standard, because of balooning gold production, there were not many countries losing gold to an extent that adversely affected employment and output. Put differently, the universal inflow of gold allowed virtually all nations to gain gold and to grow by feeding off the new supply rather than off each other. This new gold was the money machine that kept all nations growing, even with a fixed exchange rate that minimized national competitions, that gave gold its near-sacred aura.

When governments did follow the rules of the game by issuing additional money following a gold inflow, there were other and more complicated effects than rising prices. It was no simple case of the "quantity theory of money" wherein prices and money supply necessarily move closely together. Changes in the money supply affected incomes, employment, interest rates, capital movements, and other economic variables as well as prices. The paradox, however, was that so long as the system was fueled by new South African gold production, it worked better than might have been expected from theory. In addition to raising prices, higher money supplies raised incomes and lowered interest rates. Lower interest rates encouraged new investment, which raised per capita output and real income; higher incomes encouraged imports. Thus under the special 1900–1914 conditions, the general trend of world output and employment was decisively an upward one. But experience before and after shows the 1900–1914 period to be atypical, almost to the point of being a benign mutation with zero chance of reappearing.

Aside from the gold discoveries, the apparent success of the gold standard was favored by the economic environment of 1900–1914. This period of rapid economic growth and prosperity was also a time of great discovery and of application to industry of new science and technology. New technology was quickly used, resulting in new industries that included, among others, the steel, oil, electric power, and automobile.

The fortuitous nature of these gold discoveries is underscored when they are compared to the inrush of gold and particularly silver from the Americas during the Spanish heyday of the sixteenth and seventeenth centuries. For Spain, the result was simply a disastrous inflation and the destruction of its international position, as that nation (and that time) lacked the technological infrastructure to enable it to use the new treasure productively, as the early twentieth century could and did.

In the conventional wisdom, world prosperity from 1900 to 1914 had depended on exchange rates at fixed values, and fixed exchange rates in turn depended on the gold standard. In fact, it was not the gold standard per se or fixed exchange rates, but rather the chance discovery of new gold in South Africa that was the money machine which fueled unusually great investment opportunities with a rapidly growing world money supply. When this was invested in the new technologies, all nations could grow and have a favorable surplus in their balance of payments most of the time, despite—and not because of—fixed exchange rates.

# 2.
# The Interwar Years: Beggar Whose Neighbor?

n financial as in other history, World War I is a crucial and generally unhappy turning point. During that war, vast new supplies of printed money dwarfed the existing gold supplies, which were in any event radically redistributed. The supply of gold could not, by war's end in 1918, provide enough new reserves to keep the golden age alive. The money machine had ceased to function.

The interwar years provided a laboratory in which there were periods of fixed and periods of fluctuating exchange rates, even within the same country: France had fluctuating rates to 1926 and rigid rates to 1936; Britain had fluctuating rates from 1919 to 1925, fixed rates to 1931, and fluctuating rates again until the start of World War II. With what results?

The common, often expressed view that the interwar years were characterized by competitive devaluations of currency is simply not true. The myth that one nation devalued to gain a surplus, only to be offset by a savagely retaliatory devaluation by others, appears not borne out by the facts. This myth was virtually gospel to the Bretton Woods planners. Indeed it exists now and underlies the strong continuing antipathy in some quarters to flexible exchange rates. The antipathy is usually rationalized by vague allusions to interwar history.

In the section that follows, each interwar period is examined to find evidences of the times and the circumstances when the allegedly vicious competitive devaluations took place. Unless the point has been missed badly, they simply never did. The allusions are vague because they cannot be pinned down by fact; the myth appears to have been only that, without historic support.

To be relevant, this analysis will be confined to the major countries in international finance, those 11 now known as the Group of Ten: the United Kingdom, the United States, France, Germany, Italy, the Netherlands, Belgium, Switzerland, Canada, Sweden, and Japan. Clearly these are the important countries in international trade and finance. The tendency of UN (or League of Nations) publications to lump "Belgium and Bolivia," or the "United States and Uganda" simply confuses the significant movements. In a real sense, it makes little difference to world money what Bolivia or Uganda does. No lack of concern for small and developing countries is implied by this more realistic view of international financial development. However, one reason for the exaggerated importance attached to competitive devaluations in the 1930s arises from the tendency of the literature, particularly of international organizations, in chronicles of the time to count as equally significant the devaluations of small, often primary-producing countries. But those nations were not then and are not now the important traders. Then, as now, in many cases they resorted to persistent devaluations because their economic, monetary, and fiscal policies ranged from bad to nonexistent, as a flood of development literature has argued. In any event, their impact on world money was miniscule compared to that of the Group of Ten.

A definition is in order to interpret what follows. What are the symptoms of the dreaded competitive devaluation, instrument of "beggar my neighbor" policy?

To find positive evidence of beggar-my-neighbor policy and competitive devaluation, two questions need to be answered positively:

1. When one country devalued, was this action followed by a substantially greater devaluation by another major country?
2. If there was a substantially greater devaluation, did it result in the buildup of a foreign trade surplus?

The recognition should be made explicit that competitive devaluations were certainly not the only devices of the beggar-my-neighbor policy. These included trade restrictions of all varieties, e.g., quotas, tariffs, exchange controls, and others. The devices even included economic policies designed to reduce wages, absolutely or relatively, for competitive advantage—policies successfully engineered in England by 1925 to raise the pound's value so that it could become the reserve currency of the gold exchange standard in that day.

In recognizing these alternative or supplementary beggar-my-neighbor devices, it will be evident that devices of this type have always existed and still do. Even in the post–World War II period there have been successive and not wholly successful attempts to reduce tariffs. Quotas still abound. As recently as 1973 former Treasury Secretary John Connally, in a speech to Wharton School alumni, pointed out that it is necessary for the United States to bear a particularly heavy burden of Japanese imports because of European restrictions against them, based on quotas or outright embargoes in various categories. Consequently, he noted, the French–Japanese trade is miniscule, less than $500 million per year. Nontariff barriers also existed then and exist now, in a dizzying variety of forms. Even an innocent electric outlet in the wall is a nontariff barrier because it will not accept a foreign radio or shaver.

While recognizing the existence of all these devices to restrict trade, this analysis focuses on competitive devaluation of exchange rates because this device has been singled out by advocates of rigid exchange rates as the main weapon in the beggar-my-neighbor armory. As the subsequent analysis will show, it was not used for this purpose, whereas many of the other devices cited, notably quotas and exchange controls, were used precisely to protect or to maintain rigid and overvalued currencies, rather than as additional weapons in conjunction with competitive devaluation. For example, in 1931, after the United Kingdom had given up its reserve currency status and abandoned gold conversion, and France maintained an overvalued franc, the French were forced to use quotas extensively to protect French industrial and agricultural goods against "cheap imports." These defenses would have been unnecessary, or at least less justifiable, with generally floating or flexible exchange rates, which need not be defended in this fashion. Similarly, Germany, particularly after 1932, used exchange controls extensively as part of the Nazi isolationist technique in response to its particularly unfortunate history.

History can never be rerun. But if it could be, it would appear that the ideal policy for this period would have been freely floating exchange rates and deficit spending and/or preservation of the money supply for internal expansion—for reasons analyzed herein.

The devaluations of the 1920s and 1930s have been analyzed with these symptoms in mind. In most cases devaluations of one major country were followed by smaller devaluations of other major countries. In the small number of cases where a bigger devaluation followed, notably in the United States and Japan in 1931–1934, the greater devaluation—in these cases after the 1931 sterling devaluation—did not result in an expansion of trade surpluses. Both the United States and Japan, by simultaneous expansionary fiscal-monetary policies, actually raised imports in line with exports. Their devaluations thus did not result in a trade surplus nor did it pull reserves away from other countries, a necessary precondition for the beggar-my-neighbor theory. Belgium in 1926 and 1935 affords the other example of greater depreciation than its "lead country" —France. But Belgium, whatever its actions or their consequences, was and is too small a factor in international finance really to affect the whole, and is certainly too marginal a case on which to base a universal theory.

## 1919 to 1921

During World War I the rules of the gold standard game became impossible to follow. Trade balances moved sharply against belligerents and in favor of neutral countries. The belligerents with gold outflows—where these were permitted at all—greatly increased their money supplies, as the conduct of the war required an enormous step-up in government outlays, financed by deficit spending beyond what could be financed by taxation. Neutrals received large gold inflows. But some of them, notably the Scandinavian countries, could not accept the consequent rate of inflation and stopped following the rules of the gold standard game. They stopped accepting gold in payment for exports, preferring instead to revalue their currencies, to see their exchange rates rise temporarily. Thus World War I ended with (1) a much greater paper currency issue in most countries, and (2) a different distribution of holdings of world gold supplies.

During and after World War I the United States remained on the gold standard but also did not follow the rules of the gold standard game. The rules would have required increases in the money supply, and price increases in proportion to the gold inflow. But the Americans did not want to import Europe's inflation; instead they sterilized the gold inflow, keeping the money supply and prices well below the level that new gold stock would require under the gold standard rules. With Europe's prices remaining higher than those in the United States, the gold outflow to that country continued.

Clearly, for most of the belligerents devaluation was the only alternative after World War I. But, unlike post–World War II countries, the world of 1919 had known nearly steady exchange rates for as long as 100 years. Devaluation was not only unpopular, it was an almost unknown expedient, a course vouchsafed only to revolution-plagued Latin American countries or in consequence of the most dire circumstances, e.g. those in the United States after the long Civil War. Further, once the plunge was taken, devaluations were seen as temporary. In the dominant view of things, currencies must, should, ought to return, sooner or later, to the promised land of prewar parities.

Three reasons were expressed for the wishful thought in Europe that the lost parities would be soon regained: (1) the United States would support European exchange rates; (2) foreign capital and foreign investors, foreseeing the return of the prewar parities, would move heavily into Europe, creating great surpluses that would permit revaluation; and (3) for the Allies, and particularly the French, reparation payments, to be extracted from Germany, would restore prewar parities. Had not the reverse been true in 1871?

But none of these hopes was in fact realized. Early in 1919 the United States withdrew its support from the French franc. Unlike the post–World War II period, U.S. aid was limited to food supplies: There was no Marshall Plan. The "band of wilful men" who thwarted President Wilson saw to that. Private capital did move into Europe, sometimes as straight currency speculation, but never in sufficient quantity for the restoration of prewar parities. And reparations, far from restoring currencies, became a major currency destabilizing force, as Keynes was later to argue eloquently.

In early 1919 the currencies of most of the belligerents were significantly below their 1914 exchange rates. In view of worldwide shortages of raw materials, all major currencies showed further losses relative to the dollar between January 1919 and December 1920. Table 2 shows the extent of these moves.

But in all records of the 1918–1920 period, there is no suggestion that countries deliberately devalued their exchange rates to gain trade advantages. The devaluations were regarded as temporary and at best as necessary evils. All countries welcomed the turnaround in exchange rates that began in early 1921, when most major currencies, except the mark, began to appreciate.

Table 2

Percentage changes in exchange rates, January 1914–January 1919, and January 1919–December 1920 (U.S. cents per unit)

|  | January 1914– January 1919 | January 1919– December 1920 |
|---|---|---|
| U.K. | − 2.07 | −26.72 |
| France | − 4.81 | −67.74 |
| Germany | −82.18[a] | −67.61[b] |
| Italy | −17.90 | −77.80 |
| Belgium | −34.89[a] | −49.88[b] |
| Netherlands | + 5.19 | −26.84 |
| Switzerland | + 7.50 | −25.51 |
| Sweden | + 7.80 | −32.19 |
| Canada | − 1.97 | −11.89 |
| Japan | + 4.29 | − 3.16 |

[a]January 1914–September 1919
[b]September 1919–September 1920.

Source: U.S. Federal Reserve System, *Banking and Monetary Statistics,* 1943.

# 3.
# The Gold Exchange Standard and After

he major currencies other than the German mark, whose unique history is summarized below, and the yen (with a small further devaluation) appreciated between December 1920 and June 1922, thus regaining a substantial part of what had been lost between January 1919 and December 1920. Table 3 shows some detail of these moves.

**Table 3**

Percentage changes in exchange rates, December 1920—June 1922 (U.S. cents per unit)

| | |
|---|---|
| United Kingdom | +27.5 |
| France | +48.1 |
| Germany | −76.8 |
| Italy | +42.2 |
| Belgium | +31.6 |
| Netherlands | +25.1 |
| Switzerland | +23.7 |
| Sweden | +31.7 |
| Canada | +14.5 |
| Japan | − 5.2 |

Source: U.S. Federal Reserve System, *Banking and Monetary Statistics*, 1943.

The end-1920 to mid-1922 appreciation of currencies reflected the beginnings of economic recovery in Europe, the lower prices of food imports after 1921, and some counteradjustment from the oversold European currency markets in late 1920. Hopes for currency stabilization were again high, especially in view of the pervasive nostalgia for the long period before 1914, in which the gold standard was given credit—whether accurately or not is immaterial—for having accomplished two things: holding all currencies at fixed exchange rates, and simultaneously permitting economic growth and prosperity in all countries. Completely forgotten were the periods of monetary stringency under the gold standard, as in the United States between 1879 and 1900.

But after World War I, the value of world gold supplies was much less than the amount of paper money currencies swollen by wartime deficit financing. To reduce currency supplies and thus restore depreciated currencies to prewar gold parities would, in countries with depreciated moneys, require a push-down of prices, including wages, to prewar levels. This was simply not politically feasible. In an attempt to restore "something like" the prewar gold standard, a new system called the *gold exchange standard* was set up in the Genoa Agreement of 1922. This system differed from the gold standard in that governments and central banks in each country would hold, as part of their reserves, not only gold but gold-backed currencies as well. The gold value of the gold-backed currencies would be maintained so that they would, in theory, be "as good as gold." Like reserves in a banking system, the gold-backed currencies—also called *reserve currencies*—would be gold convertible, i.e., readily exchangeable for gold. Governments would follow the rules of the gold standard game with respect to both gold and the gold-backed currencies: As gold or gold-backed currencies came in, they would increase the money supply; and as gold and gold-backed currencies went out, they would reduce the money supply.

But while the gold exchange standard was in principle widely accepted at the Genoa Conference, it took three years for the system to commence effective operation. Having accepted the new view that international money should revolve around one "key" or "reserve" currency, world central bankers, in setting up the gold exchange standard, faced two unanswered questions: (1) What would be the world reserve currency? (2) What would be the parity of each other currency with respect to the world reserve currency?

These questions were answered with the restoration at its prewar level of the British pound in 1925 and the stabilization of most other major currencies in the years shortly following. For much of continental Europe, however, 1923 to 1927 was a period of renewed and wider currency fluctuations.

## The Fall of the Mark

In the period between mid-1922 and 1927 there was overall currency appreciation for the British, Dutch, Swiss, Swedish, and Canadian currencies. The Japanese yen devalued by about 15 percent in 1924 as a result of the earthquake, but by 1927 had regained its 1922 level. It was a different story in Germany, France, Italy, and Belgium, where currencies continued to fluctuate widely, even wildly. In Germany the old currency became worthless and was stabilized only after a new unit, the reichsmark, was created.

The political tragedy that overtook Germany with the rise of the Nazi system, and all that followed, had its origins in the economic events of the 1920s. The depreciation of the currency that commenced in 1914 continued unabated through 1923. In the end the mark was worthless, eventually to be restructured (devalution is here a meaningless term) on the basis of one new reischmark for 1 trillion old marks.

Barter replaced other commercial dealings in the early 1920s, and despair was so widespread among the population that food riots were frequent. The middle classes and pensioners were probably the heaviest losers; they saw their savings wiped out. But the drop in real wages was a hard blow for the working classes as well.

The near-pathological fear of inflation in Germany also had its origins in this period. As the fear of unemployment in the Anglo-Saxon countries, particularly England, explains much of the inflationary thrust in the postwar period, the German fear of inflation is an often unstated key to its financial and monetary behavior. While inflation was wreaking havoc with the masses, a few businessmen and industrialists made large profits and bought up bankrupt enterprises. Speculation was rife, and those with debts to pay off, mainly farmers and landowners with mortgages on their land, gained immensely.

This extreme inflation began during World War I when the German government, faced with budgetary deficits, issued more and more paper money to meet its expenses. The practice was continued after the war, and the value of the mark declined steadily, mainly because of reparations payments but also because of the flight of German capital abroad, the obstacles to the revival of German foreign trade, and the consequent adverse balance of payments. The result was a runaway inflation more severe than in any other part of postwar Western Europe.

The Treaty of Versailles did not specify an amount for reparations to be paid by Germany, but it held Germany responsible for vast sums: damages to nonmilitary property and to civilians, and pensions for veterans. Various conferences in 1920 determined amounts that Germany should pay, which Germany promptly declared she was unable to meet. The 1921 London Conference then fixed reparations at 132 billion gold marks to be paid in installments of 2 billion marks annually plus an amount equal to 26 percent of Germany's annual exports. In 1923 Germany defaulted on these payments, and French and Belgian troops occupied the Rhineland. The German government tolerated, if not ordered, passive resistance to French and Belgian attempts to get the mines and factories working, and a ban on all reparations deliveries ensued. The occupation forces in turn arrested and deported some Germans and, by means of a crippling economic blockade, cut off the Ruhr, together with the greater part of the occupied Rhineland, from the rest of Germany. Dispossessed of this important territory, Germany was unable to make payments, and each attempt to convert marks into foreign currency drove down their value. Within Germany there was resort to sabotage and guerrilla warfare, and for a time the army high command believed that the situation in the Ruhr might lead to open war, a view which led them to encourage the clandestine recruitment of irregular forces to form a Black Reichswehr. The legitimation of underground violence was later to play a terrible role in Germany's political development.

The blockade dislocated the whole economic life of the country and gave the final touch to the depreciation of the currency. The mark, which had already fallen from 162 to more than 7,000 to the dollar by 1922 (the pre-1914 rate had been 4.20 marks to the dollar), plummeted in 1923 to 160,000 to the dollar on July 1; 242,000,000 on October 1; and 4,200,000,000,000 to the dollar on November 20, 1923. The price of a single copy of a newspaper, to take one instance, rose to 200,000,000,000 marks.

Finally, by the end of 1923 the mark was stabilized. An independent central bank was established under the ubiquitous Dr. Hjalmar Schacht. To be sure the new reichsmark was worth a trillion of the old, but about 23.02 cents (and 0.35842 grams in fine gold content), or near the prewar mark value to the dollar. This stability and the Dawes Plan of 1924 brought new capital into Germany, which experienced a few years of growth until the stock market crash in the United States led to capital withdrawals in 1931–1932. The Locarno Treaty of 1925 was to lead to the withdrawal of French troops and a reduction in reparations payments, which were met in the later 1920s; the *quo* for this *quid* was German agreement to renounce claims on Alsace—and other political agreements, all soon to be broken by Hitler.

France, in insisting on impossibly high reparations, also hoped thereby to restore the French franc to some approximation of its prewar value. During World War I France had financed war expenditures by printing quantities of paper money; the French governments expected, and assured their people, that reparations from Germany would restore the purchasing power and exchange rate of the franc. Perhaps believing that the precedent of French indemnity payment to Prussia after the Franco-Prussian War would be reversed on a grand scale, the French people gave this promise far too much credence. In the early postwar years French politicians could not tell the terrible truth, that reparations from Germany could not finance war losses and thus offset the wartime inflation and postwar currency devaluation. John Maynard Keynes in *The Economic Consequences of the Peace* (1919) had eloquently attacked the reparations demands on Germany, but had little influence on the policies of the Allies. The huge reparations "agreed to" in the Versailles treaty were scaled down in the London Conference of 1921, but were still at impossible levels.

There were two direct consequences of the massive depreciation of the mark. France, disillusioned with reparations, saw its exchange rate fall badly after 1923. Secondly, the mark was stabilized at its new value, and as a result, other currencies, notably the British pound, also stabilized.

But in 1933 Hitler could convince Germany that "we are the result of the distress for which others are responsible," in large part because of this history.

## The Last of the "Latin Bloc"—France, Belgium, Italy

In the later part of 1922 and in 1923, the increasingly negative prognosis for the mark was also a negative prognosis for reparations to France in sufficient amounts to restore the French franc to prewar parity. With the end of reparations illusions, the French franc fell steadily, declining by 37% from 8.76 American cents in June 1922 to 5.52 cents in November 1923. Then the famous 1924 bear raid began, and by February 1924 the franc had dropped to 4.42 cents, losing an additional 20%. Speculators who had sold the franc short believed that the government would be unable to pay its debts to the Bank of France. However, the speculators turned out to be wrong and experienced a crushing bear squeeze. The Bank of France was able to borrow $100 million from Morgan and Lazard Frères. Between February and April the franc gained 39%, rising to 6.16 cents.

But the February–April bear squeeze was not the end of the rocky road for the French franc. In May 1924 the government of the more conservative *bloc national* was succeeded by the more left-wing and less stable *cartel de gauche*. The new government shook confidence in the franc because of (1) proposals for a capital levy, which encouraged French citizens to switch to other currencies; (2) deficit spending for the Riff war in Morocco; and (3) political instability —there were six finance ministers in 1925. The franc dropped 60% from 6.16 cents in April 1924 to 2.47 cents in July 1926. At this critical juncture, Poincaré, the former premier and wartime president, was able to form a strong government with broad financial powers,

Library
I.U.P.
Indiana, Pa.

332.45    K644g
c.1

including higher taxes. Confidence in the French franc revived. Between July and December 1926 the franc was up 60% to 3.95 cents, at which level it was de facto stabilized (later de jure in June 1928). Stabilization of the French franc at 3.95 cents was a victory for Moreau, then governor of the Bank of France, over Poincaré and President Doumergue, who wanted a higher parity closer to the prewar level. Moreau opposed a higher value of the franc, realizing that such a move would hurt France's competitive position.

For volatility—both up and down—among major currencies, the French franc from 1923 to 1927 would surely lead the league in the whole interwar period. Two questions arise: (1) Were the devaluations adverse for French prosperity? (2) Did other countries overreact with competitive devaluations in response to declines in the exchange rate of the French franc? The answer to the first question is no. To the second the answer is also no, except possibly for the Belgian devaluation of 1926. Between 1923 and 1927 French industrial production shows a close covariation with exchange rate devaluations. Industrial production was at a 5.7% average annual rate of increase between 1922 and 1927, and a closer look at the data, shown in Table 4, indicates on the whole a covariation —probably a correlation as well—between devaluation and rising industrial production, certainly when devaluation exceeded 10%. On the other hand, 1926–1927, the year of appreciation, showed a 10.9% decline in French industrial production.

How did other countries react to the French devaluation? Actually

**Table 4**

French revaluations (+) and devaluations (−) compared with industrial production: percentage increases (+) and decreases (−) in yearly averages, 1922-1927

|           | Exchange rates | Industrial production |
|-----------|----------------|-----------------------|
| 1922–1923 | − 25.9         | + 8.4                 |
| 1923–1924 | − 13.9         | + 23.8                |
| 1924–1925 | − 9.0          | − 3.1                 |
| 1925–1926 | − 32.0         | + 13.6                |
| 1926–1927 | + 21.0         | − 10.9                |

Source: U.S. Federal Reserve System, *Banking and Monetary Statistics*, 1943; Industrialization and World Trade (Geneva: League of Nations, 1945).

in the period between June 1922 and end-1926 among the Group of Ten, only Belgium and Italy had depreciating exchange rates. As the "Latin bloc," these nations had traditionally been tied to France. Germany, for the special reasons noted, had its currency virtually destroyed until 1924 when it was restabilized as the reichsmark at some 23.02 cents. All other currencies in the Group of Ten appreciated with respect to the dollar. Thus it remains to consider the Italian lira and the Belgian franc and how they performed in relation to the French franc. This tale is told in Table 5.

In every year from 1922 to 1926 when France devalued, Italy devalued less; when France appreciated in 1926–1927, Italy appreciated more, hardly symptomatic of "competitive devaluation." Similarly, in the 1922–1926 period, Belgium devalued 56.1% compared with 60.5% devaluation in France. However, in 1926–1927 when France appreciated 21.0%, Belgium again devalued by 15%. In 1935 Belgium would again adopt a strong devaluation. These actions were explicable by its small size and high dependence on exports. If this "competitive devaluation" may be hung on Belgium, that nation was certainly too small to have qualified the world as the site of the exchange war some have imagined to have occurred in the 1920s and 1930s.

Is France itself not the classic case of competitive devaluation that gave rise to the later obsession against that phenomenon? On the whole the French experience would seem not to qualify for that designation.

First it was obviously deeply involved with misconceptions relat-

**Table 5**

Exchange rate percentage depreciation (−) or appreciation (+); France, Italy, and Belgium, 1922–1927 (yearly averages)

|  | France, | Italy | Belgium |
|---|---|---|---|
| 1922–1923 | −25.9 | − 3.2 | −32.1 |
| 1923–1924 | −13.9 | − 5.3 | −11.0 |
| 1924–1925 | − 9.0 | − 8.7 | − 2.5 |
| 1925–1926 | −32.0 | − 2.2 | −31.2 |
| 1926–1927 | +21.0 | +32.6 | −15.0 |

Source: U.S. Federal Reserve System, *Banking and Monetary Statistics*, 1943.

ing to the capacity of German reparations to undo the excessive currency issue of World War I. When the reparations illusion vanished, it was obvious that the French currency must adjust, and the period at hand is in fact that adjustment. It will soon be seen that at a later period, from 1931 on, the French maintained a rigid and overvalued franc as leaders of the "gold bloc," with quite different results. Secondly, and more important, the French experience did not precipitate a round of competitive devaluations.

It is the countervailing rounds of devaluation that are feared in beggar-my-neighbor policy. If one nation alone devalues, or even if its devaluation is followed by that of one or two closely tied currencies, this can be symptomatic of needed adjustment; but it is hardly competitive devaluation rippling like a snake through the system. And this scenario seems to have characterized the French action in the period from 1922 to 1926.

Perhaps significantly it was France alone among the Group of Ten which consistently devalued its currency in the post–World War II period as well, during the heyday of the rigid exchange rate belief. Paradoxically, having devalued six times after World War II, as late as 1957, 1958, and 1969, the French became the greatest advocates of fixed rates and monetary orthodoxy. The conclusion is inescapable that French financial behavior is unique and has been so throughout. But the conclusion is also inescapable that French behavior did not, in the 1920s, precipitate the round of countervailing devaluation so feared.

## Britain's Return to the Gold Standard

In 1925, before the de facto stabilization of the French franc in 1926, Britain had returned to the gold standard; its currency was widely used as reserves by other countries, with an implicit understanding that sterling could be exchanged for gold. Thus the gold exchange standard had come into operation, based on the pound sterling as the reserve currency. In the 1922 Genoa Conference, most of the world had looked to England to return to the gold standard, so that this was a move favored by almost everyone. But Montagu Norman, then governor of the Bank of England, while anxious to return Britain to gold, had delayed because he believed that the pound should be restored to its prewar gold value; this might be difficult because United Kingdom prices had climbed above the United States levels. Norman's hand was forced, however, by developments outside Britain.

With the demise of the mark, it became evident to Britain and the United States that German reconstruction was a prerequisite for German reparations payments. In spite of French objections, the so-called Dawes loan to Germany was organized in 1924. The outlook for the German economy improved, and in October 1924 the new currency unit, the reichsmark, was stabilized in terms of gold.

The stabilization of the mark had been preceded by stabilization in Sweden, and there were reports that Holland and Switzerland would soon follow. The feeling grew that the worst of the postwar gyrations were over and stability would be restored. To the ruling classes, the gentlemen of the rentier class, this meant the possibility of restoring exchange rates to their prewar value so that their assets—mainly bonds—would also return to their traditional and pre–World War I value. Winston Churchill, then chancellor of the exchequer and a leading Conservative, of course shared this rentier view. In addition, however, he saw restored stability as a potential threat to British financial leadership in the world and especially in the empire. He feared the possibility that some currency other than the pound would become the reserve currency under the Genoa gold exchange standard, and that the banking and other invisible income as well as the prestige implicit in that position would be lost to Britain.

He sought to restore British financial and banking supremacy. The pound and gold would be tied, with the pound as a "universal money." Other currencies—notably the dollar—and other bankers would be forestalled from occupying this central role. As Churchill put it in a speech before Parliament (April 28, 1925):

> ... if we had not taken the action the whole of the rest of the British Empire would have taken it without us, and it would have come to a gold standard, not on the basis of the pound sterling, but a gold standard of the dollar.

Banking is a profitable business, the rentier class the backbone of the Conservatives, and the City important in London. But when the benefit of being a reserve currency is offset by the loss of industrial production and employment because of an overvalued currency, the costs to the rest of the country override the benefits. Nevertheless, this same scenario appeared again when sterling was overvalued in the 1950s and 1960s.

Keynes, in *The Economic Consequences of Mr. Churchill*, brilliantly attacked the return to the prewar gold sterling parity. He and a few others warned that an unrealistic exchange rate for sterling would lead to stagnating exports, low economic growth, and rising unemployment. But his, in those days, was still a maverick position. The return to gold was advocated by all parties, Conservative, Labour, and Liberal alike, and by a substantial majority of informed public opinion in the United Kingdom. Moreover, it had the full cooperation of monetary authorities in the United States and most of the rest of the world.

Nevertheless, it is now clear that the return of sterling to the prewar parity was one of the worst monetary mistakes of the twentieth century. Keynes' warnings were fully realized in six years of stagnation in the United Kingdom. To maintain the overvalued pound, the United Kingdom adopted a tight money policy. There was no significant change in currency circulation between 1925 and 1926. Wage reductions in 1926 led to the seven-month coal strike and the nine-day general strike. In the period 1925–1929 industrial production in the United Kingdom gained much less than in most other major countries. Among major countries the United Kingdom was lagged only by Italy (see Table 6).

**Table 6**

Percentage increases in industrial production, 1925–1929, major countries

| | |
|---|---|
| Japan | 46.9 |
| Belgium | 39.9 |
| Canada | 39.7 |
| Sweden | 33.8 |
| Netherlands | 32.1 |
| France | 24.8 |
| Germany | 23.6 |
| Switzerland | 23.0 |
| United States | 22.1 |
| United Kingdom | 16.2 |
| Italy | 15.4 |

Source: *Industrialization and World Trade* (Geneva: League of Nations, 1945).

After 1929 the effects of the overvalued pound were complicated by the Great Depression. Stagnation of the United Kingdom in the late 1920s was inevitable in view of the overvalued pound, but there were additional complications. Cotton exports suffered from the growth of Japanese textiles and the development of a domestic textile industry in India, which had formerly imported textiles from the United Kingdom.

Moreau had persuaded Poincaré to stabilize the franc at a probably undervalued level of 3.95 cents and successfully resisted efforts to raise the value of the franc to prewar levels. The French balance of payments improved, drawing gold and foreign exchange away from London. If the political background had been different, Moreau might have cooperated more closely with Norman to give the United Kingdom some relief from its gold outflow problem. But at that time political relations between France and England were strained over (1) United Kingdom advocacy of an easier policy on German reparations and (2) rivalries for financial leadership in eastern Europe. As in the 1960s, France used international monetary policy as a political and diplomatic weapon.

Stagnation of the British economy was a liability for the Conservative government; the unwillingness of the Bank of England to give out complete information on external claims against sterling raised further doubts. The Labour Party, under Ramsay MacDonald, came into office in June 1929. In November 1929, the famous Macmillan Committee was appointed to study Britain's international finances. The committee report, issued on July 23, 1931, announced that despite the enormous sacrifices Britain had made for financial solvency, it had more than a billion dollars of short-term liabilities to foreigners—several times as much as its gold reserves. This was against a background of bank failures in Austria and Germany which it was widely feared would spread to England. Although Britain borrowed over $400 million between July 23 and September 19 to defend the pound (by buying pounds in the foreign exchange markets), reserve losses in the same period were nearly $1 billion. More loans from abroad would have required guarantees that Britain reduce its budget deficit. Philip Snowden, the Labour chancellor of the exchequer, was ready to meet this requirement with a 10-percent cut in the dole to unemployed workers and reduced salary payments to government servants and the armed forces. But such actions against the already depressed unemployed ran counter to the social philosophy of a large faction of the Labour Party, led by the foreign minister, Arthur Henderson. The Labour government resigned on August 24, to be replaced by a coalition government under the same MacDonald and Snowden. Further attempts were made to cut public spending and secure loans from abroad. But the exchange rate had become a subject of public debate. On September 15 sailors of the Royal Navy raised a protest against pay cuts. This was widely reported as a mutiny and further shook confidence in sterling. Indeed, the spectacle of the Royal Navy sitting idle off Scotland in protest against pay cuts could hardly have had any other effect. On September 21, 1931, Britain allowed the pound to float. Its value in relation to the dollar declined 30 percent by the end of 1931.

In most of the world, England's abandonment of the gold standard was viewed as an unprecedented disaster. But, freed of the burden of an unrealistic exchange rate, the economic results in England were favorable. Between 1931 and 1936, United Kingdom manufacturing production climbed 44.5 percent. Much less progress was made in countries that went back to the gold standard.

Many have noted the parallels between Britain's inability to maintain convertibility in 1931 and that of the Americans 40 years later. Professor Robert Triffin argues this is inherent in the gold exchange system, and indeed had predicted events correctly because the system could lead nowhere else. Proposed reforms of the Bretton Woods system, to be discussed later, aim, inter alia, at replacing any single national currency with a new international money as the basic reserve. The Special Drawing Rights (SDRs), which are to serve this purpose, are not insignificantly called "paper gold."

The theory—myth is more appropriate—of competitive devaluation would require Britain's 1931 devaluation to result in much greater devaluations amongst its trading partners. The French-led gold bloc nations devalued not at all in consequence. Among nations related to sterling, only Japan's devaluation greatly exceeded Britain's, as Table 7 shows. Japan's cumulative depreciation was over

65% from 1930 to 1935, half again as great as the United Kingdom, Canada, Sweden, or, parenthetically, the United States.

But the Japanese devaluation was not necessarily an artificially induced one to promote exports to stimulate the economy, the second criterion of competitive devaluation. It was probably an equilibrium rate in view of the enormous import needs of Japan in the 1930–1935 period, when industrial production climbed 55%. The rise in Japanese output was not due to an export-led boom, but rather to government deficit expenditures, including a heavy component of armament outlays as the military in the 1930s became more influential. The national debt nearly doubled from 6 billion yen in 1931 to about 12 billion yen in 1937. Because Japanese labor was readily available and timid about asking for wage increases, the expansion of the economy in this period was achieved with no overall inflation from 1930 to 1935. As a result of the rapid expansion in output, however, the need for imports was very great. In spite of the hefty devaluation, the trade account was in deficit during all but two of the eight years between 1931 and 1938, as Table 8 shows. The need for imports to fuel the growth of the economy was accentuated in view of the rise in import prices compared with export prices. By 1937 the "terms of trade" ratio of Japanese import prices compared with export prices (1928 base) was up 65%.

It is thus concluded that Japan's devaluations in the 1930s were the consequence of its domestic expansionary policy, rather than an

**Table 7**

Annual percentage changes in currencies in relation to their gold parities, United Kingdom, Canada, Sweden, Japan, and the United States, 1930–1935

|           | U.K.   | Canada | Sweden | Japan  | U.S.   |
|-----------|--------|--------|--------|--------|--------|
| 1930–1931 | − 6.7  | − 3.5  | − 6.0  | − 1.1  | 0      |
| 1931–1932 | −22.7  | − 8.5  | −26.9  | −42.4  | 0      |
| 1932–1933 | − 5.4  | −16.9  | − 6.4  | −28.4  | −19.3  |
| 1933–1934 | − 9.3  | −17.8  | −10.4  | −11.9  | −26.1  |
| 1934–1935 | − 3.2  | − 1.8  | − 3.1  | − 3.9  | − 0.3  |
| 1930–1935 | −40.1  | −40.8  | −44.1  | −65.5  | −40.6  |

Source: U.S. Federal Reserve System, *Banking and Monetary Statistics*, 1943.

**Table 8**

Japanese foreign trade, 1931—1938 (millions of yen)

|      | Exports | Imports | Trade surplus (+) or deficit (−) |
|------|---------|---------|------------------------------------|
| 1931 | 1118    | 1206    | − 88                               |
| 1932 | 1362    | 1383    | − 21                               |
| 1933 | 1827    | 1883    | − 56                               |
| 1934 | 2134    | 2244    | −110                               |
| 1935 | 2454    | 2427    | + 27                               |
| 1936 | 2631    | 2702    | − 71                               |
| 1937 | 3125    | 3732    | −607                               |
| 1938 | 2668    | 2641    | + 27                               |

Source: *Statistical Yearbook of the League of Nations* (Geneva, League of Nations, 1940).

attempt to use competitive devaluation to spur the economy with a trade surplus. In fact it can be argued that the Japanese foreign exchange policy in the 1930s was one of the most reasonable. It avoided the deflationary policies seen in the United States in 1932, the rigid exchange rate policies of the gold bloc countries, and also the extreme exchange controls of Germany. Unfortunately the benefits of Japan's policy were used mainly in the military buildup, but this does not affect the validity of its economic methods for achieving its goals.

## FDR's Devaluation

After 1931, Britain was off gold—sterling floated, to Britain's economic advantage. Germany tightened the exchange controls that had already been imposed earlier in 1931. In the United States, discount rates were raised to stem the outflow of gold to buyers who could no longer obtain it in London, or who feared that the United States would follow the United Kingdom in devaluation, but who were still free to buy in the United States.

On the Continent the central bankers of France, Belgium, the Netherlands, Switzerland, and Italy looked at their balance sheets.

Most of them had taken losses, some quite heavy, from the devaluation of the sterling they had held under the gold exchange standard. The losses of the Netherlands Central Bank, for example, exceeded its entire capital. The bank was unable to convert its pounds into gold, its pounds were devalued, and the governor of the bank was forced to resign. In 1826 Canning had sent from the Foreign Office one of the classic dispatches of all time, which began:

> In matters of commerce the fault of the Dutch
> Is offering too little and asking too much.

In post-1931 London, a cruel paraphrase ran through the City:

> In matters of gold the fault of the Dutch
> Is asking too little and trusting too much.

Large losses were also incurred by the French, to whom the phrase "perfidious Albion" developed yet another and financial meaning.

It is therefore not surprising that in the 1950s and 1960s some countries have shown an enormous penchant for the accumulation of gold and have striven for an export surplus to acquire it. They have been quick and consistent to convert. The consequences of earlier history may be seen. One result has been an uneven distribution of gold among the nations' reserves. The United States in 1971, as the reserve center, had almost all its reserves in that metal, while Japan had only some 4.6 percent. The Europeans lie between these extremes. In round figures, in 1971, Holland had 62%, Belgium 56%, France 48%, Italy 4.%, Switzerland 42%, Germany 24%, and Sweden 20% of reserves in gold. Canada had some 15% and the United Kingdom less. These data are not precise in the sense that they measure gold as a percentage of certain reserves. Reserves can be defined with some elasticity, and a refined definition would change these percentages somewhat. Nevertheless the emphasis and the trend are quite clear. Some nations more than others, but almost all continental European nations, have taken gold very seriously, have operated within the IMF rules to acquire it, and are reluctant that it should be relegated to the status of a "barbarous relic," as many Anglo-Saxons, using Keynes' term have suggested.

In 1931 as now, the continental Europeans (except Germany,

which was already en route to the controls and isolation that were to characterize the whole Nazi period) focused more on gold. They formed (along with a few Eastern European nations) the "gold bloc" paced by France. The gold exchange standard was repudiated. They decided that—even if they had to skimp on reserves, limit imports, and slow economic growth—they would not be caught again holding someone else's depreciable currency, as they had been caught with devalued sterling. They would instead rely on gold alone as the reliable monetary reserve. And their prayers were that the United States would join them. If President Hoover, a believer in the gold standard, had been reelected in 1932, their prayers might have been answered. Before its defeat in 1932, the Hoover administration, following its orthodox impulses, condoned the Federal Reserve action in raising the discount rate. A later generation, steeped in monetarist or Keynesian rules of economic management, would see that action as horrendous in failing to be contracyclical. But in the early 1930s such ideas had not yet been formalized into "modern" theory, although deficit spending had been an established technique even in ancient Greece: Pericles built the Parthenon with public funds to absorb unemployed artisans, as well as for holier purposes.

The adverse effects on the United States economy of the rise in the discount rate and consequent tightening of the money supply have been described by Milton Friedman and Anna J. Schwartz in their *Monetary History of the United States, 1867–1960*. It is quite likely that the United States depression might have ended two years earlier if a more expansive monetary policy had been followed. As the money supply was reduced, banks were forced to demand liquidity when there was none, with ensuing rounds of bankruptcy, unemployment, bank failures, and incredible suffering.

Franklin Delano Roosevelt was elected in November 1932 and took office on March 4, 1933. Without delay, on March 6, 1933, the United States went off the gold standard via an embargo on gold, a prohibition on private holdings of gold, and, incidentally, a proclamation closing all banks—the famous "bank holiday." These were initially thought to be temporary measures, because the New Deal administration had not decided on an international currency policy. But the right of citizens to own monetary gold was prohibited from the enactment of the Emergency Banking Act in March 1933 up to the present. In 1973 a Senate committee would recommend the restoration of that right, against the advice of many economists.

This prohibition has perspective significance. In contrast to Europeans, Americans have not for 40 years seen or used gold or relied on it as a final store of value. Nor, to be fair, have Americans ever had to flee across a border, needing as refugees do some compact, universally acceptable medium of exchange in lieu of blocked or worthless currency. In both psychological and real terms, the metal is not the same in the Anglo-American and the European view.

Before the new United States government could make international monetary decisions, it was necessary to act upon decisions made under the previous administration. The Hoover administration had become convinced that world economic recovery depended on stabilization of exchange rates. Thus it was anxious to lead the World Economic Conference, scheduled for June 1933, to a new set of rigid exchange rates. Of paramount importance would be the "restoration of the gold standard in the key countries, England and Germany." This Hoover goal was welcomed eagerly by the gold bloc countries, which wanted company in their adherence to gold and consequent suffering from overvalued currencies. But alas for them, it was not Hoover but Roosevelt who sent the United States delegation, under Cordell Hull, to London with quite different ideas.

Sentimental internationalists who believed that a vaguely defined "international cooperation" would cure the Great Depression were loud in their criticism of Roosevelt for allegedly wrecking the World Economic Conference. But the gold bloc wanted only one kind of cooperation, to stabilize the dollar and sterling at levels that Roosevelt, overriding the advice of his more orthodox advisers, could not accept. He opposed even a watered-down resolution on currency stabilization, instead urging the conference to find other remedies, notably in trade liberalization and a synchronized program of government spending, to beat the Great Depression. But these ideas appealed to neither the gold bloc nor Britain's national government. Since the London conference had been publicized as a conclave to somehow bring back prosperity, its breakup was a widespread disappointment. It might have been a greater disappointment if the United States had allowed its monetary expansion, essential to whatever economic recovery did take place, to be hamstrung by the rigid ties of the gold standard.

In January 1934 Congress gave Roosevelt power to fix the value of the dollar, i.e., to devalue it in terms of gold. He devalued by 40.9 percent, setting the dollar price of gold at $35.00, up from $20.67 per ounce.

The overvalued gold bloc currencies thus became more overvalued. But Roosevelt's action was not inspired by a beggar-my-neighbor philosophy. Rather he was strongly influenced by the highly dubious theory of George F. Warren, professor of farm management at Cornell University, that raising the gold price would —by a mysterious, unexplored mechanism—raise prices generally. A key element in the early New Deal was to get prices up—witness the National Recovery Act (NRA) and the Agricultural Adjustment Act (AAA). Roosevelt's stated aim was the restoration of prosperity "by reestablishing the purchasing power of half the people," including, of course, the beleaguered farmers. John Blum's *From the Morgenthau Diaries* (pp. 69–70) is explicit:

> But Roosevelt, imperturbable, set his objectives for January 1st, 1934, as 10c. cotton, 50c. corn, 90c. wheat. To start to reach these prices he intended during the next week to raise gold to $33.02. His schedule called for putting the price on Monday up to $31.98 and then adding daily for five days 28c., 12c., 28c., 20c., and 16c. He considered this schedule sufficiently erratic to confuse speculators, sufficiently high to affect world gold and monetary prices.

Roosevelt stuck close to this plan, but on one of the days when there had been deviations from the intended price, he suggested 21c. Roosevelt remarked, "It is a lucky number because it is three times seven."

Morgenthau's comment on the chance number is often quoted by those anxious to denigrate Roosevelt:

> If anybody ever knew how we really set the gold price through a combination of lucky numbers, etc., I think they would be frightened.

Actually in a later passage, Morgenthau realized that Roosevelt had once again relieved a tense and grim moment by humor. But FDR had also, his frivolity notwithstanding, hewed closely to the plan he had set earlier, and he continued daily to raise the price.

Two further comments may be in order on Roosevelt's behavior in this period. His differences with the gold bloc were not merely differences in monetary theory. They were differences in the trade-offs among social values. Roosevelt wanted to raise American incomes and employment. To do this he was willing to take risks that there would be some losers in the money game. But the whole emphasis of the financial elite in the gold bloc countries (and in the United States where FDR was a "traitor to his class") was the preservation of capital. Income and employment were secondary values. Results of this perverse trade-off are still evident in sharper class cleavages in post–World War II France, and as Nicholas Davenport has argued in *The Split Society*, in the United Kingdom particularly, as a consequence of the 1925 return to gold.

It should be stressed that the United States devaluation did not produce beggar-my-neighbor effects, nor was it intended as a "competitive devaluation." United States imports climbed faster than United States exports from 1934 to 1937. This process might have continued if the 1937–1938 recession had not slowed United States import growth (see Table 9). A competitive devaluation, by definition, implies a will to increase a trade surplus in order to stimulate domestic income and employment at the expense of other nations. The stimulus for growth in the United States was from government spending and revived confidence of private investors. Without the devaluation, it is possible that the United States trade balance might have become a drag on United States growth in 1933–1936.

## The End of the Gold Bloc

With the devaluation of the dollar, the full burden of currency overvaluation shifted to the gold bloc countries. The story of economic stagnation in England, with an overvalued pound in 1925–1931, was repeated with minor variations in the gold bloc countries between 1931 and 1936. This bloc centered in France, and

**Table 9**

U.S. imports, exports, and trade balance, 1933–1938 (millions of dollars)

|       | Exports | Imports | Trade surplus (+) or deficit (−) |
|-------|---------|---------|------------------------------|
| 1933  | 1647    | 1433    | + 214                        |
| 1934  | 2100    | 1636    | + 464                        |
| 1935  | 2243    | 2039    | + 204                        |
| 1936  | 2419    | 2424    | − 5                          |
| 1937  | 3299    | 3010    | + 289                        |
| 1938  | 3057    | 1950    | +1107                        |

Source: *Statistical Yearbook of the League of Nations* (Geneva: League of Nations, 1940).

its important members were Italy, Switzerland, and Benelux, as well as some East European adherents—but not Germany.

In the 1925–1931 period the gold bloc countries had undervalued currencies; in spite of the Great Depression, they showed remarkable growth in manufacturing production. On the other hand, countries moving more or less in line with sterling—the United Kingdom, Canada, Japan, and the Scandinavian countries—showed significant stagnation or less than their full growth potential. The opposite applied in 1931–1936, when the gold bloc currencies were overvalued and the currencies moving with sterling were undervalued.

All of the major countries in the gold bloc showed declining rates of growth in industrial production in the years when their currencies remained overvalued. On the other hand, the United Kingdom and the countries that devalued had higher rates of economic growth in 1931–1936 compared with the 1925–1931 period when their currencies were overvalued. These comparisons can be seen in Table 10.

In France the 1931–1936 scenario was, in its early stages, similar to that in the United Kingdom in 1925–1931. With an overvalued franc, overseas markets were lost. Where import controls were not applied, domestic industries faced severe competition from imports;

Table 10

Average annual percentage changes in industrial production

|  | 1925–1931 | 1931–1936 |
|---|---|---|
| Sterling related currencies |  |  |
| United Kingdom | – 0.8 | + 7.6 |
| Canada | + 1.6 | + 3.8 |
| Sweden | + 4.7 | + 7.0 |
| Japan | + 4.4 | + 10.9 |
| Gold bloc currencies |  |  |
| France | + 1.2 | – 1.1 |
| Belgium | + 1.3 | + 0.8[a] |
| Netherlands | + 3.5 | + 0.9 |
| Italy | – 1.3 | – 2.4[b] |
| Switzerland | – 1.2 | – 3.9 |

[a]1931–1935: Belgium devalued in 1935.

[b]1931–1934: Italy adopted exchange control in 1934.

Source: *Industrialization and World Trade* (Geneva: League of Nations, 1945).

tourist earnings suffered. But even more so than in England in 1925–1931, there was almost no support for devaluation. The French were convinced—quite erroneously but to England's benefit—that devaluation of the franc would result in inflation and loss of asset values, as in World War I. But more important, the French were so bemused by maintaining the tie of the franc to gold that they were willing to suffer the consequences. All the major political parties, from the Communists to the far right, wanted a stable franc. All economic classes (incl. ding exporters) opposed a franc devaluation. The only significant exception was Paul Reynaud, a right-wing politician, who was largely ignored.

But toward the close of the period of overvaluation, in France as in England, attitudes changed. Stagnation in the British economy in 1925–1931 had been a key element in the success of the Labour Party in the 1929 election. Likewise in France, the more left-wing Popular Front government under Léon Blum was brought into power in the election of May 1936. Although in the election campaign Blum had opposed devaluation of the franc, he found it unavoidable; in

October 1936 the franc was devalued 26.4 percent. But the damage of long years of stagnation had taken its toll in sharp social divisions within France. Sit-down strikes and widespread labor unrest led to higher wages and shorter working hours, which nullified the benefits of the Blum devaluation. In 1937 the franc was again under pressure, and Blum resigned. The Chautemps government that followed permitted the franc to float. But if France was mesmerized by the idea of fixity from 1931–1936, at least it learned. For never again, as is clearly demonstrated by its policies after World War II, did France follow a policy of excessive exchange rate rigidity. More than any country since 1945, it has used devaluation to achieve economic and political ends while urging stability on others, with no sentimental nonsense about the glories of the franc.

In April 1937 a more conservative government under Daladier came into power. In November he appointed Reynaud, the early advocate of devaluation, minister of finance. Daladier and Reynaud again devalued the franc and, in May 1938, tied it to sterling. This, however, became a formality with the coming of World War II and the adoption of exchange controls in most of the belligerent countries.

Had competitive devaluation really existed, one would expect to see other countries in the gold bloc devaluing during the 1935–1939 period to a greater extent than France. However, none did so, as Table 11 shows. Italy, Holland, and Switzerland devalued to a lesser extent. Belgium, which had devalued in 1935 as well, might be considered the exception, but it is too small a country to have made a substantial difference to world trade. Nor did the sterling connected countries, in consequence of French action, undertake countervailing, greater depreciations, as the beggar-my-neighbor theory would hold with respect to exchange rates. Table 11 again is explicit. An overall view of the movement of exchange rates between the wars is presented in Chart 1.

**Chart 1**

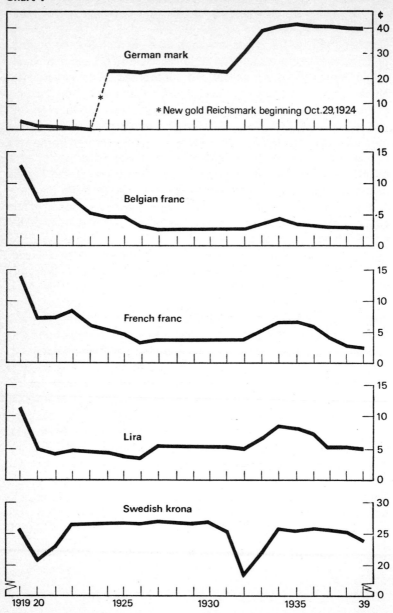

German mark

*New gold Reichsmark beginning Oct. 29, 1924

Belgian franc

French franc

Lira

Swedish krona

1919 20          1925          1930          1935          39

Source: Based on League of Nations and Federal Reserve
Board statistics.

# Foreign exchange rates between the wars
### (In U.S. cents per unit, yearly averages)

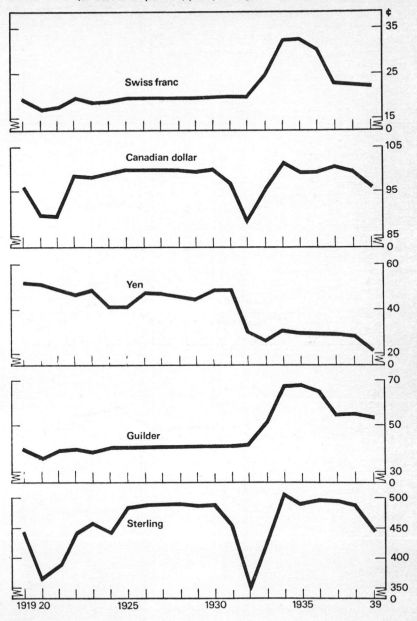

**Table 11**

Major percentage changes in the currencies of the Group of Ten: yearly averages in relation to the U.S. dollar, 1935–39

|  | France | Italy | Belgium | Netherlands | Switzerland | Canada | Sweden | Japan | U.K. |
|---|---|---|---|---|---|---|---|---|---|
| 1935–36 | – 7.4 | –11.6 | –8.2 | – 4.8 | – 7.1 | 0.4 | 1.4 | 1.1 | 1.4 |
| 1936–37 | –33.8 | –27.9 | –0.2 | –14.6 | –24.0 | 0.1 | –0.5 | –0.7 | –5.4 |
| 1937–38 | –28.9 | 0 | 0.1 | – 0.1 | – 2.9 | –0.6 | –1.1 | –1.2 | –1.1 |
| 1938–39 | –12.8 | – 1.2 | –0.3 | – 3.0 | – 1.5 | –3.4 | –4.8 | –8.7 | –9.3 |

Source: U.S. Federal Reserve System, *Banking & Monetary Statistics*, 1943.

# 4.
# Some
# Conclusions

an the somewhat dizzying array of events and numbers that are required to portray the interwar years be pulled into some conclusions? If, as we have argued, the period was not characterized by competitive devaluation, what was going on? Why has it been misinterpreted?

To analyze the period broadly, a reiteration of the symptoms of competitive devaluation may be useful: A devaluation in one major country is followed deliberately by a *greater* devaluation in a "competing" major country, with a resulting increase in the trade surplus (and possibly reserve position) of the follower.

Bearing the criteria in mind, the dramatis personae of the interwar years amongst the nations comprising the Group of Ten are the following:

1. The group of countries linked to and moving with the British, including Canada, Japan, and Sweden.
2. The gold bloc countries moving in concert with France, including Italy, Benelux, and Switzerland.
3. Germany, whose role was unique and tragic, with massive inflations, devaluations, and reparations problems in the early 1920s. After 1931, Germany became increasingly isolated and con-

trolled, at first concerned with domestic recovery and later with war preparations—the prelude to destruction by 1945.

4. The United States, which also played a somewhat lone hand—in the immediate postwar years by abandoning the gold system rules, and after 1932 by the efforts of President Roosevelt to reflate the domestic economy.

In a real sense, the major protagonists in the interwar years were the first two blocs, based on England and France respectively. Prior to 1931 there is no evidence whatever of a desire to devalue at all, let alone for competitive reasons. On the contrary the drive in both blocs is to reestablish a gold parity for its currency close to the prewar level, and to return to the prewar gold standard. Both blocs could agree to establish a replica of the gold standard in the Genoa Conference. Prior to 1925, the French are frustrated in their desire to appreciate their currency by the events in Germany: The reparations payments that were to have reestablished the gold basis to the franc, inflated by World War I printings, could not be paid by Germany. It was the United Kingdom therefore, less inflated than France by World War I and less dependent on reparations, that was first able to appreciate its currency, return to gold, and become the reserve currency of the gold exchange system in 1925. Churchill, then chancellor of the exchequer, was eager to do so lest another currency be first. But the debate in France makes it clear that from 1923 to 1927 the maintenance of the value of the franc was the highest goal of French financial policy.

The modern mind finds this effort to return to prewar parity hard to understand. The dominant concern of the post–World War II generation is with the effects of the exchange rate on income and employment. If devaluation means more exports, more jobs, more income, is this not good? To understand the interwar years, the contemporary mind must understand the interwar values. And except for mavericks or radicals like Roosevelt or Keynes, the dominant motif in the interwar years was not welfare but rather the restoration of the value of capital assets.

If a gentleman of the rentier class had a bond worth 100 francs (or pounds) earning 4 francs (or pounds) per year fixed interest, and the

World War I printing-press inflation raised prices so that 300 francs was needed to buy what 100 francs had previously bought, the gentleman was impoverished or wiped out. The value of the bond, or any similar capital asset, and its respective yields were reduced in purchasing power. The bondholders and asset owners were, in an interwar society still much closer to its Victorian origin than to the modern world, the wielders of power. Politicians might represent, or be recruited from, one or another wing of asset owners, but their concern was with the interests of the propertied classes above all others. The politicization of the masses, the primacy of concern for mass employment and income, phenomena that the contemporary mind no longer considers radical or even terribly liberal but rather the common goal of all parties, had not yet come.

The restoration of the values of fixed-income securities, damaged by inflation, was identified in the interwar period with pushing down inflated prices and pushing up depreciated currencies. Today a discussion of exchange rates leads almost immediately to an analysis of trade and balance of payments. This was not the main line of thought in the 1920s and 1930s. Then, because of the wartime and early postwar experience, exchange rate depreciation was intellectually tied to inflation on an almost one-to-one basis. The leading—now almost forgotten—theory of exchange rate determination was "purchasing power parity": As prices in a country rise relative to world prices, its currency will depreciate. Conversely, the restoration of a currency parity, or at least the stabilization of a parity, would enforce discipline against inflation and perhaps even force down relative prices—as Britain had done in the early 1920s. Thus rigid exchange rates were viewed as the guardian of price stability and consequently of the real income of the rentier class.

The drive to restore the franc or pound to its prewar parity was therefore a drive to restore the value of capital assets. Nor was this a case of simple economic royalism, as FDR called it. Never before in modern history had inflation wiped out the savings of the rich and the middle class, or indeed the savings of any class. This shocking state of affairs had to be temporary, to be overcome as soon as possible. When, during World War I, French politicians had promised the restoration of asset values (restoration of the prewar value of the franc) to be paid for by German reparations, they meant it. They believed this could be accomplished and had their own experience after Bismarck in 1871 as precedent. Hence the effort to collect reparations earlier described, which now appears so obviously self-defeating.

Inflation hedges in property, stock markets, depreciable oil, or cattle assets, now standard concepts to savers, are the result of inflations that Europe, and especially France, witnessed for the first time after World War I. Fixed securities bearing interest, the classic victims of inflation, were still the classic forms of savings. To restore the currency meant to restore their value.

In *The Economic Consequences of Mr. Churchill,* Keynes had argued that the 1925 restoration of the pound to its prewar parity would entail deflation, depressed wages and prices, strikes, and a permanent contraction of Britain's heavy industries. He therefore favored continued fluctuating exchange rates and the maintenance of wages. But this view was before its time. By 1931, Britain's industrial production index stood at 80% of the 1924 base of 100, down from a 1929 high of 113. After the pound was again floated in 1931, the index rose to 88 by the end of 1931, to 90 by 1932, to 127 by 1935, and employment rose with it. Small wonder that the view of Keynes was to conquer England, to use his phrase, as the Inquisition had conquered Spain.

England had not devalued (or floated) competitively in 1931; it had been forced off gold by its inability to continue conversion, i.e., by overvaluation. And in 1931, the "poison cup" of overvaluation passed to France and the gold bloc. By 1936, in consequence, French production stood depressed at 93% of its 1931 base of 100. And it was in this period, to protect the overvalued franc, that import tariffs were increased by France, and quotas and other trade restrictions adopted on some 60% of its imports. Other countries soon retaliated. With the election of the Popular Front government of Léon Blum in 1936 and the consequent devaluations, the link of the franc to gold was broken. After 1937, French output began to rise.

The classic review of this period is Ragnar Nurkse's *International Currency Experience—Lessons of the Interwar Period,* published in 1944 by the League of Nations. Nurkse concludes that as each currency floated off gold, this "was followed by a domestic expansion of investment and national income." Nor was this evidence of competitive devaluation at someone else's expense.

Countries with depreciated currencies increased their exports, mainly to other countries with depreciated currencies. This was a natural result of the expansion of production and money income which accompanied devaluation. ... Any export gains obtained by devaluation at the expense of countries that had not yet devalued were short lived and relatively unimportant. (pp. 129–130)

In each case, he found this tended "to stimulate foreign trade all around." Moreover, after all the rounds of currency devaluations, the relations of currencies were not very different from before, as shown below by Nurkse's data. The conclusion is inescapable that had there been floating currencies in the interwar years, rather than successive attempts to preserve overvaluation, the net result would have been expanded world trade and employment. Nurkse has this table, showing exchange rates in relation to the dollar, on page 129 of his book:

|         | 1930 | 1932 | 1934 | 1936 |
|---------|------|------|------|------|
| Britain | 100  | 67   | 102  | 101  |
| France  | 100  | 100  | 168  | 119  |
| Italy   | 100  | 100  | 162  | 100  |
| Sweden  | 100  | 67   | 95   | 94   |
| Belgium | 100  | 100  | 168  | 119  |

Parenthetically Nurkse notes that in the 1930s (as now) "dirty floats"—interventions by the central banks to distort the true, i.e., market-determined, value of a currency for some political reason —were prevalent.

But *freely* [emphasis in original] fluctuating exchanges were by no means common. The changes were either controlled, or, after brief intervals of uncontrolled fluctuations. were followed by a measure of stabilization at a new level." (p. 210)

The difficulty of the 1930s, Nurkse suggests, lay in lack of proper and hopefully coordinated monetary policies among the nations, a conclusion that would still be relevant:

If the leading industrial nations had initiated, by whatever methods ... a simultaneous policy of monetary expansion in, say, the spring of 1931, they would probably have had little difficulty in keeping their mutual exchange rates stable. (p. 130)

Nurkse's final chapter, in which he espouses fixed exchange rates, is often cited by those who support fixity, and was said to be influential in the Bretton Woods planning. One of Nurkse's objections to fluctuating rates was the cost, "if obtainable at all," of forward market hedging, i.e., insurance against loss from currency fluctuations, which "adds to the cost of trading." But perhaps the most significant development of the late 1960s and early 1970s has been precisely a good forward market, the cost of which is in fact relatively very little. Indeed currency fluctuations of the 1970s have been acceptable to, and even popular with, businessmen for this reason. One wonders whether Nurkse's conclusions might have differed had there been developed forward markets when he wrote.

The importance of restoring bond or other asset values as a primary motive in the continuous struggle to revalue currencies to prewar levels has been emphasized—perhaps too often—in these pages to compensate for the fact that it is so often neglected in other analyses of this time. There is a tendency to project contemporary motives back to the past.

But the interwar years can be seen clearly only if the motives then dominant are recalled. Similarly it is too easy to forget the political importance of the asset holders and the relative weakness of the new (at the time) views of Keynes and FDR. In contemporary times, full employment and economic growth have been accepted as the overriding priority by all governments and by all political parties. But this was not so in the interwar years. And in emphasizing these motives it is not suggested that they were the sole motives. Certainly Churchill's desire to restore world supremacy to the pound—and with it, to British banking—was important in his 1925 decision. Similar considerations of prestige affected French policy decisions. A strong currency then, as now, was considered a strength in international esteem. But these motives—the preservation of assets, the esteem of a strong currency, the banking income—all militated in favor of overvalued currencies. Certainly devaluations occurred, but they were usually forced on the country by external circumstances and were not willful acts. Nor is there any evidence from the foregoing of competitive devaluations, i.e., deliberate undercuttings of a competitor's exchange rate in order to increase the trade surplus.

It therefore follows that a second reason for the misinterpretation of interwar history, for the insistence that the period was plagued, and the depression worsened, by competitive devaluations, was lack of history itself. A clearer view of 1919–1939 might have emerged if more economic history had been written. But since 1939 and the outbreak of war, most economists have been occupied with the complications of economic policy, with such immediate concerns as reconstruction and monetary stabilization of domestic economies. Newer methods of demand analysis or econometrics or model building consumed the energies of the bright young men of the field. Studies of financial history, never numerous, were neglected. In some major universities, economic history vanished as a discipline or was consigned to part of the general study of history by scholars whose economic sophistication was limited.

In part this represents the belief widely held among the younger economists that the past in any case was a comedy of errors, too ridiculous to merit study, from which lessons should certainly not be drawn, and unlikely to repeat itself now that we know so much more. The idea that the interwar years had been consumed by, and reeked with, competitive devaluations was accepted as an article of faith, and never seriously reexamined. On this faulty historic assumption, sophisticated superstructures were built. Those who accepted it, when pressed, usually refer to the Nurkse study cited earlier. Yet another reading of Nurkse indicates that while he supported fixed exchange rates, he did not support the competitive devaluation thesis. On the contrary, his statement that devaluations resulted in greater trade with other countries that were expanding because they had also devalued, or because they were engaged in what Keynes called "expansion under the aegis of public investment," seems a patent denial of the competitive devaluation thesis.

Nurkse is often cited as the source of the antipathy to exchange rate flexibility amongst Bretton Woods planners. And this in itself is rather strange, for his book appeared in 1944, the year of Bretton

Woods, well after the various plans for discussion there had been prepared by the British Treasury group under Keynes, or by its American counterpart, or by others. It is unlikely that Nurkse's views could have sunk in so deeply and so rapidly. This is particularly true since his views by no means support the thesis that the thread of competitive devaluations runs through the debacle of the interwar years.

Increasingly there is a tendency toward revisionist history of the interwar years as it becomes apparent that these years again are being used as a horrible example of what might happen with more flexible rates. Those who feel that flexible rates are the essence of reform are in this sense forced to think through the lessons of the interwar years far more than those who rely on the conventional wisdom that cites their shortcomings. Revisionist views of the interwar years are beginning to appear, particularly in newspapers and other journals where publication follows fast upon the writing. For example, the *Wall Street Journal* of March 21, 1973, carries a thoughtful piece titled "The Current Uneasiness of Business" by Alfred Malabre Jr.

> Visions of the 1930s era, with its unsettled currency rates and its beggar-thy-neighbor economic policies, cannot be totally disregarded. . . . But, we submit, the likelihood of a 1930-style scenario remains exceedingly remote. . . . Against the background of Mr. Nurkse's study of the 1930s, today's situation begins to take on a startlingly new and far from distressing appearance. It can be argued that the time of "maximum danger" when governments struggled to preserve fixed rates for their currencies is already behind us.
>
> Indeed, if the current monetary situation does contain a serious danger, the record of the 1930s suggest that danger isn't today's unstuck currency exchange rates. Rather, it would appear to be the possibility that governments, including the United States government, may intervene too strenuously in coming months to "stabilize" rates. (p. 20)

Malabre assigns this danger more specifically to central bankers in what he calls a cynical view.

> One may presume, for instance, that central bankers tend to be energetic fellows, eager to have work to do and power to exert. Obviously, such people might regard as relatively unappetizing a monetary system in

which central bank intervention to fix a currency's value is rarely practiced, or practiced not at all.

Doubtless other scholars will contest the views we have put forward in this section and those of Malabre as well. And if this leads to a realistic appraisal of what actually happened in the 1930s, that will be all to the good.

A third reason for misinterpreting the interwar years and seeking surcease in fixed exchange rates from the woes of that time flowed from the views purveyed by some of the latter-day Keynesians, often more zealous and less judicious than the master, as disciples tend to be. No one expressed these views better than Joan Robinson.

In times of general unemployment a game of beggar-my-neighbour is played between the nations, each one endeavouring to throw a larger share of the burden upon the others. As soon as one succeeds in increasing its trade balance at the expense of the rest, others retaliate, and the total volume of international trade sinks continuously, relative to the total volume of world activity. Political, strategic and sentimental considerations add fuel to the fire, and the flames of economic nationalism blaze ever higher and higher.

... The principal devices by which the balance of trade can be increased are (1) exchange depreciation, (2) reductions in wages (which may take the form of increasing the hours of work at the same weekly wage), (3) subsidies to exports, and (4) restriction of imports by means of tariffs and quotas.

The very fact that the modern Keynesians' model could envision the use of competitive devaluation as a device to score off one's neighbors led them to project back onto the statesmen of the 1930s these motives. Put differently, the false vision, based on models which never existed, to explain the years 1919–1939 fitted only too well into the analytic schemes fresh from the drawing boards of the new breed of model builders. The concept of competitive currency depreciation fitted the Keynesian theory of income and employment, and it also fitted the theory of oligopoly as well. The idea of declining exports postulated to arise from some other country's devaluation was an extension of the multiplier theory. The idea of retaliation of exchange rate cutting was cast in the image of modern duopoly.

Such a logically beautiful concept simply had to exist; if the facts were otherwise, the facts had to be related to the model.

There was no need to prod traditional conservatives—not those of the Chicago School variety but those who disliked change simply because it was change. These conservative views, now strengthened by those of the latter-day Keynesians, became (from both sides, so to speak) the apparatus with which students were trained. The idea that the interwar years had to be unstable because of competitive devaluation fitted both sets of prejudices, despite the fact that many elements of Keynes's own thought had militated otherwise.

This combination of views, taken in conjunction with the fact that no one had bothered to look at the interwar history for a very long time, served to create a bogeyman which had the net effect of arguing against flexible rates—for very much the wrong reasons.

The myth that competitive devaluation prevailed in the 1930s is so great that the most astute students of economics—even the best proponents of flexible exchange rates—slip into it. Thus Harry Johnson, writing in the University of Chicago *Journal of Business* (January 1973) on the "International Monetary Crisis of 1971" says:

> ... the major countries were forced one by one to recognize a choice between domestic deflation of incomes and employment and the attempt to avoid deflation either by devaluating their currencies and passing the burden of unemployment on to other countries ... or by imposing restrictions on their imports and subsidizing their exports. Both were "beggar-my-neighbor" policies, in Joan Robinson's famous phrase ...

The time has come to set the record straight, even if in the course of doing so new models must be built. The world is still haunted by the specter of the depression, turmoil, and, ultimately, fascism of the interwar years. It is a history no one wishes to repeat. But if we are to gain new insights from this period, it should be recognized that its ills arose not from competitive devaluation but rather from three glaring errors of the era. First, the reparations policy against Germany, which set the period on a disastrous path from which it never recovered. Second, the failure of governments to use fiscal and monetary policy, optimally coordinated internationally, to achieve and maintain high levels of employment. Third, the adherence to rigid exchange rates and the repeated push to overvalued currency levels, by the United Kingdom in 1925 and France in 1931.

The world has learned that two policies, reparations and rigid adherence to balanced budgets, are now defunct. But the world is indecisive and ambivalent about exchange rate rigidity, for which reason this question continues to loom large in the sections to follow.

# The Rise and Fall of the Bretton Woods System

# 5.
# The
# Bare Bones
# of Bretton Woods

he end of World War II found the American economy strengthened, operating at full capacity with great efficiency, producing and using leading technologies. In contrast, most of the belligerent countries were destroyed in varying degrees, Germany and Japan most visibly, and all were hungry for goods available almost exclusively from the United States. The American balance of payments position reflected this strength. In the four-year period 1946–1949, the United States trade surplus—the excess of its exports over imports—totaled no less than $32 billion. Through the Marshall Plan and other aid and loans, the United States disbursed some $26 billion in this period; this still left a net surplus of some $6 billion, which was added to American reserves largely in the form of such gold as remained to the former belligerents.

The Americans were well aware of this strength before the war's end. American initiative had laid plans for a United Nations, the parliament of man, to commence functioning immediately peace should be restored. The financial wings of the United Nations, planned at the Bretton Woods, New Hampshire, conference of 1944, were to be the International Monetary Fund (IMF) with which these pages are centrally concerned. In addition there would be the International Bank for Reconstruction and Development (IBRD, or later "World Bank") and, relatedly, the General Agreement on Trades and Tariffs (GATT). Like the UN, the IMF included developed and developing nations, but uniquely the IMF weighted voting strength by initial subscription, so that about two-thirds of the votes were controlled by the industrialized nations, later to be known as the Group of Ten (G-10), and the majority of these by the combined votes of the United States and the United Kingdom.

Histories and treatises on the IMF and the Bretton Woods system abound. It is not the intention here to repeat history but rather to interpret it, focusing on the thrust and purpose of the Bretton Woods system in a perspective view. Seen in hindsight, it would appear that Bretton Woods was a system that never, or hardly ever, worked. And this is surprising, for under its aegis the free world has prospered as it had not since the pre–World War I gold standard days. The fact is, however, that the prosperous path on which the postwar world was set reflects much the same force as had characterized the pre-1914 world. A new money machine—this time the flow of dollar and gold deficits from the United States, and to a lesser extent from the United Kingdom—fostered a growth of exports and a rise of liquidity in the other G-10 nations that fueled their recuperation and growth. Before this machine could operate, massive currency depreciations against the dollar were required; these were completed (except for France) by 1949. And the basis for this massive growth abroad took place in the first phase of Bretton Woods, to 1958, a period here called the "beneficial disequilibrium" during which the rules of the system were virtually suspended by general agreement. This suspension permitted the recuperating nations to employ exchange controls and a variety of lapses from free trade and investment—the purpose of Bretton Woods.

After 1958, the system may be said to have been operative in a period here called "revelation." By this time the basic disequilibrium of the system was already evident. Massive and alarming gold flows from the United States began; the system operated under an increasing sense of unease and with controls and props instituted in the United States itself. The final phase, disintegration, commenced about 1965 and ended in 1971 with the suspension of gold convertibility and with floating exchange rates, not unlike the fate of the gold exchange system under British leadership in 1931.

The bare bones of the Bretton Woods system will not be unfamiliar, for in essence the planners opted to restore the gold exchange system devised in Genoa in 1922 and operative from 1925 to 1931. Thus tired old gold became again the backbone of the new system. Each nation was to hold its reserves in this metal, but also in a reserve currency, which would be freely convertible to gold. The dollar was of course the major reserve currency, although the pound continued to be used by some countries, mainly in the British Commonwealth. The value of the dollar was set in terms of gold at $35 per ounce, and the value of each major currency was set in terms of the dollar, with a definable—if derivative—gold content.

The Bretton Woods planners understandably wanted to rectify the horrors of the 1930s. Believing that competitive devaluations had been the bête noire of that era, with more fervor than historic justice they opted, in both rules and spirit, for fixed exchange rates. But the rules, thanks largely to Keynes' insistence, also permitted the right to devalue if needed to a new "peg," 10 percent freely and additional amounts with IMF concurrence. The rules even contained a "scarce currency clause," providing legitimated tariff punishment for nations that had a persistent surplus and should have revalued but failed to do so.

Keynes had also proposed that "bancor" (bank gold) be issued as the central reserve unit, rather than gold or any national currency; at the outset American treasury officials put forward a similar plan, based on "unitas." Both ideas would have moved away from the gold exchange system, possibly in memory of the fact that the system had failed initially when the quality of the currency (the pound at that time) became suspect as the quantity outstanding outran the gold backing. But to many it seemed inconceivable then that this chain of events could ever overtake the dollar, based on the powerful American economy and its technological superiority. This early arrogance was the particular province of members of Congress, who intervened in the planning, overriding the Treasury and of course Keynes, whom they saw as a wily British debtor. Later, in the 1960s, the Special Drawing Rights plan would in many respects reconstruct

Keynes' bancor vision, but only after Bretton Woods had paralleled in its failure the earlier gold exchange system.

Fixed but movable exchange rates were thus to prevent competitive devaluations like those widely (but erroneously) believed to have dominated the 1930s. The GATT rules against discriminatory tariffs were to prevent the misuse of those devices to beggar one's neighbor. Greater tariff or quota reductions and the elimination of nontariff barriers were to be left to future agreements, some of which have taken place in the Dillon and Kennedy rounds of negotiations, with more to be discussed starting September 1973. Freedom of capital movements was never spelled out fully; the Havana Charter of 1948, which attempted to do so, proved abortive.

If the purpose and working of reserves is understood, the outline of the system is complete. The rational purpose of reserves for a nation is rather like savings for an individual; they provide needed liquidity for a rainy day. The nation's rainy day arrives when it incurs a deficit in international payments. Then the supply of its currency in the foreign exchange markets exceeds the demand for it. If supply and demand forces were free, the price (or par value) of its currency would fall (devalue) to clear the market. But the fixed exchange rules provided further that no nation could allow its currency to fall (or rise) more than 1 percent from its par value, i.e., its relation to the dollar. If the supply-demand forces threatened a price change beyond this narrow band, the nation must "intervene"—i.e., buy back its currency from the market with its reserves of dollars or gold until the supply-demand price again comes within the permissible band. And if that reserve proved inadequate, credits were available from the IMF to assist, up to a limit; later the General Agreement to Borrow would supplement IMF credits, particularly for Britain, to keep the pound from devaluing and keep the rigid exchange rate system alive. There is an irrational aspect of reserves as well: their acquisition and hoarding as dollars or gold, beyond any conceivably needed working balances.

Obviously the dollar was different, or "asymmetrical," in the jargon. An excess of dollars in foreign hands was met by the convertibility route; excess dollars were "bought back" by the United States with its large gold reserve, as long as that lasted. Since the expectation, especially of congressmen, was for perpetual American surpluses, any danger to the gold hoard seemed academic in the 1940s and through most of the 1950s. The burden of adjustment must fall on deficit nations. They must use reserves to buy back their currencies pending deeper adjustments, including induced recession to reduce their income and their relative costs and prices, to import less, export more, and come back to equilibrium or surplus. Interest rate manipulation could also be effective; if raised, interest rates would not only slow the rate of economic growth but also attract foreign deposits and investments, thus helping the balance of payments. If nations other than the United States ran surpluses, they faced no adjustment problems. Surplus and virtue were increasingly equated, and the "scarce currency clause" never used.

In the course of time, with no change in the rules, the idea grew that devaluation was symptomatic of weakness or poor economic management. The British devaluation of 1967 was considered a major defeat after a long and costly battle to avoid it. Even the IMF, meant to administer the Bretton Woods rules, urged members against devaluation. Except for France, which devalued six times in the post–World War II period, others tried desperately to avoid this route. At the same time the maintenance of full, even overfull, employment became a priority goal, making internal adjustment even more difficult.

The dollar became a true universal currency, never replaced even during its time of trouble in the 1970s. It was used to settle accounts among private traders or manufacturers, who turned all or part of their dollars into their banks for local currencies. The remainder they retained as deposits in the United States, abroad, or later in Eurodollars. From the exporters and banks, dollars eventually found their way to the central banks, the residual holders, as reserves or for intervention purposes, or to exchange for gold. In part the dollar's universal acceptance and use bespoke confidence; even when confidence waned in the 1960s, there was no alternative transaction, intervention, or investment currency to replace it.

Rules and administration apart, two other broad perceptions characterize Bretton Woods. First, it was a national system. Each nation adjusted against each other nation, primarily through the trade balance. The idea of integration through direct investment of the international corporations or through the Eurodollar markets could not have played a part in Bretton Woods thinking, as such things hardly existed in the 1940s. Nor did the system envision a Common Market or European currency. Second, and more important, Bretton Woods was an equilibrium system. Equilibrium is a central and deceptively simple concept. Defined most simply, it has been called a state which if attained will be maintained. The analogy to celestial physics is apparent. It has both a national and international context.

To be in equilibrium a nation ideally would have a net zero balance. It should have neither surplus nor deficit over any extended period. The total of its payments—its outgo for imports, tourism, aid, military expenditures abroad, foreign investment—all the things for which a nation's citizens and its government spend abroad, should just equal the amount that foreigners spend in it. Since the two —income and expenditures—are rarely if ever equal, reserves are used to tide a nation over when its income is below its outgo. But eventually income and expenditures must match; adjustment mechanisms equilibrate income and outgo. An asymmetry exists as a deficit country must adjust lest the reserve kitty runs out, but a surplus country is really under no such pressure and is indeed at some unconscious level considered successful and virtuous. To be sure, a surplus can be inflationary, but internal offsets such as higher taxes, steps to increase savings, or monetary policy are available.

Basically, the adjustment mechanism for the deficit country consists of cost-price reduction of its goods (or, more realistically, a rate of inflation slower than that of its trading partners). Action to depress its economy is required—measures which will have a price effect and an incomes effect, lowering both relatively. Recession may also be induced by raising interest rates, thereby theoretically attracting capital flows and further assisting the balance of payments position. The more serious is the nation's commitment to full employment and growth, the more difficult the steps. If all these steps fail, "fundamental disequilibrium" exists, and the currency might be devalued. Thus the rules recognize devaluation as tantamount to, and a substitute for, cost and price reduction; but the ethos considers it failure, evidence of weakness.

This internal concept of "equilibrium" is a reflection of the external internation concept of equilibrium that underlies all other assumptions of Bretton Woods. The internal equilibrium described above is designed to keep the nations in relatively fixed relation to each other. Equilibrium between countries implies that one country's gain is at another's expense and is necessarily short-lived. Only when a money machine adds liquidity, as South African gold did prior to 1913 and as American deficits did after 1949, can equilibrium be sustained in which all other countries grow in the same direction and at a proximate rate. After World War II, none wanted a static equilibrium. All wanted recovery, implying faster growth, in Europe and Japan. Thus there was a basic conflict between the goals of equilibrium and growth. The conflict was resolved in favor of growth by the "beneficial disequilibrium" from 1944 to 1958, based on American (and lesser British) deficits. How was it accomplished, and at what cost? And what does it have to say about the future?

# 6.
# 1949-1958:
# Beneficial
# Disequilibrium

he enormous American surpluses from 1946 to 1949, some $32 billion, have been noted. Bretton Woods thus commenced with rules favorable to surplus earners when in fact the war's devastation cast only the United States in this role. The 1940s' belief in the American capacity to remain economically dominant lay behind the willingness of the United States to distribute vast Marshall Plan aid, without so much as a return IOU, meaningless at the time, but capable in retrospect of delaying the fall and devaluation of the dollar for another decade.

This same certainty of American economic superiority also engineered the vast depreciations of other currencies against the dollar which took place, at American insistence, by 1949. The view evolved in the United States that aid would be wasteful to countries that could neither produce nor compete at predepreciation exchange rates. The United States forced the nations to devalue extensively, simply by threatening to suspend Marshall Plan aid if they did not do so. The Bretton Woods rules, to be sure, allowed for percentage-point devaluations, but the initial postwar illness required deeper surgery: a restructuring of exchange rates against the dollar rather than devaluations in the 10–15 percent range.

Thus in 1949, Britain devalued by 30.5% and Sweden did the same. Holland devalued by 30.1%; Belgium, 12.3%; Canada, 9.1%. Depreciations of even greater magnitudes took place in the defeated axis nations. In 1948 West Germany recalled all its currency and for each 100 reichsmarks issued seven new deutschmarks. There were some variations in the rate of issue (corporations, for example, received a different rate), and some money was issued to those who had none at all. But this reconstitution of currency approaches a 93% depreciation. Nevertheless, in 1949 the deutschmark was devalued an additional 20.7% against the dollar. From the end of World War II through 1949, the total depreciation of the Italian lira was 63.9%, 8.5% of it in 1949. The prewar (1941) Japanese yen had been worth some 23.4 U.S. cents, or just over four yen to the dollar. The postwar rate was set at 371 yen to the dollar, a 98.4% devaluation. France, theoretically a victorious nation, had devalued its currency 66% from the war's end through 1949. In 1949 alone, by Federal Reserve reckoning which differs slightly from that of the IMF, the devaluation was 38.7%.

It is less surprising in the light of these figures that the defeated nations particularly became the "miracle" economies of the postwar period, with export-led booms pacing and forming development. In 1964 Paul Samuelson would write that if history could be rerun, the postwar depreciations might well have been smaller. But rerun it can never be. The world has rightly applauded the incredible generosity of the Marshall Plan. A correct assessment of the past would give virtually equal credit to these devaluations for the economic revival. The United States in this period was far less concerned with the competitive potential of those it so revived than with the ability, particularly of the vanquished, to resist new political extremism, now including communism, and to flourish under the democratic regimes they had so recently and so haltingly adopted. To the United States, economic considerations were secondary to those of a geopolitical and strategic nature. In any event, the great strength of the United States, its industrial and particularly its technological lead, made American deficits seem a far-off worry. Even when they appeared in 1950 and for the first eight years thereafter, they were taken lightly as a redistribution of chips, necessary for the game to go on.

The consequences of these depreciations were swift, profound, and lasting. In 1950—the following year—the United States went into overall deficit with a jolt. A $5.3 billion surplus on trade in 1949 —exports over imports—declined to $1.1 billion in 1950. The total U.S. deficit on the official reserve transactions reckoning was $3.3 billion in 1950.

The currency realignments were, to be sure, not the only contributor to this jarring change; the 1950 Korean War helped, both by direct purchases and by stimulating a more rapid American inflation. Because most U.S. trade at that time was with Canada, which had devalued only 9 percent, and with Latin America, which devalued not at all, Europe was not the major recipient of the dollar windfall. But the depreciations set the stage for a continually strengthening European competitive position, which would result in consistent American deficits every year thereafter except 1957 and 1968–1969, for special reasons in each case: the Suez invasion, and inflows through the Eurodollar market, respectively.

An undervalued currency has been compared to being downwind in a sailing ship race; once downwind it is almost impossible to be caught. Tantamount to a reduction in costs and prices, devaluation makes possible greater exports, hence greater profits in the export industries; in addition, capital resources and the best labor flow to those industries, which can pay for them. Devaluation also makes imports more expensive.

Unless this advantage is wiped out by inflation and rapidly rising costs and prices in the devaluing nation, it will stay downwind, experience an "export-led boom," and accrue surpluses of dollars and/or gold. In the case of most continental countries—particularly Germany and Italy—this was the precise course of events. The absorption of unemployed labor as the economy expanded—some 8 million East-zone refugees in Germany and farm labor in Italy —assured continued low wage rates in those countries. If France lacked these advantages, it did not hesitate in subsequent years to devalue frequently (1957, 1958, 1969) to stay downwind.

The desire to accrue reserves and gold is reminiscent of mercantilist behavior, when the object of economic statecraft was the accumulation and protection of a gold hoard, considered vital to military strength. If mercantilist gratifications dominated Europe, there were other benefits to the United States in this period. First there were strategic and foreign policy gains: increased power and tangible economic success, under United States leadership, for the non-Communist world. Secondly, there were whatever benefits accrue to a reserve currency—"debts without tears," as the French put it—and some invisible earnings in banking from the use of the dollar. The mercantilist preferences run deep and still continue. A subsequent chapter considers the consequence in more detail.

As the strong center of the West, the United States did not view its deficits with any great alarm until the end of the 1950s. On the contrary, the Americans saw the redistribution as necessary to the rebuilding of the European economies, the real barrier to Communist inroads. And the 1950s proceeded in a happy symbiosis—the European economies growing in size and competitive strength based on low labor costs, undervalued currencies, and updated technology, provided first by the Marshall Plan and later by multinational corporate investment and abetted by native developments. American deficits fueled this growth. The process was encouraged by American self-confidence that it could, if need be, turn this all around at will by reducing Agency for International Development (AID) funds and that in any event the process provided a needed redistribution of reserves.

Despite the deficit in trade, no lack of confidence was felt in the dollar abroad. The gold supply still far exceeded accumulated reserves of other industrial nations. Through 1957, these totaled $8.9 billion, of which over half, $5 billion, went to renascent Germany. The "dollar shortage" was taken as a fixture of life and appeared to be a long-run prospect. As late as 1957, an important British economist could publish a book entitled *The Dollar Shortage*. American importance, even dominance, was unquestioned.

The pattern of the 1950s, from the American balance of payments perspective, may be seen in Table 12 below. The first column shows the annual average balance-of-payments results by categories of receipts or expenditures for the seven-year period 1950–1956. In terms of exports and imports of goods, the United States ran a persistent surplus averaging $2.6 billion in these years. Another important private sector activity is investment income. This is mainly the result of past investments abroad in plant and equipment, i.e., direct investment by multinational corporations which in this period were mainly oil and mining companies, some manufacturing plants, and utilities—for the most part in Canada and Latin America. The great movement of the multinationals to Europe had not yet begun. Investment income also includes dividends and interest on foreign stocks and bonds owned by Americans. This surplus averaged $1.8 billion in these years. The outflow or deficit figures associated with the private (i.e., nongovernment) sector were relatively small, some $900 million from private investment, which would of course return future dividends, and $100 million from "travel and transport," which includes tourism. On balance, private business activity earned surpluses for the United States.

These private sector surpluses, however, were consumed, so to speak and bypassed by government expenditures. Among the more important are some $2 billion for military expenditures abroad, and another $2.2 billion for "U.S. government grants." Not all of this was net deficit: Some military and aid expenditures returned to the United States as matériel purchases. But by far the bulk did not. The net result, using the "official reserve transactions balance," the more acceptable of the several varieties of balance of payments reckoning in use, was an average deficit of $1.2 billion per year or $8.4 billion total over the years. Of this total, some $1.7 billion was taken by the surplus earners as gold, the balance as dollars into reserves, over half the total going to Germany.

The trade-off of dollar deficits for security through military expenditures and aid was, in these years, questioned by only a few. But as the American deficits continued and could not be stopped, many have increasingly questioned the wisdom of such expenditures.

As late as 1971 as firm a conservative as Treasury Secretary John Connally said in a Munich address:

> I find it an impressive fact, and a depressing fact, that the persistent, underlying balance of payments deficit which causes such concern is more than covered, year in and year out, by our net military expenditures abroad, over and above the amounts received from foreign military purchases in the United States.

Table 12

U. S. balance of payments, 1950-1971 (in billions of dollars)

| Items (net) | 1950-1956 | 1957 | 1958-1959 | 1960-1964 | 1965-1967 | 1968-1969 | 1970 | 1971 |
|---|---|---|---|---|---|---|---|---|
| Merchandise trade | 2.6 | 6.3 | 2.3 | 5.4 | 4.2 | 0.6 | 2.1 | − 2.9 |
| Military expenditure | −2.0 | −2.0 | −3.0 | −2.4 | −2.7 | −3.2 | −3.4 | − 2.0 |
| Travel and transportation | −0.1 | −0.2 | −0.7 | −1.1 | −1.5 | −1.7 | −2.0 | − 2.2 |
| Investment income | 1.8 | 2.4 | 2.5 | 3.9 | 5.5 | 6.1 | 6.3 | 7.0 |
| Other services and transfers | −0.5 | −0.5 | −0.6 | −0.6 | −0.7 | −0.8 | −0.8 | − 0.7 |
| Balance on goods, services, and remittances | 1.8 | 5.2 | 0.5 | 5.2 | 4.0 | 1.0 | 2.2 | − 0.8 |
| U.S. government grants | −2.2 | −1.6 | −1.6 | −1.9 | −1.6 | −1.6 | −1.7 | − 2.0 |
| Balance on current account | −0.4 | 3.6 | −1.1 | 3.3 | 3.0 | −0.6 | 0.5 | − 2.8 |
| Long-term capital | | | | | | | | |
| Official | −0.3 | −0.9 | −0.6 | −1.0 | −1.8 | −2.1 | −2.0 | − 2.4 |
| Private | −0.9 | −2.9 | −2.1 | −3.0 | −3.4 | +0.6 | −1.5 | − 4.1 |
| Balance on current account and long-term capital | −1.6 | −0.2 | −3.6 | −0.7 | −2.2 | −2.1 | −3.0 | − 9.3 |
| Short-term capital | 0.1 | 0.3 | 0.8 | −0.5 | 1.3 | 5.8 | −6.5 | −10.3 |
| Errors and omissions | 0.3 | 1.0 | 0.3 | −1.0 | −0.6 | −1.5 | −1.1 | −10.9 |
| Allocations of SDRs | − | − | − | − | − | − | 0.8 | +0.7 |
| Official reserve transactions balance | −1.2 | 1.1 | −2.7 | −2.2 | −1.5 | 2.2 | −9.8 | −29.8 |

Source: Bank for International Settlements, *Annual Report*, 1971.

... we today spend 9 percent of our gross national product on defense—nearly $5 billion of that overseas, much of it in Western Europe and Japan. Financing a military shield is a part of the burden of leadership; the responsibilities cannot and should not be cast off. But twenty-five years after World War II, legitimate questions arise over how the cost of these responsibilities should be allocated ... the nations of Western Europe and Japan are again strong and vigorous, and their capacities to contribute have vastly increased.

The pattern set in the 1950s thus continued into the 1970s. When the private sector surplus could no longer offset government and particularly military expenditures, the deficit became too large for the system to bear.

Over the years, various plans had been put forward for "burden sharing," zero foreign-exchange cost of military spending, and the like. But to no avail. The military refused to countenance balance of payments limits to its expenditures, and no administration could be persuaded to reduce this burden. In 1973, President Nixon proposes to tackle the problem "honorably" by seeking balanced force reduction, so that both United States and Russian forces in Europe can be numerically reduced.

Fritz Machlup, in a fascinating historical foray, has shown that in other times, other nations have undertaken similar, although always lighter, burdens. In each case the nation was forced to suspend gold convertibility or devalue its currency in the end as a result. Machlup reckons foreign military and aid payments as 3 percent of U.S. GNP from 1949 to 1964, or 48 to 63% of the export earnings that had to service them. This burden was some four times as great as that of Britain after the Napoleonic wars, over twice as heavy as French reparations after 1871, and five to six times the size of German reparations after the first world war, the consequences of which have been described earlier.

To complete the period, a word on 1957. The Suez invasion and the closing of the Canal boosted U.S. export earnings to $6.3 billion, overcoming all deficits. But 1957 remains unique as the *only* year of American surplus, until another random occurrence in 1968–1969. And in 1957 the overall surplus was only $1.1 billion.

On the whole, then, the period through 1957 is one of "beneficial disequilibrium." Continental Europe and Japan busied themselves with growth and burgeoning export industries. The United States ran persistent deficits as a result of government spending. Was the dollar even then overvalued? Some would argue no, since private business could earn surpluses on exports and investments. But some argue that it was: To do *all* the things the United States sought to do—to aid and arm the free world as well as do business with it—the private earnings had to be even greater. And greater exports and fewer imports, presumably through a cheaper dollar, were required to do so. The exact time at which the dollar became overvalued is only of academic interest, except to note that freely fluctuating exchange rates might have given an early warning that fixed rates could not. But prior to 1958, Europe worked happily behind a barrier of exchange controls and with inconvertible currencies, piling up reserves in the belief that the dollar shortage was real and permanent. This delusion was to end abruptly in 1958.

# 7.
# 1958-1965:
# Revelation

he first American anxiety—prescience of the basic difficulty of the system—came after 1958. In that year convertibility was restored among European currencies. All discovered that their rush to stockpile American dollars as reserves had in fact been excessive. They discovered that they did not need as many reserve dollars as they had in fact acquired. The "dollar shortage," which had dominated the thinking of the 1950s, had become a "dollar glut." The 1972 Economic Report of the President states, with retrospective wisdom, that there had been "uninterrupted concern with the excess of U.S. payments abroad over receipts since 1959."

The term "convertibility" is confusing, since it is used in two major senses in monetary jargon. The obligation, under Bretton Woods rules, of the United States to exchange "excess" dollars in the hands of foreign official institutions (central banks and treasuries) for gold is one type. The free (or relatively unrestricted) exchange (purchase and sale) of currencies, one for another, is another concept of convertibility. Few Europeans permitted the latter type before 1958. But in that year the two types of convertibility tangle. Currency convertibility led to discovery by many nations that the dollar shortage was over; they had more dollars than they needed. This in turn led to a rash of conversions, i.e., cashing in of excess dollars for gold. Between 1958 and 1960 U.S. gold reserves were reduced an alarming $5.1 billion through such conversions. But the convertibility of currencies also inspired a much freer world economy in investments as well as trade. A U.S. company earning a profit abroad could now—with currency convertibility—remit profits in dollars to the parent, or otherwise use its foreign-gained currency in virtually any way it pleased. No longer would companies be forced to trade blocked francs for blocked lira for Italian hairpins to import to the United States for dollars. Coincidentally, in 1958 too, the Rome treaty became effective, opening the economic space of the Common Market behind a unified tariff barrier. American "multinationals" began to invest heavily in production facilities in this market, i.e., ownership of plant and equipment, including factories, distribution facilities, even banks and advertising agencies.

In 1958, American corporations had owned some $25 billion (book value) of direct investments abroad. Over two-thirds, or $17 billion, was located in Canada and Latin American. The largest investments ($13.5 billion) were in extractive industries (oils and mines) and public utilities. By 1966, the total would more than double to $54 billion. And manufacturing would bypass all other industries as a magnet for foreign direct investment to become $22 billion of the total, now equal in size to all extractive and utility investment. Moreover, the geographic shift was marked; Europe became by 1966 the recipient of $16.2 billion, second only and barely behind Canada.

To the other elements of deficit were thus added long-term direct capital outflows, further increasing dollar earnings in Europe and leading, in turn, to conversion (to gold) of more "excess" dollars. In the long run this investment would yield handsome dividends to the U.S. balance of payments, but at the outset the direction was, necessarily, out.

The year 1958 has been marked as a turning point because the restoration of convertibility that year revealed the weakness of the dollar. The year has been likened to the continental divide. As the rivers change their flow from east to west, so the European desire to obtain dollar reserves changed to a desire to get rid of excess dollar surpluses—the change from "dollar shortage" to "dollar glut." Table

13 traces the movement of gold from the United States to the rest of the world, taking account of newly mined gold as well as the acquisitions of official institutions like the IMF. The aforementioned $5.1 billion drain in 1958–1960 may be seen here. In contrast, the outflow before 1958 had been only $1.7 billion. The outflow began to bother the after-dinner speakers: "too many chips changing hands." Still, general confidence in the dollar remained high. Europeans and Americans alike were still convinced, but less invincibly so, that the powerful United States was being indulgent and could change course if it wished.

In France there appeared the first proposal to "solve" the problem by doubling or tripling the price of gold, thereby providing increased liquidity (a greater gold hoard) so that the convertibility rules as prescribed in Bretton Woods could continue—and, coincidentally, those who had acquired gold would gain a windfall profit as well. The United States was criticized because it ran "deficits without tears," exported inflation, and bought European assets "with our own money." The ideas were put forward by Jacques Rueff —among others—who argued, not without logic, that the greatest beneficiary of a gold price jump would be the United States, whose gold assets still totaled approximately $20 billion. With a hoard revalued to $40 or $60 billion, faith in the dollar, i.e., in its gold backing, would be unequivocally and "eternally" restored. Convertibility would be unquestioned. But the idea moved from the relatively arcane world of economic theory to the arena of power politics, where it became important in the Gaullist anti-American fusillade. The French tradition of using financial devices in diplomatic strategy was old and familiar to the mandarins who provided French leaders a choice of policies. The American response was negative —genuine hurt. Stunned by the "ingratitude" of the view, the Americans violently rejected a new price for gold. The general and vague American antipathy to gold as a "barbarous relic" sharpened. Gold was being used as an instrument to push the Americans around and to question—as de Gaulle did—their qualifications for world leadership. Those who concurred in the Gaullist view on gold, including some Americans, were assailed as "gold bugs." Handled differently and more diplomatically by the French, the fate of

**Table 13**

Changes in official monetary gold stocks (in billions of U.S. dollars)

| Periods | Total (=new monetary gold) | United States | International institutions | Rest of the world |
|---|---|---|---|---|
| 1950–1957 | +3.6 | –1.7 | – | +5.5 |
| 1958–1960 | +1.7 | –5.1 | +1.0 | +5.8 |
| 1961–1965 | +2.7 | –4.0 | –0.8 | +7.5 |
| 1966–May 1968 | –2.8 | –3.3 | +0.8 | –0.3 |
| June 1968–July 1970 | +0.8 | +1.5 | –0.4 | –0.3 |
| August 1970–August 1971 | – | –1.7 | +2.9 | –1.2 |

Source: Bank for International Settlements, *Annual Report*, 1971, page 17.

gold—and of the system—might have been different. But once the question was set in this context of conflict, many Americans were unrelenting in the pursuit of a reduced, even phased-out, role for gold.

As behooves the outs, John F. Kennedy's 1960 election campaign focused attention on the balance of payments, and particularly on the gold outflow, as another sin of omission of the Eisenhower administration. "He kept us out of space," one speaker said, and "will soon run us out of gold as well." Abroad, the response to the Kennedy rhetoric was to raise the expectation that the United States might devalue its currency, thereby increasing the price of gold, which the French and others wanted. Consequently, in October 1960 the first gold crisis occurred as an upsurge of private demand, reflecting both diminished confidence in the dollar and the possibility of a devaluation, sent quotations as high as $40 per ounce on the free, unofficial London gold market. This break in the then official price of $35 was shortly to result in a gold pool of the major nations, with the U.S. contribution at 50 percent, designed to feed gold to the private markets and thus keep the private near the official price. Still later, in 1968, the pool would cease to function, as the huge rise in the private gold price meant the pool's efforts had failed. The 1960 break in the official price constitutes yet another turning point in the Bretton Woods system.

The Kennedy years are singled out for a close view because in these years three elements come into play. First, the development of ideas. The flow of ideas was stimulated in part by an apparent intellectual receptivity, coincident with the shock to Americans occasioned by the revelation in 1958 of the dollar glut and by the subsequent heavy gold drain. Ultimately, but not until the 1970s, the ideas advanced by academics at the time—particularly for more flexible exchange rates, implying dollar devaluation—would become the basis for an official American proposal for reform of the system. Secondly, administrative steps, consisting of controls over certain flows of capital, were chosen to combat the persistent U.S. deficits. Until the breakdown of the system in 1971, they remained the major weapons in the American armory. Finally, despite—possibly in response to—the academic pleas for greater flexibility, the myth hardened that exchange rates must never, or hardly ever, be changed, particularly by the "responsible" reserve currency countries. Fixed exchange rates were required, went the argument, for business and trade to prosper. The uncertainty of flexibility would stunt international trade and economic growth. Look at the interwar years.

In 1960–1964 the American economy was growing more slowly than the European, and, by some measures, was in recession. The consumer price index in the United States (1958 = 100) rose only to 107 by 1964, compared to 113 in Germany and 142 in Japan. The then new measure of the degree of recession, the gap between potential and actual GNP, reflecting the degree of unemployment of capital and labor, was in the vicinity of $30 to $35 billion per year, a total GNP loss of $190 billion from 1957–1962 and a loss in federal tax revenue of nearly $70 billion. The Kennedy administration saw its prime economic target as reflation, to "get the country going again."

To do so risked a worsening of the balance of payments. In the 1950s, the cumulative American deficit had been over $12 billion, with signs of stronger competition ahead. In the early 1960s, this deficit was to double—and European surpluses with it. Under Kennedy a major concern was to forestall this sequence. An internal expansion, it was recognized, would mean increased imports from abroad and therefore an even worse balance of payments prospect. To find guidelines for action in the field, President Kennedy inspired a number of studies, perhaps the most influential of which was that prepared by the Brookings Institution in 1963. In the briefest summary, that study put some of the fears to rest. Because the U.S. inflation was less than the expansion in Europe, the study looked to an increasing surplus in the trade balance in the years ahead, leading to a surplus in the total balance of payments position by 1968, if existent trends continued. Implicit in this view is the renewed possibility of "dollar shortage." If this were to happen, some new and hopefully managed form of reserve would have to supplement gold and the then decreasing dollar reserves, for a steady growth of reserves is necessary in order to keep the world economy growing. But the study was sufficiently cautious to suggest that if the trends changed and surplus did not come to pass, some increased exchange rate flexibility—implying dollar devaluation—might be in order.

Nor was the report without prophetic value under the reigning conditions. Referring back to Table 12, in the years 1960–1964 the average merchandise trade surplus increased substantially to $5.4 billion yearly average, from $2.3 billion in the pre-Kennedy years (excepting 1957). Nevertheless, even this increase in the trade balance could not overcome the deficit items, so that the total deficit averaged $2.2 billion from 1960 to 1964, nearly double the 1950s rate. To the normal military and government drains, there was added some $3 billion per year for private investment. Multinational corporation as well as private portfolio investment rose as American investments poured into the Common Market, with its new-found economic space and convertible money, behind its heightened tariff walls, to participate in its growing markets.

Short-term capital movements began to increase and shifted on average from a source of strength to weakness as interest rates abroad were persistently above U.S. levels. But "hot money" flows could be quickly reversed. Growing attention was therefore paid to the basic balance (i.e., the balance on current account and long-term capital transactions). The view began to jell among economists that if the largest element of the U.S. payments position, merchandise trade, could be improved while the exodus of long-term multinational corporate, or private portfolio, investment could be kept in bounds, the American position might become increasingly tolerable.

From the pens of the professors there also came ideas that made little official impression at the time, although they were volubly argued, particularly in academic circles. These looked to longer-run solutions to the problem than had the Brookings study, doubtless because they were not limited in their terms of reference, as the Brookings study had been. They fell into two basic categories: improvement in the liquidity system, and improvement in the adjustment mechanism.

In 1959 there came the prophetic warning from Professor Triffin that the gold exchange system would not last and that new liquidity devices were in order. Trade and investment had outrun the pace of reserve creation, which depended on the very limited and quixotic supply of new gold and on national currency deficits, mainly the dollar. But the dollar provided liquidity to the system only when the United States was in deficit. If the deficit were to continue to grow, he warned, the quality of the dollar would be questioned as its outstanding quantity increased; in the end, impossible demands for conversion to gold would collapse the system as it had in 1931 when England was its center. And since 1932 had followed 1931, dire consequences might be expected. On the other hand, if the United States should return to surplus, reserves would be withdrawn from the system, thus inhibiting the expansion of world trade. The remedy lay in the replacement of gold and the dollar with a new reserve unit, managed and issued as the requirement of liquidity indicated. The similarity of this new idea to Keynes' bancor plan, rejected in 1944, is obvious. Most of the reform discussion focused on the liquidity question.

The second basic reform notion was improvement of the adjustment mechanism. And normally, advocates of this type of reform had in mind greater exchange rate flexibility. To be sure, the Bretton Woods scheme had provided for exchange rate moves, but the nations had been demonstrably unwilling to use even the Bretton Woods provisions. This reflected, said the adjustment reformers, their arbitrary rather than automatic nature. To move an exchange rate, central bankers or governments had to decide and to act; this discretionary power had been misused, because needed changes were in fact not made. If the exchange rate moves could be automatic, in response to some "trigger" or in reflection of the forces of supply and demand in the foreign exchange markets, with no (or minimal) intervention, the kind of growing disequilibrium then visible could be overcome painlessly. Studies estimated the U.S. currency to be overvalued by some 10 percent by the early 1960s. More flexible exchange rates would automatically have devalued the dollar by this amount without capital controls, import restrictions, enforced unemployment, higher interest rates, or other illiberal or uneconomic devices.

The "peg" system of Bretton Woods also inspired speculation through "hot money" flows that precipitated the feared changes. A big move, say 10 percent, from one peg to another invited unsettling currency movements, particularly since pegs were moved only after it had become clear that they must be, after the required devaluation or revaluation had been resisted to the bitter end, giving speculators plenty of time to act and signals to attract them. More gradual changes in the value of currency could eliminate this problem, it was argued.

The purest and best case for exchange rate flexibility came from Professor Milton Friedman and his many monetarist followers. Rather than try to fight the market, constant and daily small adjustments in the price of currency were in order, in response to the free foreign exchange markets ruled by supply and demand rather than by fallible central bankers. The monetarists argued that the movable peg was in any event awkward. It vested authorities with excessive discretion which they were often bound, even with the best of intentions, to misuse. They could not be expected to guess precisely the correct new value of the currency. Only market prices could do that. New rules were necessary. With flexible rates the need for reserves would be substantially reduced. Mercantilist behavior would be visibly irrational. Intervention need be minimal. And the classical medicine of underemployment, used to match national costs and prices to an arbitrary and usually erroneously chosen exchange rate, would be unnecessary.

Fixed rate advocates countered that exchange rate unpredictability would make trade and investment difficult or impossible and would inspire controls and tariff wars as was alleged to have occurred in the 1930s. How would a future contract or a bond of 20-year maturity be priced without fixed rates? The monetarists' answer was that once real—i.e., market—equilibrium was attained, it would change only slowly and in fact be highly stable. Absolute predictability of the future was never possible in any event, but forward markets could be used to insure against potential losses from currency changes. In fact forward markets have grown enormously from the late 1960s for just this purpose.

But the fixed rate advocates retorted that even if flexibility was more efficient, discipline would vanish; any nation could inflate and devalue without limit. Fear of reserve loss, replied the monetarists, has demonstrably failed to stop inflation. The pre-Friedman monetarists, notably Henry Simons, had also espoused flexible rates, but had stated clearly that price stability was a necessary concomitant. Except for sporadic moments, stability of prices has been notably lacking in the entire industrial world. In the monetarist view, the failure to control the domestic money supply was at the root of persistent inflation. Again, fixed rules of money supply growth, rather than the authority of central bankers, were required for internal policies as well. Nevertheless, even for some reformers, pure flexible rates were too much. Into the argument came a host of semiflexible rate schemes. Wider bands, crawling and gliding pegs, and other elegantly conceived schemes were proposed to meet the objections to pure flexibility. All were designed to provide the benefits of flexibility in an orderly and controlled manner, lending the psychological perception of stability to the procedure. At the same time all were meant to minimize speculative "hot money" flows, which threatened to become unsettling, and in the late 1960s proved decidedly so.

Nor were the proposals for greater exchange rate flexibility restricted to the professors. As noted, the Brookings report kept the idea alive as an ace in the hole. From the Joint Economic Committee of Congress came *Guidelines for Improving the International Monetary System*, a 1965 report with similar sentiments:

> Substantial improvements are needed in the adjustment process which brings international imbalances to an end.

Intellectual hopes ran high for a vast reform of the adjustment mechanism—a reform that would constitute an effective alternative to the cumulative and now evident disequilibrium in the system without imposing a straitjacket of controls over capital movements or trade, or both.

But all to no avail. As it turned out, there was not the slightest willingness on the part of the major nations to reform the adjustment mechanism at this time. It is difficult to pinpoint historic turning points, particularly when ideas or conceptions are involved. But if the attitude toward greater exchange rate flexibility can be summarized, incorporating later events with the clarity of hindsight, the thread might follow this line: the Kennedy era could still believe that an improvement in the American trade balance—Brookings-style—plus some capital controls might yet restore the dollar; the spending for Vietnam and the Great Society programs and the consequent inflation in the United States during the Johnson administration destroyed the Brookings scenario. Sometime in the course of the Johnson administration it became increasingly clear to an increasing number of influential people that greater exchange rate flexibility—or in plain English, dollar devaluation—was required. This was particularly true after the futile efforts to defend the overvalued British pound ended in 1967 with the pound's devaluation and great losses by the British Treasury to the "speculators." Such discussions or feelers as were put out by the U.S. Treasury during the latter days of the Johnson administration to the other nations, proposing a conference or other means of deliberation to improve the adjustment mechanism and to devalue the dollar, seem to have proved futile. It is of course difficult to document these feelers, as there is no public record. Nevertheless, the failure of the major nations to agree on greater flexibility had become so evident by mid-1968 that a preelection task force could induce the Republicans to accept the policy of "benign neglect"—of which more later. This policy, rather than agreement, forced the dollar devaluations and greater exchange rate flexibility of the 1970s. Thus an idea engendered in academic discussion, and at first scorned by the practical men of affairs, became in successive but unrecorded steps the policy of the United States and the practice of the international monetary system more than a decade after its serious proposal.

Back to the Kennedy era. The main weapon to contain the overall deficit was capital controls. Construed as "temporary" at the outset in 1963, the controls were designed to reduce long-term capital outflows from the United States. Through the Interest Equalization Tax (IET), the use of the New York capital market for foreign borrowing through bond issues or the sale of shares was reduced and effectively denied to Europeans. Technically no American could be denied the right to lend to foreigners or invest in foreign issues. But a tax of up to 15%, later increased to 30%, was imposed, effectively reducing interest or share yields and discouraging such investment. The IET burden fell heaviest on European borrowers;

Canadian, Japanese, and developing-country issues were untaxed or taxed at a lower rate. At the same time, pressure was put on the American underwriters to abstain from European issues.

The first effect of IET was dramatic. New issues of foreign securities in the United States declined from $1.9 billion in the first half of 1963 to $0.6 billion in the second. Trade in outstanding securities switched from $302 million outflow in the first to $204 million inflow in the second half of that year as well, and the success was sustained into 1964. But the secondary effects were, or should have been, more sobering. The fluidity of capital began to be demonstrated. Since interest rates abroad were higher, banks increased their foreign lending from $322 million to over $1 billion by the third quarter of 1964; other financial institutions followed suit. The controls had therefore to be extended to banks through the Gore Amendment in 1963, and extended again under the Johnson administration. Eventually this and later capital controls were to create parallel (to New York) financial markets abroad, out of reach of all controls, the consequences of which are discussed in Chapter 11.

Although the Bretton Woods rules had said little about capital flows, they had clearly intended that trade and investments be free. In lieu of an appropriate adjustment mechanism, the Kennedy administration had set the nation on a "drift to controls." If the administration and its coterie of economists considered this a practical victory, others excoriated the drift. The Joint Economic Committee's *Guidelines* summarized this view:

> It is one of the ironies and inconsistencies of modern life that to protect fixed exchange rates—the means—we have compromised freedom of capital movements and, to some extent, trade—the ends—which the fixed exchange rates are intended to serve.

When in 1964 Mr. Johnson was elected, not much more had been accomplished.

# 8.
# 1965-1971:
# Disintegration

lected in 1964, President Johnson escalated both American participation in Vietnam and the "Great Society" programs by 1965, with enormous inflation the consequence, leading to a steady erosion of the American balance of payments position, of confidence in the dollar, and of the viability of the Bretton Woods system. Periodic arrests of this erosion proved temporary as the fundamental trade strength of the United States waned.

The volume of imports rose and their composition changed. Superimposed on this weakening base, moneys flowed faster among the industrial countries, stimulated in no small measure by the very capital restrictions the Americans had imposed in a vain attempt to save the system. Taken together, the policies of this period could hardly have been better designed to make clear the unbalancing consequences of previous actions and the inability of the system to right itself, given the prevailing attitudes.

Those who would have saved the system can find a positive note in this period in the successful efforts of the U.S. Treasury to create and launch Special Drawing Rights, known as SDRs or, colloquially, as "paper gold." These IMF-issued units of value were designed to provide additional liquidity in the monetary system and lessen the world's reliance on both gold and dollars as the major reserves, in line with the ideas of Professor Triffin and Lord Keynes before him, noted earlier. The initial issue of SDRs in 1970 in the amount of $3.5 billion was hailed as a milestone in international cooperation. Unfortunately, they appeared when the world was figuratively drowning in excess dollar liquidity and when reform in the adjustment mechanism, rather than in liquidity creation, was most needed. But this cannot detract from the accomplishment that SDRs were agreed upon and issued at all. More units were issued in 1970 and 1971, pursuant to an original three-year agreement, bringing the total to some $9.5 billion by 1972, when their issue ceased—theoretically temporarily—in recognition of excess liquidity.

Inflation is largely a statistical matter, and a few numbers can save many words. If 1963 is taken as a base, the price of manufactured exports in the United States rose to a level of approximately 128 by early 1971. Its competitors' prices for export goods rose less swiftly after 1965, reflecting the relatively greater inflation in the United States. Partly as a result of price increases, the American trade surplus declined and virtually disappeared by 1968. The trade surplus had averaged $5.4 billion in the 1960–1964 period; in continual decline, it averaged only $2.5 billion from 1965 to 1970. The year-to-year decline shows the trend more clearly. In 1964 it had been $6.8 billion; 1965, $4.9 billion; 1966 and 1967, $3.9 billion; 1968, some $600 million; and 1969, some $700 million. In 1970 it rose again to $2.1 billion but declined sharply to a deficit, for the first time in the century, of $2.9 billion in 1971. In the same years, imports rose dramatically from $18.6 billion to $45.7 billion, wiping out the trade surplus. In 1970 U.S. exports were 51 percent higher than in 1964, but all U.S. imports were 90 percent greater. Manufactured goods, formerly a source of American strength, were 140 percent greater.

This shift is due in part to inflation, in part to a change in the composition of imports. The only U.S. export category to increase markedly was capital goods, machines to make machines, which of course served to further increase the efficiency and productivity of foreign firms. But foreigners increased their sales to Americans in all categories. Shipments of small cars quadrupled in value. Less than

6% of all auto sales were imports in the early 1960s; by the end of the decade, nearly 17% were. In addition, the imports of auto parts from Canada were enormous, pursuant to the provisions of the Auto Agreement of 1965 between the United States and Canada.

Had the structure of imports not changed, American imports might have increased in some proportion to relative price movements and/or in proportion to the increase in American income. But, as Chart 2 shows, they increased by a much greater proportion. The elasticity of demand for imports relative to American income, i.e., the percentage change in each, doubled in the post-1965 period. In 1960–1964 imports and GNP rose by about the same amounts, 5.3% and 5.9% respectively. But after 1965, while GNP rose 7.3%, imports rose 13.4% to 1971, as the elasticity changed from 0.9 to 1.8.

The rapid inflation in the United States wiped out the possibility of the type of return to an American trade surplus which the Brookings study had foreseen, had the trends evident in 1963 continued. To some extent the Kennedy administration had delayed any other action in the hope that the Brookings premises might come to pass. Since inflation was preventing this, what steps did the Johnson administration take to control it? The most obvious antidote would have been an increase in taxes to offset the increase in government expenditures, particularly for the Vietnam War. But no attempt to do so was made until 1968, when additional taxes were levied. But by then the money supply and the price-wage escalators were running at an increasingly furious pace. It has been said that President Johnson had been restrained from asking higher taxes for a variety of political motives. The cost of the Vietnam War, without proper tax-offset, was disastrous in its inflationary consequences for the United States and in its ultimate destruction of confidence in the dollar and the international monetary system. Many have wondered how economic planners as astute as those who could venture to run the "fine-tuned economy" in the mid-1960s could have permitted the inflation to run so far out of hand. The ultimate story of the internal relations between various sectors of the government in the latter 1960s may have to wait the candid memoirs of some of those who were privy to inside decisions. In the interim, however, Chapter 27 of David Halberstam's *The Best and The Brightest* gives an outsider's,

**Chart 2**

# Import elasticities

United States: Gross national product and merchandise imports ($ billion)

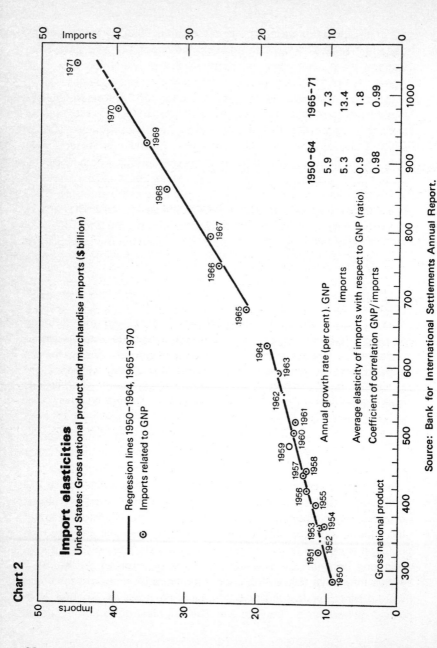

— Regression lines 1950–1964, 1965–1970

⊙ Imports related to GNP

| | 1950–64 | 1965–71 |
|---|---|---|
| Annual growth rate (per cent). GNP | 5.9 | 7.3 |
| Imports | 5.3 | 13.4 |
| Average elasticity of imports with respect to GNP (ratio) | 0.9 | 1.8 |
| Coefficient of correlation GNP/imports | 0.98 | 0.99 |

Gross national product

Source: Bank for International Settlements Annual Report.

but nonetheless widely credited, version that lays the blame on President Johnson himself and virtually exonerates the economic planners.

Back in 1954 when President Eisenhower was being urged to continue the fight with the Vietminh that the French had lost, he refused to do so because General Ridgeway's estimate of a $3.5 billion cost would have created too large a budget deficit. Lyndon Johnson was not so deterred.

Halberstam tells us that by early 1965 the Joint Chiefs of Staff were fully aware how expensive the Vietnam War would be and were

> ... pushing for special funding for the war. ... The Chiefs wanted a wartime footing which included traditional wartime budgetary procedures —invariably meaning higher taxes—and they lost that fight in July 1965 when Johnson decided to go ahead and make it open-ended, without really announcing how open the end was. ... Lyndon Johnson would not give accurate economic projections, would not ask for a necessary tax raise, and would in fact have *his own* military planners be less than candid with *his own* economic planners, a lack of candor so convincing that his economic advisers later felt that McNamara had seriously misled them about projections and estimates. The reasons for Johnson's unwillingness to be straightforward about the financing were familiar. He was hoping that the worst would not come true, that it would remain a short war, and he feared that if the true economic cost of the war became visible to the naked eye, he would lose his Great Society programs. The result was that his economic planning was a living lie, and his administration took us into economic chaos: ... the failure to finance the war honestly, would inspire a virulent inflationary spiral which helped defeat Johnson himself. (pp. 603–604)

Halberstam reports that in the critical fiscal year 1966 (ending June 1966) Senator Stennis and Representative Mendel Rivers estimated the cost of the war at about $10 billion. Gardner Ackley, chairman of the Council of Economic Advisers, did not wish to believe this figure. To reassure himself that his estimated maximum cost of $3 to $5 billion was correct, he sought guidance from the White House. Defense Secretary McNamara is alleged to have assured him that the cost was relatively low, nowhere near $10 billion.

So Ackley went ahead, and unfortunately the figure finally was about $8 billion, far closer to the Stennis–Rivers estimates than to the McNamara estimates.

But that was a marginal miscalculation compared to what was in store. ... With an overheated economy already on hand, and a war and major domestic legislation just ahead, they [the Council] felt it was time to move for a tax increase. On December 10, 1965, they sent a message to the President to that effect.

... Ackley was telling the President he could not have three things: the war, the Great Society and no inflation. If he wanted all three, then he would need a tax increase. ... The President feared that if he went to the Congress for the tax increase, he might blow the whole thing. ... So the President ... decided ... he would hold back on the real estimates of the war for a year—perhaps Hanoi would have folded—meanwhile he would push very hard to get the Great Society legislation through by early 1966, and then, once it was passed, he would concentrate on the war. (pp. 605–606)

Some council members could express their doubt with humor. To the frequent government-memo legend "for internal use only," Halberstam reports that the able Arthur Okun at one time added, "But not to be swallowed." For fiscal 1967, when members of the council confronted McNamara

... they found [him], usually so sure, usually so filled with certitudes, very reluctant to come down with a hard figure for the cost of the war, and he gave three figures: high, low and medium ... $17 billion ... $15 billion ... the low was $11 billion. Eventually the figure came to $21 billion ... (p. 607)

The inflationary effects of the Vietnam War could have been avoided by raising taxes at an earlier stage. By 1967 it was too late. It has remained a mystery for many years why the business community, which suffered the direct consequences of the excessive cost of the war since the administration's only defense of the dollar was via controls on capital and on foreign investment, never objected openly to the procedure. Halberstam gives us one insight.

In May 1967 Ralph Lazarus, President of the Federated Department Stores and a member of the Business Council, held a press conference and publicly criticized Johnson's war budget (he estimated that government spending on the war for the next fiscal year would be $5 billion higher than the government estimate of $21.9 billion). He was immediately telephoned by no less an economic authority than Justice Abe Fortas, who asked Lazarus to tone down his estimates because they were inaccurate; indeed, Lazarus had upset the President very much with his erroneous projections. Unfortunately, the cost turned out to be $27 billion, which meant that Lazarus was right on the nose. Similarly, the deficit for the year was about $23 billion, closely paralleling the cost of the war. (p. 609)

Halberstam adds that the inflation, ironically, added to the country's internal divisions, which Johnson had tried so hard to heal. The inflation exacerbated the tensions between blue-collar whites and blacks. Cities, hospitals, and schools found themselves caught in destructive labor disputes caused by the inflation.

The irony of it all was that the cost of the war itself was not enough to destroy the economy; it never cost more than 3 5% of the gross national product, and there were never any real shortages. It was not the war which destroyed the economy, but the essentially dishonest way in which it was handled. (p. 610)

Finally, by 1968, the decision to put a ceiling on troops for Vietnam was as much economic as political or strategic.

In late 1967 General Westmoreland made a request for additional troops. When it came in, the White House sent it to the Council of Economic Advisers for a reading on what the economic realities were. It was the first time Johnson had ever done it, and the Council was very pleased to render its quite negative findings, though there was a general feeling that it was all very late. (p. 610)

Actually, Halberstam's account of deceived economists unanimous in their demand for higher taxes might have been accurate insofar as official Washington was concerned but was not entirely true for the country at large. Many traditional liberals feared that a tax increase could plunge the nation back into the recession from which war and other federal spending, on top of the 1964 tax cuts, had rescued it. *The New York Times* editorials of this period so argued, with better rhetoric than economic logic. Since this view corroborated Mr. Johnson's decision, it was regarded as Delphic in the executive corridors. In a full-page advertisement in *The New York Times*, another group of eminent academic economists excoriated the war as immoral and unjust, and so also opposed tax increases. The creation of a "fiscal surplus" for such an evil purpose, they argued, could set a terrible precedent for future military adventures without congressional approval but with congressional validation if taxes were voted to pay for it all. Presumably the alternative to the "fiscal surplus" was to be a roaring inflation, which would in the end discomfit the nation, visit on it fiscal retribution, and stop the war.

By 1968, the inflation was roaring. In November unemployment bottomed at 3.4 percent, factories operated at 90 percent of capacity (hence inefficiently), prices rose, and the gap between potential and actual GNP was literally negative. The nation was producing beyond its potential, straining its labor and machine resources to do so.

In addition to a declining trade balance it can be seen from Table 12 (p. 72) that the post-1965 years were also characterized by rising military expenditures, which had been cut back in the Kennedy years. From $2.4 billion average in 1960–1964 they rose to an average of $3.2 billion by 1968–1969; while the costs of military actions in Vietnam must rise, they were not reduced in Europe.

The natural consequence of this declining trade position was a similar decline in confidence in the dollar abroad and in the possibility of the United States stanching the already excessive flow of dollars to foreign coffers. It is difficult to pinpoint turning points in a generally deteriorating situation, but surely March 15, 1968, qualifies. On that particular day, gold buying in Europe reached frantic proportions. The United States lost $2 billion to the gold pool, which tried to calm the panic by supplying the markets with gold. The unofficial expectation was for a gold loss of $5 billion more on the next day, and consequently the pool was closed. The result of this was the birth of the "two-tier" system: the then official price of $35 per ounce, and a free market price which fluctuated. By mid-1973, the latter was to rise to over $120 per ounce. Communication as well as purchases and sales between the official and unofficial gold markets ended. On the same Ides of March, European tradesmen refused to accept American dollars or travelers checks; the first of the American strandings took place. Within the United States, the

Senate voted by only 39 to 37, after a heated debate, to support the administration's plea to eliminate the 25 percent gold cover for the U.S. money supply, thereby freeing the remaining available gold for foreign use. A fortnight later President Johnson announced his desire not to seek reelection, and confidence in the economic and political judgment of the United States was at a new low.

With a Brookings solution out, with a clearly deteriorating status of the dollar, with a rampant inflation, something had to be done. The major, and indeed the sole, reliance for some improvement in the American balance of payments fell again on the capital controls of the Johnson era. The Interest Equalization Tax, introduced in 1963, had effectively closed the New York capital market to foreign borrowers. This logic was extended. In 1965 the Interest Equalization Tax was extended to cover lending by banks and by such nonbank financial corporations as insurance companies. The immediate impact of these regulations was salutory in the sense that the levels of foreign lending fell very sharply. Encouraged by this performance, the government extended the logic to American business as well. "Voluntary" and "temporary" guidelines were established for the total foreign payments and receipts of multinational American business to reduce the flow of direct investment from the United States to foreign subsidiaries. Administered by the Office of Foreign Direct Investment of the Department of Commerce, these are known as OFDI controls and are further discussed below. The restrictions fell mainly on the right of companies to send additional money abroad and proved temporary in the sense that they became mandatory on January 1, 1968, and were extended in scope and severity.

To these policies there were, of course, objections from the business sector, but they were mild and ineffective. Very occasionally a head-on attack was made by responsible businessmen. This acquiescence is surprising, for what was involved was no less than a policy trade-off favoring continued military and other government spending deficits at the expense of foreign lending and direct investment by multinational business.

One reason—in addition to the variety of government threats and pressure, implicit and explicit—for the relative lack of protest by business was its ability to borrow abroad to obtain the funds that could no longer be sent from the United States. Large and well-known companies, in particular, found this feasible. Government spokesmen had argued that they were not opposed to investment abroad, provided it did not add to the net dollar drain. Thus they aided the growth of parallel financial markets abroad, which in the end boomeranged. These markets, particularly the Eurodollar, were to become a powerful magnet for funds formerly lodged in the United States, whose exodus was perhaps the precipitating factor of the 1971 breakdown. Through these markets, vast and unregulated sums could cascade—to the discomfit of central bankers and governments. Exchange rates were virtually indefensible when the cascade moved into or out of a suspect currency. National monetary policy became difficult to sustain under these circumstances. The result was a retreat by 1971 to a new network of exchange controls throughout the advanced countries—even in Germany, heretofore the bastion of the free market. These developments were far removed from the intent of Bretton Woods and were further testimony to its decline. The development and consequences of the Eurodollar and related markets deserve fuller examination and will be treated in Chapter 11.

In the United States, on March 30, 1968, Mr. Johnson announced his decision not to seek reelection. His party's successor candidate inherited the Gordian knot that was Johnson's legacy. If Mr. Humphrey had a clear position on the increasingly perplexing and unhappy questions of the dollar and the international monetary arrangements, it was never fully clarified to the electorate.

In the Republican camp, however, there commenced one of the most unexpected and effective strategies ever devised in financial history. Its purpose was to devalue the dollar. It was known as the policy of "benign neglect."

Prior to its adoption, candidate Nixon's advisers had apparently accepted the view of an increasing number of American economists that the dollar was hopelessly overvalued and must be depreciated. The view was by no means universally held, however. Most government spokesmen and some economists rejected the idea for a variety of reasons. But such attempts as were made to persuade other governments to permit the United States to devalue unilaterally had failed. Other major nations threatened to follow in devaluations, nullifying its effect to improve the American trade balance. The United States trade surplus had fallen to near zero ($611 million surplus) by 1968, from the $5 to $6 billion level a few years earlier.

To be sure, there were some rather fortuitous gains for the United States in 1968–1969. In response to rising interest rates and a severe credit shortage, American banks borrowed extensively from the Eurodollar markets through their branches abroad. This served to reduce foreign, including government (official), holdings of dollars, easing for a while the "dollar glut." The short-term capital inflows produced the first overall (official settlements) surplus the United States had enjoyed since 1957. If these factors were bound to be temporary and reversible, they nevertheless had an effect in 1968–1969. And in May 1968, the fall of President de Gaulle in France had lessened resistance to cooperation with American policies. Under these circumstances, the SDR plan mentioned earlier was agreed upon, with French concurrence, and even with "front loading," i.e., a larger issue of SDRs in the first year of operation, 1970.

But if SDRs might prove some longer-run help as supplement or substitute for the dollar, the acute problem of the fallen trade balance, reflecting an overvalued dollar, remained.

Acknowledgment by the United States of the strength of the mercantilist-surplus view in Europe and Japan lay behind the first Nixon administration's policy of benign neglect. That policy has been assailed, especially in Europe, as heartless, a deliberate violation of the Bretton Woods rules, and later, under Treasury Secretary John Connally's ministrations, as "malign neglect," or two-gun Texas diplomacy. In Japan a new word, "Nixonshock," came into the language to describe, pejoratively, the cumulative effects of benign neglect, including the actual 1971 devaluation.

Yet in this recording of events the policy of benign neglect must be accounted a brilliant stratagem, not only because it has succeeded, but because at the time it was virtually the only strategy that could work.

The time is not yet ripe for extensive official disclosures of all the facets of the benign neglect policy, but occasionally abbreviated accounts do appear and are useful. Harvard Professor Houthakker, a former member of President Nixon's Council of Economic Advisers, presented one in the *Wall Street Journal* of March 16, 1973. The policy, he wrote,

> first formulated by a Republican pre-election task force in 1968 under the chairmanship of Professor Gottfried Haberler ... was aimed at forcing a depreciation of our overvalued dollar. At that time there was no possibility of devaluing the dollar unilaterally, since several other countries had made it clear they would devalue by an equal amount, thus nullifying our move. These countries therefore had to be persuaded by a continuing accumulation of inconvertible dollar balances. (p. 10)

While some powerful Europeans were agitated about the "flood of dollars" and talked of "dethroning" the dollar, they still did not want to lose their trade advantage implicit in the dollar's overvaluation, threatened to match an American devaluation, and had no realistic alternative solutions to offer. From France there continued to come the suggestion to raise the price of gold. By now the suggestion was more than annoying, as it missed the problem. Since the American hoard was now down to the $10 billion range from $26 billion in 1950, even a tripling of the gold price would not match gold assets to dollar liabilities.

Into this breach stepped the benign neglect tactic, a kind of policy that was never easy to use. Houthakker notes:

> It could not be publicly explained and was therefore widely misunderstood not only abroad but also by several influential newspapers in the United States It put a considerable strain on the international monetary system, and even so results were slow in coming. (p. 10)

It was Treasury Secretary Connally's 10-percent import surcharge in 1971 that proved to be the key negotiation weapon to permit dollar devaluation and to break the exchange rate pattern. This had made him very unpopular abroad. Of this Houthakker writes:

> The drastic actions taken by John Connally were a departure from the tactics, though not the strategy, of "benign neglect." (p. 10)

Later, after the Smithsonian devaluation of December 1971, United States authorities intervened to some extent in the foreign exchange markets to support the dollar—by buying some off the markets with borrowed marks—but this concession was a temporary deviation from benign neglect. As late as the weekend of March 13, 1973, when European finance ministers demanded that the United States raise interest rates, Secretary Schultz is reported to have responded that "our interest rates are determined by domestic considerations. ... " Houthakker comments:

> Such statements are of the essence of benign neglect, and so was the announcement that we will phase out capital control programs by the end of 1974. (p. 10)

The essence of the benign neglect policy was simple: Do nothing. As dollars poured out of the United States, the government would not intervene to stanch the flow or to support the dollar in the foreign exchange markets. Nor would it wring its hands publicly or call for great new conferences to reform the system when Europe and Japan were resisting the key elements of reform, dollar depreciation and future flexibility, and profiting from this resistance by the additional acquisition of reserves.

The fate of the dollar was left in foreign hands, or to the forces of foreign exchange markets. As dollars accumulated in foreign hands, the supply of dollars exceeded the demand. To prevent the price of dollars from devaluing, or the price of other currencies from rising vis-à-vis the dollar, the foreign central banks themselves would have to "buy" (i.e., accept) the unwanted dollars, piling up additional reserves. The price of dollars would differ in each foreign exchange market: In London, for example, the supply of dollars was less, relative to demand, than in Tokyo, which had in these years an enormous trade surplus, or in Bonn, where dollars came in both through a trade surplus and through Eurodollar or other financial channels. And by 1970 an enormous pileup of dollars abroad began. While the banks had borrowed from Europe in 1968–1969, they repaid these borrowings in 1970 as credit conditions eased in the United States. The short-term capital account shifted from a positive (inflow) $5.8 billion average for 1968–1969, to a negative $6.5 billion in 1970 (of which over $5 billion was the result of the banks' repayment of last year's loans), a swing of nearly $12.5 billion, most of which the foreign central banks had to absorb. And while United

States credit conditions eased and interest rates fell in 1970, the opposite happened in Europe. Germany, to fight inflation, raised its discount rate from 6 to 7½ percent in 1970. Thus, as funds flowed out of the United States, the main recipient was Germany, to which they were attracted by higher interest rates and the prospect of capital gain on the mark rising against the dollar. In the last nine months of 1970, German reserves rose no less than $5.8 billion, $5.1 in short-term capital. For 1970, the United States deficit reached a new high: With a basic external deficit of $3 billion (despite a $2.1 billion trade surplus), the aforementioned short-term capital outflows raised the total to $9.8 billion.

The crisis of 1971 started early in the year. United States banks repaid an additional $5 billion in the first quarter, as domestic interest rates continued to ease; the trade balance was clearly inadequate, and the deficit for the quarter was $5.5 billion. Benign neglect or no, the United States attempted to reduce the impact of the outflow by the issue of some $3 billion of Treasury and Export-Import Bank notes to the foreign branches of American banks, and by increasing the use of "swaps" with other central banks, particularly the German. The Germans also intervened by purchasing dollars forward in the exchange markets, to reduce the covered interest rate incentive for the inflow of funds, and by buying dollars at the "spot" (current) price. Forward and spot purchase together by the Bundesbank totaled $3 billion in April alone.

Nevertheless, dollars poured into Europe in May 1971, and particularly to Germany, partly because of the expectation that the mark would be floated up, a course recommended by some leading research institutes there. On May 3–4, 1971, $1 billion flowed into the Bundesbank and an additional $1 billion in the first 40 minutes of trading on May 5, at which point the Bundesbank suspended trading. When it reopened on May 10, it also suspended the trading limits, allowing the mark to float, i.e., to rise. Those who had converted dollars to marks were rewarded by handsome capital gains. The Dutch followed the German pattern while Austria revalued some 5%, and Switzerland 7%.

Two factors in August 1971 completed the rout of the dollar. The first was the release of the second quarter United States balance of payments data, which showed a continuing deterioration in the trade position. Associated with it was the announcement of a further run on American reserve assets, mainly gold.

Second, and more important, the issue of a report on August 6, 1971, by the highly respected Reuss subcommittee of the Joint Economic Committee of the United States Congress created shock waves in Europe, although it was barely noted in the United States. For this report, measured and accurate as the Reuss committee reports always were, indicated that the United States could not continue with an overvalued dollar, and suggested devaluation and a basic reshuffling of the exchange rates. Noting that even herculean reductions in military expenditures could not, at this point, produce the required balance of payments improvement, the report suggested instead that the United States "may have no choice but to take unilateral action to go off gold and establish new dollar parities."

The impact on Europe of the Reuss report ought not be underestimated. For example, the *Economist*, in its August 14, 1971, issue, said that dollar devaluation " . . . was all too inevitable once Mr. Henry Reuss's cat . . . had been let out of the bag." The 1971 *Annual Report* of the Bank for International Settlements said:

> The August crisis proper began on the 6th day of the month when the same conviction was expressed in a report by a Subcommittee of the United States Congress. . . . During the week that followed, the flight from the dollar into other currencies added $3.7 billion to other countries' reserves, the largest . . . being $1.7 billion into Swiss francs.

Demands for gold conversion also compounded the American troubles in 1971. The BIS *Annual Report* stated:

> To meet requests for conversion of, or exchange guarantees on, the dollars purchased by central banks, the United States drew down its reserves by $1.1 milliard [billion] in the first half of August, bringing its total reserve loss since the beginning of the year to $3.1 milliard. It also drew $2.4 milliard on the Federal Reserve swap network. But, as the situation had become untenable, President Nixon announced on Sunday, 15 August, the suspension of convertibility to the dollar.

So ended the Bretton Woods system.

# 9.
# Transition

here was a tendency, and a will, to believe that the suspension of gold convertibility on August 15, 1971, was a temporary measure—that somehow the United States would again resume its obligation to restore convertibility, and that one way or another Bretton Woods, perhaps modified, would be restored and the past continue.

From August 1971 into mid-1973, at this writing, there has been a marked transition of views. Transition to what? It is impossible to outline in full the new view, as it is still in formation. But several distinct characteristics of a new outlook may be distinguished.

First, despite all the shocks to the system, the "great wheel" as Adam Smith called the international monetary organization, did not grind to a halt. On the contrary, world trade and investment continued at ever increasing levels of activity. There arose, to be sure, a spate of controls on short-term capital movements, to try to block the waves of money flows that had forced so many of the changes the authorities tried vainly to resist. But these may prove a temporary obsession as equilibrium among exchange rates is restored. In any event, the much-feared trade war, complete with tariffs and countertariffs and a "return to the competitive devaluations of the 1930s"—a state of affairs that never was—these horror scenarios did not come to pass. On the contrary, new negotiations will commence in September 1973, at American initiative, seeking even further reductions in the existing tariff barriers.

Second, the dollar was not "dethroned." The world is on a pure, inconvertible dollar standard, and it is alive and well. The use of the dollar strengthened even as its reputation declined. Europe did not unite to produce a competitive currency unit, although plans aplenty continue to be put forward to that end. It may well be that as equilibrium is further restored and the dollar strengthens, these plans will seem less pressing. In any event, there has appeared no alternative to the dollar; it is still world money.

Third, there has developed a new set of attitudes toward the world monetary system, particularly in the United States and the United Kingdom. Both countries, rather than dying of shame because of devaluations, are very satisfied with the procedure, even though results have been slow in coming. Indeed, in the United Kingdom, and to an increasing extent in the United States, the idea that freely floating currencies may well be the appropriate *system* has taken hold. Put differently, there is a new respect for the ability of free market prices to find the best and quickest "right" answers. Concomitantly, there is recognition that fallible finance ministers, striking poses and bargains, cannot do nearly so well. Economic cooperation among central banks and nations is, of course, desirable, but free markets are a smooth method for organizing and giving direction to cooperation.

Finally, much of the world has also concluded that it cannot look back, cannot patch up the past, but must find new forms to fit the new realities. The ubiquitous John Connally expressed this view with his usual clarity, addressing the Wharton School alumni on April 26, 1973.

> The era of American supremacy in international finance that began in World War II is finished. The monetary and trading system that provided the basis for the postwar era has collapsed. There is no point in kidding ourselves about it, that it is just shaky, that we will reconstruct it. It's gone.

This transition of views was forged in the smithy of experience after August 1971. This chapter examines some of the salient facts and ideas of that period.

When on August 15, 1971, President Nixon suspended convertibility, he also announced wage and price controls, and a 10-percent surcharge on imports.

Wage and price controls were intended to destroy the domestic inflationary psychology and particularly the heavy wage demands, so-called cost-push inflation motivators, which in fact reflected past inflation. The control also served notice of intent that United States costs and prices were to be contained, and international competition sharpened. In the 18 months following, American inflation was in fact less than that in other industrial nations. Price controls were ended in early 1973, although reinstated on some items later in the year. The attempt of the administration expressed in late 1972–early 1973 to contain government spending was a further anti-inflation measure meant to give the dollar additional strength.

The import surcharge was bitterly assailed abroad as a violation of the GATT rules, as wiping out all the tariff reductions so laboriously negotiated under the Dillon and Kennedy rounds, and destructive of the liberal spirit the United States had espoused. But the surcharge was early recognized in the United States as a bargaining pawn to attain some longer-term reform in the world money system, as well as immediate relief for the beleaguered trade balance. Nevertheless, its early repeal was urged, not only by foreign critics but also by many Americans who feared retention could produce the feared trade and tariff war.

Many in Europe thought the breakdown of the system would finally precipitate European monetary cooperation. Professor Triffin of Yale, Belgian born and reflecting strong continuing ties to Europe, is illustrative. In "How to Arrest the Threatening Relapse into the 1930s," published by the Bulletin of the National Bank of Belgium in November 1971, Triffin spoke with authority as a long-time prophet of the inevitable collapse of the gold exchange system:

> The present situation is untenable ... a simple return to the past unthinkable for political as well as economic reasons. ... It is therefore essential to negotiate with all urgency ... a viable international monetary order which will take account ... of the establishment of a European Fund

... for monetary cooperation ... and give the European community ... a consistent and effective policy ... in relation to the rest of the world, especially the dollar area.

At the same time Triffin assailed American "mistakes" and the "supersovereignty of the dollar," now "a paper currency, inconvertible, not only into gold but into any other currency, special drawing rights, or any other generally acceptable instrument." He also took issue with Secretary Connally's position in favor of "clean floating" to permit the markets to determine the true value of exchange rates. "It is doubtful whether such a recommendation will be universally followed."

Nevertheless, into this tense and fearful atmosphere intimations of the reestablishment of "order" began to appear. In the corridors of the IMF meetings in September 1971, rumor had it that a deal had been made to revalue the yen some 15 percent and other currencies less along a declining gradient, which in total would effectively devalue the dollar some 12 percent against its major competitors. And as early as August 28, 1971, the *Economist* (p. 10) reported that "the IMF staff wanted a 15% upvaluation for the yen, just over 12% upvaluation for the mark and about 7% upvaluation for the pound and the franc."

But the *Economist* article also warned, prophetically, that any new fixed exchange rate pattern would probably be wrong. Only markets could determine the proper exchange rates, by free floating. The *Economist* added that

> The staff of the IMF derive their jobs and their degree of power from policing fixed exchange rates, and through laying down conditions (of varied quality) when granting IMF credit to countries that foolishly borrow to protect overvalued rates. (pp. 9–10)

The world should not fall into this trap again, certainly during a period of transition when the true overvaluation of the dollar might prove greater (or less) than even the best econometric estimates could divine.

Perhaps the news that a currency deal was in the making calmed the world's money managers enough to prevent the feared panic and trade war in the fall of 1971. In any event the rumored pattern did come to pass, roughly, in the Smithsonian Agreement of December 18, 1971. In this meeting leaders of the major industrial Group of Ten nations agreed to a new pattern, indicated in Table 14 below. The agreement was, as usual, based on compromises. The United States would legally devalue its currency some 8 percent and thus raise the official price of gold to $38 per ounce. The "pivotal currencies," franc, lira, pound, would remain at their predevaluation parity to gold (i.e., to the predevaluation dollar) and the successful Japanese, German, Swiss, and Dutch currencies would rise. Implicit in this pattern is the view that the French franc was rightly priced, and American devaluation a form of contrition. The gold price matters little under inconvertibility; foreign-owned dollar reserves were marked down 8 percent, gold up 8 percent, both nominally.

This compromise in turn reflected another. The Americans had argued, from econometric models, for enough revaluations (hopefully without any dollar devaluation) to give them a $13 billion annual turnaround in the United States balance of payments. The 1972 *Economic Report of the President* explains the reason for this figure: to overcome a projected $4 billion deficit on current account in 1972; an additional $6 billion of government grants and credits plus private long-term capital outflow; an allowance of $1 billion for "Errors and Omissions"; and finally an allowance of $2 billion to create a surplus, replenish reserves, and serve as a margin of safety. The Europeans argued for a lower turnabout figure, based on the more reserved econometric analyses of the Organization for Economic Cooperation and Development (OECD) and the IMF. Since both models were projections of an uncertain future, either could be justified by a reasonable appeal to assumption. In the end, something closer to the European model prevailed. If American policy had not achieved market-determined parities through clean floating of currencies, it had at least achieved some form of the needed currency reshuffle.

In addition, the permissible margins of fluctuation around parity were increased from 1% plus or minus to 2¼%. Thus a currency could swing as much as 4½% before intervention to preserve its value was required. It was hoped that much of the incentive to speculate against currency repegging had thereby been destroyed. As it turned

**Table 14**

Realignment of leading currencies, May 5–December 18, 1971

| Currencies | Change against gold | Change against U.S. dollar | New central or middle rate for the dollar | New lower and upper limits against the dollar |
|---|---|---|---|---|
| | | In percentages | In currency units per U.S. dollar | |
| Japanese yen | +7.7 | +16.9 | 308.00 | 314.93 – 301.07 |
| Swiss franc | +7.1 | +13.9 | 3.84 | 3.9265 – 3.7535 |
| Austrian schilling | +5.1 | +11.6 | 23.30 | 23.82 – 22.78 |
| Deutsch mark | +4.6 | +13.6 | 3.2225 | 3.295 – 3.150 |
| Belgian franc | +2.8 | +11.6 | 44.8159 | 45.8250 – 43.8075 |
| Dutch guilder | +2.8 | +11.6 | 3.2447 | 3.3175 – 3.171875 |
| Pound sterling | – | + 8.6 | 2.60571* | 2.5471 – 2.6643* |
| French franc | – | + 8.6 | 5.1157 | 5.2310 – 5.0005 |
| Italian lira | –1.0 | + 7.5 | 581.50 | 594.6 – 568.4 |
| Swedish krona | –1.0 | + 7.5 | 4.8129 | 4.920 – 4.705 |
| U.S. dollar | –7.9 | – | – | – |

*Dollars per pound sterling

Source: Bank for International Settlements, *Annual Report*, 1971; p. 30.

out, this hope proved false. The extent of dollar overvaluation had been greater than the new bands. The 10% surcharge was duly removed, the bargain having been struck.

Despite forecasts that the United States Congress would debate devaluation endlessly and never agree to a new gold price, and that Americans would be humiliated by devaluation, Congress in fact concurred with hardly a murmur. On April 3, 1972, the president signed the bill authorizing the new $38 per ounce gold price, reporting it to the IMF on May 5, 1972, when it took effect.

In its logic the December Smithsonian Agreement was a return to a fixed rate system, the root of the troubles. It would have been the wildest coincidence had the exchange rates chosen by the Smithsonian finance ministers coincided with market prices. To be sure, the new "central values" (no longer called parities) reflected the result of floating in the brief four months prior, but a very dirty float in which central banks intervened heavily by buying dollars to keep their exchange rates down.

One result of the events from 1970 through 1972 was a huge shift in the reserve position of nations, illustrated in Chart 3. Cumulative American deficits had, of course, resulted in larger reserves abroad prior to 1971—Chart 3 shows the growth from 1950 to 1964 as well. But the huge addition of dollar reserves, particularly in Japan and Germany—hence in the European Economic Community (EEC) total—is accounted for in large measure by "dirty floating" procedures, which continued into 1972. The results are particularly striking in EEC Europe, which through the 1960s had taken the bulk of their surplus earnings in gold, as the chart shows. The addition of dollars, far in excess of reserve needs, created the "dollar overhang" problem. This new supply of dollars in foreign hands would create major problems for the future reform of the system. They would also find their way into Eurodollar and other deposits, moving quickly through the system, as described in Chapter 11.

Underlying the events was an enormous change in the attitude of Americans toward exchange rate flexibility. Connally in his Wharton School alumni speech recalled the rites of passage:

When I was Secretary of the Treasury, I was sometimes accused of chauvinism—being too rough and too crude and too undiplomatic in my

Chart 3

## Shifts in reserves among nations

1950, 1964, 1972 (end of year)

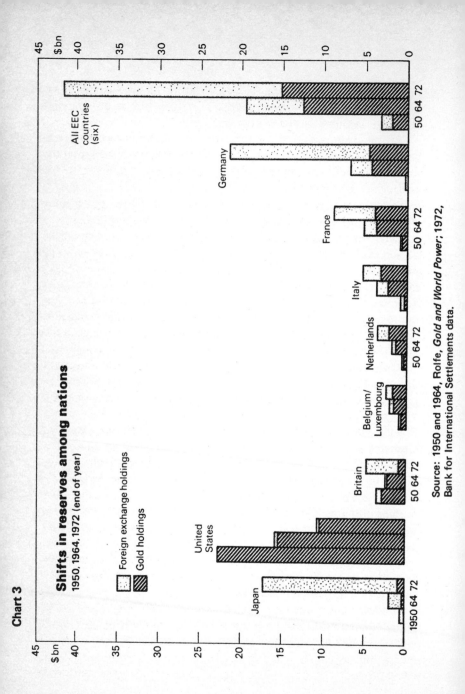

☐ Foreign exchange holdings
▨ Gold holdings

Source: 1950 and 1964, Rolfe, *Gold and World Power;* 1972,
Bank for International Settlements data.

negotiations. But let me tell you, we frankly had the task of not only saying to the rest of the world that the old days were gone and an era had ended and we were entering a new day, we had the problem of convincing our own people in this country and particularly in government. Everyone in government thought, well, we can give them a little monetary magic and we can restore the things back to the way they were. Nonsense—we can't do it, and we are not going to do it.

The United States had actively, even adamantly, supported the fixed exchange rate idea and the existent pattern throughout most of the 1960s. American support was instrumental in the costly British defense of the ($2.80) pound, ending in 1967. The widespread academic attack on rigid support of an overvalued pound and dollar was officially denied or ignored. Fred Hirsch, in the *Economist* of August 5, 1972, has put forward an interesting analysis that ascribes the change of American attitude to the importance of the manufacturing section of the "policy-forming elite," in the Nixon Camp David counsels. Specifically, Mr. Peter Peterson, later to be secretary of commerce and still later to leave the 1973 Nixon administration, was the key economic adviser "whose analysis underlay the Nixon–Connally decision to force a devaluation of the dollar in August 1971. ... " (p. 62)

Peterson had been president of Bell and Howell, which Hirsch describes as a "midwest corporation ... driven out of its original photographics by Japanese competition." This sector of the "manufacturing elite" was most insistent that its international competitive position should stay strong. While most of its spokesmen, for example the Emergency Commission Against Tariffs (ECAT), had deliberately ducked the issue of the monetary system and devaluation, relying instead on "free trade" arguments alone, Peterson faced it. His logic was widely persuasive in Washington. A number of distinguished senators began to warn that the United States was not yet prepared to become a service industry nation "taking in each other's washing," but must have manufactured (and agricultural) goods competitively priced. If an overvalued dollar precluded competitive prices, the dollar must be devalued. Nor were they willing to accept the argument that eventually American investment abroad would produce a capital reflow surplus to overcome persistent trade deficits, not unlike Britain of the Victorian heyday. The agreement crossed party lines.

Peterson's attitude is contrasted by Hirsch with the British banking elite's policy, which urged an all-out fight to keep the overvalued $2.80 pound in 1964–1967. Hirsch writes:

> The key financial advisor who did all he could to prevent a devaluation of the pound in the first half of the 1960s and thereby avoid a further blow to the international role of sterling and prestige of the City of London, was Lord Cromer, ex-managing director of Baring Brothers, a firm which owes its modern existence to the confidence commanded by the Bank of England. (p. 62)

Professor Houthakker has earlier been cited on the difficulties of publicizing "benign neglect." It is noteworthy that an observer as astute as Hirsch did not emphasize the continuity of that policy from 1968 to explain the Nixon administration's position, as Houthakker had. The new view of the dollar and the role of the United States was also a departure from the we-can-do-anything view dominant through the Johnson years. It conformed to the Nixon-Kissinger recognition of the new strength of other political–economic power centers, and a lower profile for the United States abroad. Books and articles with titles like "America in Retreat" have greeted this change. More appropriately they might have been called "America in Reality."

Despite the Smithsonian devaluation, the United States continued to experience formidable deficits in 1972, although improved from 1971. The trade deficit was $6.4 billion, and the total deficit $10 billion. Chart 4 shows the course of United States deficits since 1960, and by the two most common measures, its total deficit by quarters from the end of 1969 through 1972.

Because of the continued troubles in 1972, some doubted the efficacy of devaluation. But the majority of economic opinion recognized that the devaluation was having the desired effect, although it takes a long time for the full effect to be visible. It took Britain nearly two years to reach surplus after 1967; it must take the giant United States at least this long. The United States economy was expanding in 1972. The normal increase of imports during an

**Chart 4**

# United States deficits (Balance of payments $bn)

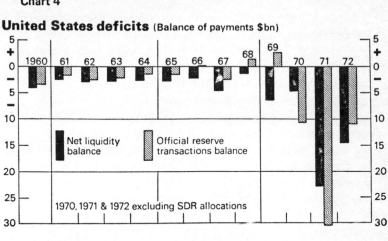

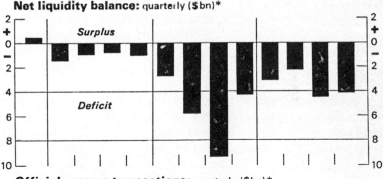

**Net liquidity balance:** quarterly ($bn)*

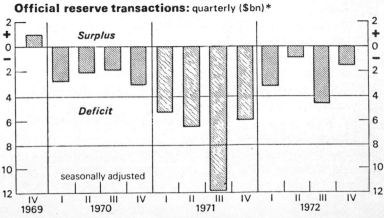

**Official reserve transactions:** quarterly ($bn)*

Source: Based on IMF data.

expansion should have resulted in a much larger deficit than in fact occurred. The American trade balance showed a smaller deficit each quarter of 1972, and into early 1973. By January 1973 exports had risen to an annual rate of near $60 billions, with imports just $300 million greater. On the financial front, the hoped-for flow-back of dollars was not taking place fast enough; money that had shifted into the hard currencies saw no reason to get out of them with conditions still uncertain.

Moreover, through 1972 United States trade deficits continued to be concentrated particularly with Japan and Canada. Chart 5 compares the United States trade position in 1964 and 1972 with that of major countries. This bilateral concentration of the trade problem was thought by some to be beyond the pale of exchange rate adjustment. The Japanese proved the dirtiest floaters of all, successfully holding their exchange rate down although it had increased over one-third against the dollar. The Canadian dollar floated with the United States dollar, and the trade problem was concentrated in automotive parts, pursuant to the Automotive Agreement of 1965 which looked increasingly one-sided to the United States.

The result of these developments was another dollar devaluation by a circuitous route in February 1973, and more currency floating subsequently. In March 1973 and again in June 1973 the German mark raised its "central rate" by 3% and by 5.5% respectively, not only against the dollar, but against all other currencies as well.

The path to the 1973 devaluation should give the orthodox something to ponder. It involved the Italians, whose trade surplus in 1972 was the highest in the world as a percent of GNP, and the Americans, whose inflation rate was less than half that of other major nations. By orthodox reckoning, neither should have been candidates for devaluation. In Italy, the failure of some labor negotiations led to a flight of capital—as lira were spirited out to be exchanged largely for Swiss francs—and a simultaneous demand for devaluation from Italian employers to stimulate profitable exports even more in order to overcome wage losses. Some internal fighting among two of the nine branches of the ruling party added to uncertainty, as "the fangs of Fanfani sank into Andreotti." This renaissance-style drama

Chart 5

## Changes in US trade (trade balances $ bn)

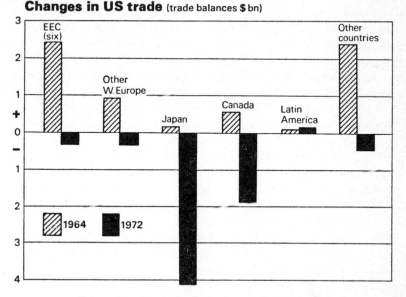

Source: Based on U.S. Department of Commerce data.

added to the demand for Swiss francs, already swollen by "window dressing" demand for balance sheet purposes. The Swiss authorities panicked and allowed their franc to float upward. The nervous with cash saw the system again collapsing, and within days some $8 billion had moved out of dollars, $6 billion into German marks that the Bundesbank bought to protect the mark. Exchange controls made the movement of dollars into yen difficult, and a weak trade balance limited the appeal of the Swiss franc. The Germans estimated that about half the inflow represented lead-lag payments by exporters, most of it by multinational companies.

After an appeal from the Germans and a week of hurried conferences, the United States agreed to devalue an additional 10 percent. Apart from its somewhat bizarre origins, the episode reveals most clearly the profound change in attitudes that had taken place.

The Germans could have revalued, but the "cross rates" among European currencies had become more important than the exchange rate vis-à-vis the dollar. Revaluation would have raised the mark's value against the other European and Japanese currencies, as well as the dollar; dollar devaluation left the European currency relations intact. This desire reflects not only some urge toward monetary union but trade magnitudes as well. Most EEC trade is "internal"—the United States is marginally important. According to the IMF *Direction of Trade* in January—August 1972 France, for example, conducted 56% of its foreign trade with the eight other members of the EEC, 21% with Germany alone, only 5% with the United States, and virtually none ($142 million of $16 billion total, less than 1%) with Japan. Similarly, 47% of German exports go to the EEC group, and 9% to the United States. Other European figures are similar.

In March, and again in June of 1973 Germany raised the "central rate" (formerly parity) of the mark against all currencies. There is great reluctance within the joint-float European countries to change relative exchange rates, for reasons cited above. This apparent contradiction arises from the fact that, despire Germany's understandable reluctance to change its exchange rate vis-à-vis other European currencies, *change* was forced upon it by the continued success of its exports and the continued strength of the mark as a magnet for capital inflows of flight capital. In March 1973 a number of European nations (with the notable exceptions of Switzerland, Italy, and Great Britain) had agreed to a joint float, primarily against the dollar. Thus they would all move up or down *en bloc* so as not to disturb their internal relationships. The Germans had revalued 3% in March in order to be at the bottom of the permissible band of fluctuation vis-à-vis other European countries. But German strength nevertheless drove the mark upward to the top of the band by May 1973 requiring another 5.5% German rise of its central rate in June.

In the United States, the 1973 10% dollar devaluation met with approval from most economists, congressmen of both parties, businessmen and bankers. Indeed it would be hard to find an influential protest. The devaluation brought the dollar closer to the pre-Smithsonian level the United States had desired. The February 17, 1973, "American Survey" of the *Economist* noted:" ... unlike their counterparts in most of Europe and Japan, there is growing support [among United States influentials] for an overt switch to a system of permanently (and cleanly) floating exchange rates for all." The long and lonely espousals of Milton Friedman had moved from far out to front and center.

Table 15 illustrates the cumulative effects of currency changes at various times, compared to the value of the currencies as of July 3, 1973. Thus, between April 30, 1971, before the currency crisis, and July 3, 1973, the German mark, for example, had appreciated by 55% against the dollar. By February 13, 1973, i.e., the second American dollar devaluation, the mark had already appreciated by about one-third, and the Japanese yen a like amount. This led many to believe that this second devaluation promised better performance for the dollar. Nevertheless, speculative activity against the dollar continued to be heavy, resulting in further appreciations of the various currencies against the dollar. The February 1973 dollar devaluation as well as the subsequent upward floating of various other currencies came against the background of an improving American trade position into 1973, although one insufficient to inhibit speculative movement against the dollar in the foreign exchange markets. The United States government did little or nothing to inhibit these movements by direct intervention. Some argue that by mid-1973 the dollar was consequently an undervalued currency; but the policy of benign neglect dictates that if this is so the correction will come through speculation in favor of the dollar in the foreign exchange markets rather than government intervention.

The announcement by Secretary Schultz in February 1973 that capital controls would be removed in 1974, presumably eliminating the Interest Equalization Tax, restrictions on bank lending abroad, and the OFDI controls, should also have an important impact on dollars held abroad, assisting their return, a matter further discussed in Chapter 11.

A second major consequence of developments in 1972–1973 was a new focus on trade. The world is still hemmed by tariffs and restrictions of all types. The United States has difficult problems,

**Table 15**

Appreciation of selected currencies against U.S. dollar as of July 3, 1973

| | May 25, 1973[a] | Mar. 16, 1973[b] | Feb. 13, 1973[c] | Dec. 18, 1971[d] | April 30, 1971[e] |
|---|---|---|---|---|---|
| Switzerland | 11.5 | 14.3 | 22.8 | 36.7 | 55.7 |
| Germany[g] | 17.2 | 18.6 | 22.8 | 36.5 | 55.0 |
| Belgium[g] | 9.0 | 9.8 | 12.5 | 25.1 | 39.5 |
| Netherlands[g] | 11.1 | 10.7 | 13.3 | 25.9 | 40.5 |
| France[f, g] | 9.4 | 11.1 | 13.3 | 25.8 | 36.6 |
| U.K. | 1.4 | 4.7 | 5.3 | −1.0 | 7.5 |
| Italy[f] | 3.0 | −0.9 | −2.8 | 1.2 | 8.8 |
| Japan | 1.9 | −2.9 | 2.7 | 17.0 | 36.8 |

[a]After the mark rose from the joint float floor.

[b]Before the beginning of joint float and 3% mark revaluation.

[c]After the second dollar devaluation.

[d]After Smithsonian Agreement.

[e]Before mark and guilder floated.

[f]Commercial rates.

[g]"Joint Float" European currencies.

Source: Based on daily 'spot' rates reported in the press.

particularly with Canada and Japan. In part, this reflects the need of the United States to absorb an unduly large proportion of Japanese exports because they are excluded from or restricted in Europe. New rounds of trade talks are set to begin in September 1973. While a full analysis of these problems is the subject of other inquiries, some of the general lines of American thinking may be seen in the following excerpts of the aforementioned talk of John Connally to the Wharton school alumni:

> No monetary apparatus, however sophisticated, can counteract the effect of basic distortions in the patterns of trade among the great nations of the world.
>
> Many of these nations impose competitive disadvantages upon us. Japan, for instance, sets very strict quotas on United States high technology products such as computers. What Japan does allow imported, they tax heavily. And Japan's restrictions on foreign investments make it all but impossible to circumvent these barriers ...
> Somehow, in spite of all its international commitments to trade, it is significant that France literally embargoes imports from Japan in 78 of its 120 industrial classifications—a complete embargo. That limits trade between the two nations to less than $500 million. If that was all the trade we had between the United States and Japan, we would be in pretty good shape, too.

Citing imbalances with Canada as well, Connally supported the proposal in the new trade bill granting the president freedom to impose or reduce tariffs at his discretion:

> He needs freedom when necessary to raise tariffs and impose quotas ... to swap cuts in United States tariffs for matching concessions from other nations ... to be able to say we'll play by whatever rules you want. ... If you want to restrict our goods we will restrict yours. If you want to allow ours in, we'll let yours in. ...

Anticipating domestic resistance, the former secretary warned:

> There are a lot of people in this country who I think live in the past too much. Their feelings are hurt because the old days are gone. Well, be that as it may, the truth of the matter is that the negotiating process which always negotiated the United States down and other countries up should be buried deep and permanent.

In the past, trade and monetary negotiations have been kept separate, for the simple reason that each is difficult enough without linking the two. But the United States is insistent that trade liberalization and monetary reforms now be linked. United States Treasury officials have asked the IMF's Group of 20 to consider the kinds of trading practices that should or should not be tolerated in a given monetary system. And the Americans have claimed that monetary reform must incorporate and reflect trade problems.

This American insistence on a link may be a new clarity. The idea is not new: the IMF has always pressed for trade liberalization, while GATT has always considered balance of payments problems a cause for justifiable trade restrictions. It may, on the other hand, be a residual obsession from the 1971 trauma, when the American trade balance went negative for the first time this century. Overvaluation and not illiberalism, or at any rate not more than traditional illiberalism in trade, may have been the root of the problem. The focus of anxiety on trade may be misplaced.

Nevertheless, it exists. Essentially the United States has three bilateral trade problems, with Europe, Japan, and Canada, each with different dimensions, each, in present official American opinion, requiring some solution before a viable money system can function.

The American displeasure with Europe focuses on the Value Added Tax (VAT), which is *effectively* an export subsidy; with the Common Agricultural Policy (CAP), which inhibits United States exports at prices above world market levels; and with the special trading arrangements the Common Market has created with 40 developing nations, which constitute a protected bloc. While the Europeans do not have very good answers on any of these matters, the three subjects for complaint are among the major accomplishments of the Common Market. They are nearly unnegotiable.

Paul Fabra, economics editor of *Le Monde*, interpreted the French position in the October 1972 *Euromoney*:

> The French are not ready to make substantial concessions on trade in order to involve the Americans in monetary negotiations. They will abide strictly by the principle of reciprocity, particularly for agriculture.

The French do not expect any monetary solutions for at least two years, in any event. They do expect the vote of the peasants to be very important in the 1976 French presidential elections.

The American problem with Japan has been noted earlier: this is the largest deficit area, a nation whose import policy, trading practice, and multinational corporate restrictions are classic. But Japan incurred a substantial overall deficit of $1.1 billion for the month of April 1973. Trade, seasonally adjusted, was still in surplus by $460 million, down nearly half from $722 million in April 1972, but still an annual surplus rate approaching $6 billion. The return flow of dollars and Japanese long-term capital investments abroad of $740 million, up from $261 million a year earlier, account for the deficit. America's problem with Japan is exacerbated by Europe's restrictions on Japanese exports. On the other hand, Japan has followed the path of economic virtue, as Chart 6 shows, so that her exports represent the end product of great saving, investment, and productivity. These advantages can be dampened by the rising value of the yen.

The Canadian-American Automotive Agreement lies at the heart of the United States deficit there. Of $9 billion of auto parts imports in 1971, $5 billion were Canadian. The net deficit on this trade, by American (but not by Canadian) reckoning, had been nearly $680 million in 1969, in contrast to a United States automotive surplus of $580 million with Canada in 1964, a swing of $1,260 million.

In the transition period, multinational companies (MNCs) also came to the fore as a subject of controversy. They were accused now of a new set of alleged evils, to fit the times—the focus of anxiety changes, the basic anxiety remains. It would be odd if the multinationals, producing goods estimated at over $300 billion per year, an amount greater than any national GNP except that of the United States—subject to no national control, perceived as a threat to sovereign power, serving to integrate the developed world's economy while its political sentiments still reside within nations—it would be surprising indeed if such a phenomenon did not arouse anxieties. In the past when the anxieties have been scrutinized, they have been found to be more apparent than real. Economic benefits have been weighed against psychological or political (i.e., nationalistic) costs. The result was a standoff: Costs and benefits

**Chart 6**

# The four cardinal virtues

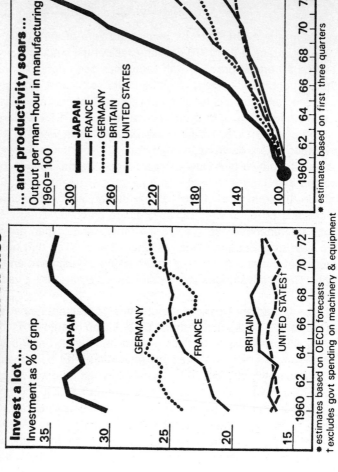

**Invest a lot…**
Investment as % of gnp

JAPAN

GERMANY

FRANCE

BRITAIN

UNITED STATES†

35
30
25
20
15

1960 62 64 66 68 70 72*

\* estimates based on OECD forecasts
† excludes govt spending on machinery & equipment

**…and productivity soars…**
Output per man–hour in manufacturing
1960=100

JAPAN
FRANCE
GERMANY
BRITAIN
UNITED STATES

300
260
220
180
140
100

1960 62 64 66 68 70 72*

\* estimates based on first three quarters

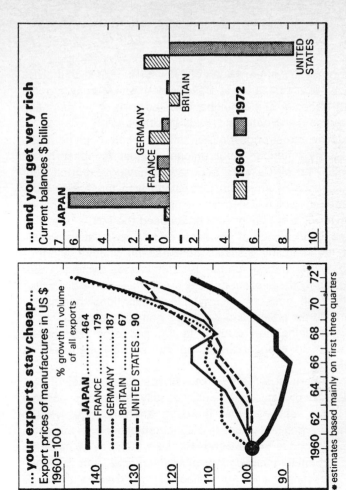

## ...your exports stay cheap...

Export prices of manufactures in US $
1960=100

% growth in volume
of all exports

JAPAN ........ 464
FRANCE ........ 179
GERMANY ........ 187
BRITAIN ........ 67
UNITED STATES .. 90

140
130
120
110
100
90

1960 62 64 66 68 70 72*

* estimates based mainly on first three quarters

## ...and you get very rich

Current balances $ billion

JAPAN    FRANCE    GERMANY    BRITAIN    UNITED STATES

7
6
4
2
+
0
−
2
4
6
8
10

1960   1972

Source: The *Economist*, April 1972.

were not denominated in the same coin. It was, as Professor Melville Watkins once put it, comparing apples and oranges. Moreover, in the past it was the specter of the multinationals as arms of the American Goliath facing so many national Davids that rankled.

Paradoxically, the strongest attack this time was mounted in the United States by American labor unions, against American-based multinationals. The MNCs were accused of having exported hundreds of thousands of American jobs, along with those very technological leads on which United States productivity and hence high wage rates were based. Labor further accused the MNCs of having hurt the American balance of payments and of speculating against the dollar in the company of sheiks, gnomes, and whatnot, and thus contributing to the demise of the Bretton Woods system. Labor proposed to rectify these alleged ills by the Burke–Hartke bill, which would inhibit (and possibly destroy) the multinational companies through punitive tax policy, and would be generally protectionist in its impact, permitting new quotas, tariffs, and other barriers to preserve "jobs" in every industry, no matter how inefficient or uncompetitive.

When the American system works well, a sudden, concentrated, determined attack on established policy usually brings in response a slower but more reasoned and thorough analysis, in which the validity of the charges and issues is weighed objectively. In this case, the reasoned response to the Burke–Hartke attack has come in the form of a report entitled *Implications of Multinational Firms for World Trade and Investment and for United States Trade and Labor.* Prepared for the Committee on Finance of the United States Senate by the United States Tariff Commission staff and published in February 1973, the document is known in these pages as the TC report. Its 930 pages are conducive neither to easy reading nor to summarizing. But for all its size and complication, the report is well worth the effort. It reveals the attack on the multinationals to have been ill-advised, and in many charges and specifications erroneous.

In briefest summary, the TC's findings give the MNCs a clean bill of health on most of the issues, from an American point of view.

Logically, the first allegation and response would relate to the MNCs impact on the United States trade balance. Do the MNCs hamper United States exports by importing from their foreign affiliates, or by using the output of their foreign subsidiaries or affiliates to supply foreign markets which otherwise could be supplied from the United States? The TC report cites an enormous export surplus accruing to the United States from the MNCs. Noting "the MNCs' 62% of United States exports of manufactured goods, which contrasts favorably with their 34% share of imports of manufactures," the TC concludes:

> The MNCs' could be affecting changes in United States exports and imports in either or both of two ways: (1) through their "direct" effect, which should be observable in their own export and import performance, in shipments from and to the United States; and (2) through their "indirect" effect, which is the substitution of foreign affiliates' production for United States exports in foreign markets. Industry-by-industry estimates of the direct effects suggest that the MNCs' performance has been highly favorable. From 1966 through 1970, they generated $3.4 billion more in new exports than in new imports, whereas non-MNC firms in manufacturing produced $3.6 billion more in new imports than new exports. Similar estimates for the indirect effects indicate a net gain in new United States exports of $400 million over the same period.
>
> Taking the direct and indirect effects together, there were sixteen industries in which net increases of United States exports in the amount of $7.3 billion appeared; there were eight industries in which net decreases (or net new imports) totalling $3.4 billion appeared—the total sample size having been reduced from 29 to 24 industries because of unavoidable combinations of industries in the course of the analysis. The overall result for all manufacturing, therefore, shows the MNCs' impact on change in United States trade from 1966 through 1970 to have been favorable by $2.9 billion in net new exports.

Parenthetically, the TC report notes:

> This "net" estimate, however, is built up from results for individual industries which vary very widely.

The Burke–Hartke bill, or any bill directed at the "multinationals," must cut across the board; it can hardly be directed at specific industries or companies. Therefore, the exporters would suffer with the importers. Most exports by MNCs go to their affiliates abroad; this traffic represents some 25 percent of all United States export shipments.

Do the foreign affiliates cause a loss of jobs in the United States?

### Has the spread of multinational business reduced American employment?

This question cannot be answered conclusively, because both the analysis and the answer must depend on crucial assumptions about:

(a) How much of the MNCs' investment abroad was made to pre-empt foreign markets that would have been lost to foreign competition anyway; and

(b) What portion of the markets now served by the MNCs' affiliates abroad could have been served by United States exports of domestic merchandise in the affiliates' absence.

Nevertheless, it is possible at least to estimate the outer bounds of what the direct employment effects of MNC activity in manufacturing may have been. The most pessimistic estimate assumes that if there were no United States plants abroad, foreign countries would not replace the output of those United States plants with local production but would import the entire output from the United States. Under these assumptions, the presence of United States plants abroad represents a net loss of 1.3 million United States jobs. A second estimate assumes that foreign countries would replace half the output of their United States plants from their own production and import the remainder from the United States. Under these circumstances there is a net loss of 400,000 jobs.

An attempt was made to frame a set of assumptions that has more realism than those of the first two estimates described. These assumptions assert that, in the absence of the United States MNCs, foreigners would not have substituted their own plants for those of the MNCs, but that United States exports could reasonably be expected only to have maintained the shares of world exports of manufactures that they held in 1960–61, rather than to have taken completely all the markets served abroad by the MNCs' affiliates. Under these assumptions, the net employment effect in manufacturing shows a gain of roughly half a million United States jobs.

### What about the balance of payments consequences of the MNCs?

The MNCs played no role in this deterioration. In the 1966–70 period, their position with respect to the "basic balance" improved by $2.8 billion. Non-MNCs in the private sector, on the other hand, showed a deterioration of $3.3 billion ... an aggregate decline for private sector transactions of $500 million.

The TC report, however, notes the concentration of the United

States deficit with Canada, chiefly because of trade in autos, which goes through MNC channels albeit pursuant to a trade agreement. With Japan, where the deficit also is large, the MNCs "improved their position—a sharp contrast against the general deterioration of the United States balance ... on non-MNC account."

Finally, what about the MNCs' speculation against the dollar through the international money markets? Citing their estimate that some $268 billion exist, traded in private markets virtually uncontrolled by official institutions anywhere, of which MNCs' affiliates control nearly half (see Table 16, pp. 150–151), the TC concludes:

> Because $268 billion is such an immense number, it is clear that only a small fraction of the assets which it measures needs to move in order for a genuine crisis to develop. The international money market, possessing such a *masse de manoeuvre* as well as an efficiency and flexibility unknown in the past (even the recent past), can focus with telling effect on a crisis-prone situation—some weak currency which repels funds and some strong one which attracts them.
>
> Because such a small proportion of the resources of the MNCs is needed to produce monetary explosions, it appears appropriate to conclude that destructive predatory motivations do not characterize the sophisticated international financial activities of most MNCs, even though much of the funds which flow internationally during the crisis doubtless is of MNC origin. Rather, the important role of the MNCs has been to provide the primary creative force in the development of the international money market, a market which is now fully institutionalized as a reality of international financial life. This is the sense in which the MNCs indeed have altered the conditions around which the policies of governments are framed.

Apart from the TC report, other sources corroborate the fact that multinationals do not do much overt speculation but do engage in lead-lag payments. German bank sources ascribed about half of the $6 billion inflow in early 1973 to leads and lags in payments. When the dollar devalued 10%, the Germans lost $600 million (10% of $6 billion purchased) trying to hold down the mark; half of this went to those who had hedged by leads and lags. The MNCs can hardly be blamed for these gifts from the Germans, whose insistence upon the protection of a fixed but wrong rate created them. A floating rate would have minimized the loss. A study by W. Mansir for the

International Chamber of Commerce and studies on financial practices by multinational companies conducted at the Harvard Business School corroborate the relative absence of overt speculation. The Harvard study finds three types of multinationals: those too big and obvious to afford being caught speculating, the medium-sized who do most of it, and the unsophisticated (usually smaller) MNCs who have neither the personnel nor knowledge to benefit from currency movements.

It is difficult, however, to see why the MNCs are so coy about speculation. The word is, after all, only a pejorative synonym for the protection or preservation of assets. A company treasurer who failed to do this could be remiss—he might make the company liable to stockholders' suits for dissipation of assets.

Nor did (or could) the TC report point out that both the expansion of multinationals abroad and labor's malaise about exports and jobs are reflections of the overvaluation of the dollar. Labor, if properly advised, would have focused its efforts to correct that overvaluation, rather than turning to protectionism which must, in the end, impoverish and not enrich the nation. Multinationals will be less prone to go abroad with a properly valued currency; on the contrary an inflow of foreign funds both for direct investment and for portfolio investment into the United States might now be expected and is indeed already visible on a considerable scale, providing additional American jobs.

Other issues remain for the future as well. The cost of military expenditures abroad continues to be an important drain. As the U.S. trade balance rises and concern with the balance of payments moves from the crisis atmosphere of the last few years to something resembling normalcy, this problem will reassert itself. Presumably payments for troops abroad can be reduced in the atmosphere of general détente with the Russians. The proposals for a balanced troop reduction have been noted earlier. There will remain to be negotiated, however, arrangements under which the remaining cost of troops will need to be borne to a greater extent than before by the Europeans and the Japanese.

The proposed unification of the European monetary system —more permanent in nature than the joint float described earlier —could present another great structural change in the international monetary system of the future. While details of plans and hopes are not worth examination since they so often fail to come to fruition, the basic principle behind the long-term thrust for European monetary unification remains valid. That principle was reflected in a talk by Italy's Dr. Ossola in February 1972.

> So long as the dollar remains inconvertible, that is probably during most of the 1970s, the problem of adjustment between the U.S. and the EEC should be solved through the free fluctuation of the dollar vis-à-vis the EEC currencies as a whole, these latter's reciprocal relations being based on relatively fixed parities.

Meanwhile, in this view, short-term capital controls and a code of conduct for long-term capital movements between large monetary areas would be needed to prevent "undesirable investment flows and unwanted changes of the respective competitive positions."

The initial thrust toward European monetary integration and fixed rates among the Europeans had been based on a desire to sustain the Common Agricultural Policy, itself an ill-conceived plan designed to subsidize European, and particularly French, farmers at the consumer's expense at prices well above world levels. But the focus on farm policy has been replaced by the longer-term needs to achieve what the October 1972 Paris summit meeting described as European unity by 1980. This goal is, of course, fraught with political peril as it involves the surrender of sovereign decisions. The prospects for monetary unification and with it for a "Europa" or alternative currency to the dollar ultimately, are, of course, difficult to assess. More impossible things have happened. The charitable view of the disruptions to date would be that they have been unpredictable, a series of unforeseen upheavals in the world currency system. The more realistic view would be that the arrangements set up by the monetary planners were doomed to failure from the start because they were founded on wishful thinking. These emphasize the benefits of unification without appropriate attention to the costs. There is in consequence little progress toward unification.

A final issue overhanging the entire monetary system is the energy crisis. This crisis arises because the United States must increase its imports of oil by about one-third to meet its present and projected energy requirements. Payments for this oil are currently projected in astronomical figures, not infrequently $30 billion per year, going mainly to underdeveloped and probably undevelopable Arab countries. To pay for this formidable total, the United States will be forced to increase its exports to the rest of the world by an amount equal to about 50 percent of its current exports, devaluing if necessary to get to this position. In the meantime its energy, and so its security, will be in the hands of the Arab world. The scenario above is based on straight line projections from the current uses and sources. It is unlikely to happen that way. There will, to begin with, have to be restrictions on the demand side, which will be forced by the increasing price of oil if nothing else. A more promising approach lies in changing the structure of the supply side of energy. What is required is something like a Manhattan project to find an equivalent for oil very soon. The 1973 energy proposals of the president have been severely criticized because they fail completely to take cognizance of this approach; instead, the alternatives he foresees are technologies that will require long-term implementation—toward the year 2000. A formidable school of opinion now exists which claims that hydrogen or related fuels can be used within a reasonably short time as substitutes for some portion of the oil demand. Some private sources are now beginning to invest sums for development of this type of technology, but it remains the responsibility of the federal government to move along these lines, and its failure to do so is apt to become a major political issue. As former Commerce Secretary Peterson warned: "Popeye is running out of spinach." It is difficult to believe that more reasonable solutions, less damaging to the future of the international monetary system, will not be found.

# 10.
# Reform

here are now two views of reform of the international monetary system. First, the conventional view, the terms of reference of which were set at the time of the Smithsonian Agreement on December 18, 1971. Here the politics of monetary reform are at least as important as the economics. The initial part of this chapter examines the elements of the conventional approach to reform, some suggested solutions, and some problems.

A second view argues that the major premise of the conventional view—a return to American-based convertibility of dollars to gold or to some other superior reserve asset—is simply not in sight for this decade. Therefore a grandiose scheme for reform may be an irrelevant exercise. This view further argues that much of the needed reform has taken place through economic and market, rather than political, forces and that to reimpose political solutions could be counterproductive. A discussion of these views concludes the chapter.

Turning first to the conventional, establishment view of reform, the Smithsonian Agreement of December 1971 not only set new exchange rates but also issued a call for a reform of the monetary system. In many respects this call involves a patching up and restoring of the Bretton Woods system rather than a fundamental rethinking toward a new system.

A broad outline of the elements to be reformed appears in the now famous last paragraph of the Smithsonian communiqué of December 18, 1971:

> ... that attention should be directed to the appropriate monetary means and division of responsibility for defending stable exchange rates and for ensuring the proper degree of convertibility of the system; to the proper role of gold, of reserve currencies, and of Special Drawing Rights and the operation of the system; to the appropriate volume of liquidity. ...

Pursuant to this general desire, there was established in the fall of 1972 a Committee of the Board of Governors (of the IMF) on Reform of the International Monetary System and Related Issues, under the chairmanship of Mr. Jeremy Morse of the Bank of England. Commonly known as the Group of 20, or G-20, it consists of senior members of the treasuries and central banks of the ten major industrial countries and of ten selected less-developed countries meant to represent the interests of the developing world. G-20 is charged with preparing a plan of reform that would eventually change the Articles of Agreement of the International Monetary Fund by the adoption of new articles by members of the IMF, pursuant to the voting arrangements of that body. The work of the committee is ongoing. It was initially hoped that the 1973 IMF meeting in Nairobi could pass on its findings, although a later date now seems more likely.

Reform did not start with G-20 but is part of an evolutionary process going on since the later 1960s when SDRs were first agreed upon. It has been noted earlier that the creation of SDRs was primarily aimed at the liquidity problem. The ever increasing volume of trade and capital would presumably require larger, and managed, predetermined levels of liquidity. Liquidity had traditionally been provided by two whimsical elements: the amount of gold that could be produced and taken into official reserves at the official price; and the deficits in the U.S. balance of payments that were reflected as growing dollar reserves in other nations' coffers. While the world was inundated with unwanted dollars from 1971 on, it was believed that at some point in the future the flow of deficit dollars must stop. At this point a more rational reserve supply will be needed.

The second major element requiring reform has been the adjustment process. A functioning adjustment process would effectively stop the cumulation of excess deficits or surpluses and bring the system back to something resembling equilibrium, i.e., to a zero net balance for all countries with all others. The adjustment provisions of the Bretton Woods system were themselves not as defective as the psychological limitations that had come to restrict their use. Nations were reluctant to devalue or revalue, as the Bretton Woods rules had provided, and consequently the system did not work.

A basic asymmetry had developed in the system. The reserve currency countries, the United States and to a lesser extent the United Kingdom, were the great deficit centers, which we have called the "money machine" of the post–World War II era. Their overvalued currencies were in patent need of devaluation from the early 1960s on. But they resisted devaluation because such action, they said, would be irresponsible, would deplete the reserve holdings of other nations, and be a basic shock to the system. Other nations were freer to use the adjustment mechanism to devalue, and at least in the case of France and the less developed countries, it was used frequently. Equilibrium also required the surplus countries, particularly Germany and Japan, to revalue. In 1961 Germany and Holland had revalued by small amounts, voluntarily, to combat the inflation to which large reserves were contributing. Not until the huge capital inflows of 1969, 1971 particularly, and 1973—under market duress, so to speak —were any significant revaluations effected. The surplus countries, bemused by mercantilist desires and under political pressure from their own exporters, were more than reluctant to move voluntarily. The "scarce currency" clause in the Bretton Woods rules, which permitted other countries to impose tariffs on perennial surplus nations and thus reduce their export capabilities, was in fact simply never used.

The two major areas of needed reform have therefore been the provision of liquidity and an efficient adjustment process. The latter had become by far the more important issue by the 1960s, but no progress could be made toward reform. The attempts by the United States to talk adjustment had been rebuffed. The surplus countries had no desire to change the status quo, and the United States had no power to make them do so until the "benign neglect" strategy flooded the world market with dollars and led to the 1971 cessation of convertibility, and the Connally import surcharge tactic forced the issue. The fact that there was some agreement in the liquidity area, SDRs, was hailed as international cooperation. And indeed it was, on the less relevant or pressing matter.

Now with reform a serious matter, how will the centrally important matter of the adjustment process—meaning, ultimately, devaluation and revaluation by all the major currencies when needed and enforcement of sanctions—be provided?

From the outset the Americans and the Europeans have taken differing positions on how to determine when exchange rate changes are necessary. Both the important speech delivered by Secretary Schultz at the 1972 IMF meetings and papers submitted to the G-20 pressed the idea developed in academic circles that changes in the level of normal reserves should lead to discussions with, and perhaps guidance from, the IMF, and eventually to exchange rate changes, if needed to restore equilibrium.

The idea of changes in normal reserves to trigger action leaves much unanswered. First, what is "normal"? The very idea suggests a static state; Europe and Japan have grown on the inflow of American reserves, the money machine of our time. A halt to the procedure cannot be attractive to them, provided the growth does not reach cancerous proportions, as it did in 1971. Secondly, the talky procedure that deviations in reserves would institute may itself be an invitation to intense short-term capital flows. If the authorities are talking to country X about its reluctance to revalue, it would be a prudent move for a money manager to be in that currency, or to lead and lag his payments in X's favor. X's currency may rise; given the circumstances, it will probably not fall. Third, what are "reserves"? The central banks gain dollars from private owners as a residual. Sizable pools of dollars in private hands can be turned in quickly for local currencies if dollars appear weak, or can be drawn from central bank reserves by private owners if the dollar appears strong (possibly even a candidate for revaluation), or can be drawn for deposit in Eurodollars, when interest rates beckon. It was alleged that in 1972 and early 1973 the Japanese central bank "persuaded" Japanese commercial banks to deposit $2 billion or more in

Eurodollar accounts. This served to reduce Japanese reserves and the pressure to revalue—and incidentally flooded the Eurodollar banks, leading to loans of reduced quality, a subject dealt with elsewhere. The point at issue is not Japan but the possibility of devices to mask real levels of reserves.

Moreover, whatever agreement is reached on presumptive rules or the trigger for greater exchange rate flexibility, it becomes apparent from the foregoing discussion that some administrative judgments will be required to interpret the trends. Analysis is required, for example, to determine whether an increase in reserves is temporary or permanent, based on real movements or on short-term capital movements that can easily reverse themselves, and so on. And when one moves away from rules to authority, presumably the IMF, with greater and somewhat more arbitrary intervention or decision-making powers than it now has, will be necessary.

There has always been something less than great enthusiasm about the International Monetary Fund. The IMF came into its own only after 1958 with the disappearance of the European Payments Union (EPU) and the end of recourse to transitional exchange controls under the IMF's Article XIV. Its resources and policies were further developed in the early 1960s. A 50 percent increase in quotas in 1959 raised its capital from $10 to $15 billion. But in 1961 the General Agreement to Borrow, providing a further $6 billion, was negotiated by the ten leading industrial nations only. The IMF was not altogether at the center of things in the first half of the 1960s. The network of central bank swaps and other credit arrangements among the industrial countries, designed to combat capital flows, was outside the IMF. Its worldwide membership, and perhaps its location in Washington, were felt during the early 1960s to make it an unsuitable forum for discussion among the countries that "mattered." Working Party Three of the OECD Economic Policy Committee was set up in 1961 in Paris and became the main forum for balance of payments questions. The Group of Ten began deliberating on world monetary reform in 1963, outside the IMF.

The IMF's prestige, however, began to rise with the creation and issue of Special Drawing Rights. It was also asked to make studies on some aspects of reform. Since 1971 the IMF has been in a somewhat ambivalent position. On the one hand, it has faced operational difficulties; it has been deprived of its foundation—the convertibility of currencies into gold. Unless convertibility is restored, either the rules must be very much rewritten or the IMF will cease to be very important. The IMF executive directors were asked to prepare a report, while the G-20 deliberations were going forth, on reform of the international monetary system. That report, published in the late summer of 1972, is not a blueprint but a discussion of the main symptoms of the present and of ways to attack them. Conflicting opinions among the major countries are clearly stated. Nevertheless, there does emerge from the report something like consensus. Briefly, SDRs should become the principal reserve asset. Balance of payments deficits should be settled in reserve assets, without running up liabilities; an exchange rate should be changed promptly and by moderate amounts, by surplus and deficit countries alike. A system along these lines would mean an enlarged role for the IMF in administering SDRs and in the procedures leading to changes in exchange parities. This report suggests not only changes in reserves as a guideline for exchange rate policy, but also changes in price levels and other guidelines.

Some students of the monetary system have expressed doubt that such an SDR system will prove viable. For example, Oxford's Peter Oppenheimer in the October 1972 *Euromoney* writes:

> ... its key weakness is the radical separation which it makes between the achievement of an equilibrium structure of exchange rates and the creation of new reserve. In other words, the conception of overall equilibrium ... maintains a "zero balance of payments" ... [with] reserve increases entirely through the creation of SDRs in the books of the IMF. ... Governments cannot manage balance of payments with such precision. If called upon to do so, they are more likely to fall back on a floating exchange rate as Britain did early this year.
>
> In contrast to an SDR system, a widespread tendency toward floating rates, whether by individual countries or by blocks, would diminish the importance of the IMF ... that is one reason why the recent Fund Report does not even consider the possibility of a block system as an alternative to worldwide reform.

Oppenheimer concludes that blocks would be messy, ill-defined, and a less elegant and streamlined system than the one based on SDRs.

But then we all know that the tortoise was less elegant and streamlined than the hare.

Despite the alleged appearance of an establishment view favoring SDRs and more flexible exchange rates, the *Financial Times* of January 26, 1973, states that Mr. Jeremy Morse, after three days of G-20 discussion

did not hide that wide differences remain, particularly over the exchange rate adjustment process which the United States wants to work effectively and decisively. ...

By mid-1973 subsequent meetings of the G-20 had failed to bring views relating to exchange rate adjustment or reserve assets beyond a "tentative stage."

Another major issue in the Smithsonian communiqué is the proper degree of convertibility. The Bretton Woods system of convertibility of surplus dollars to gold cannot be revived now. Approximately $100 billion of "dollar overhang" is in the hands of foreigners, increasingly in foreign central banks; this faces some $10 billion of "gold backing" for the dollars, an obvious discrepancy. Any convertibility undertaking by the United States would therefore require two steps: (1) the refunding of the dollar overhang, and (2) convertibility of new (post refunding) dollars for gold or some other acceptable reserve asset. This revival scenario assumes that the dollar will remain the "key" currency in the system, which it probably will simply because there is no alternative.

Refunding, in the usual formulation, would be in exchange for SDRs. The IMF would issue SDRs to those nations which have dollars in excess of working balances they wish to retain. Some question the wisdom of a sudden, large issue of SDRs: This now valued unit could experience a decline in quality as its quantity increased. Some, e.g., the Monetary Committee of the Atlantic Council of the United States, have therefore suggested instead the issue of a special IMF credit instrument that nations could use in the settlement of deficits. It would be preferable, if it were feasible without demeaning their quality, to use SDRs, which would, in the process, become the world's reserve unit, replacing or supplementing the dollar. The *numéraire* of the system, i.e., the stated relationship of one currency to another, would be in terms of SDRs.

The IMF in turn would return the dollars "refunded" to the United States for nonmarketable Treasury obligations. As an inducement for nations to refund, some have suggested that the United States guarantee through the IMF the value of the obligations in terms of SDRs against future devaluation. Similarly, interest paid by the United States to the IMF would be transferred to the owners of SDRs or the special credit instrument, probably in excess of the current $1\frac{1}{2}$ percent paid on SDRs.

Several questions appear: How big is the "overhang," i.e., how many dollars will nations want to keep in their reserves for working balances? Professor Triffin had suggested that this figure be 15 percent of reserves; others would leave the decision to each country. Since the interest rate on SDRs or the new credit instrument will presumably be lower than market, some countries will prefer to hold their dollars, earning United States money market or Eurodollar interest rates, particularly if they have confidence in the dollar's future. The size of the overhang may therefore be less than it currently appears. Once the overhang is out of the way, the United States would presumably "convert" only net, new deficit balances, after a certain date. Convert to what? If gold conversion were resumed, the drain on the U.S. gold stock would continue. For when the United States was in surplus, it could receive dollars in payment; when in deficit, it would have to pay out gold, its sole reserve. E. M. Bernstein has suggested that all nations pay, when in deficit, a balance or composite of their reserves, including gold, SDRs, and foreign exchange. Thus the United States would collect some gold—the percentage varies among countries—but always pay out a greater percentage of gold when in deficit, since virtually all of its reserves are in that metal. Many Americans object to this continual drain. Although the United States officially favors "phasing out" gold, there is considerable reluctance to phase out its own last $10 billion—as can be seen by the August 15, 1971, move abrogating convertibility.

Other problems also appear in this scenario. The present surplus nations would start the game with huge SDR reserves, in place of dollars. The United States has few. To prevent its having to pay out mostly gold, some suggest a loan of SDRs to the United States, which it would repay as it earns them through its own surpluses. Exchange rate flexibility is also central to this scenario. If in deficit, the United States would presumably be able to devalue, now in terms of SDRs, but in so doing would sustain losses because it has guaranteed its obligations to the IMF, hence to dollar refunders, in terms of SDRs. Should the United States be hobbled by this additional cost of flexibility? Would surplus nations want to refund unless they had a guarantee from the United States? What happens if the United States revalues as the dollar strengthens in the future?

The restoration of convertibility thus involves some serious departures from the old system. It is a patch job and lacks the compelling clarity of convertibility to gold. It is fraught with questions to which there are as yet neither answers nor the basis for answers. For these reasons, many believe that convertibility will not be restored in this decade. Some had earlier proclaimed that the system could not work without convertibility; the experience of 1972–1973 is that it has.

Finally, what about gold? As uncertainty about paper has increased, the private markets for gold have flourished. Its price has risen to well over $120 per ounce in mid-1973. The dichotomy between the official and private markets has remained. The American devaluations have raised the official gold price to $42 per ounce from $35 in 1971; gold is still the standard, or *numéraire*, in which par values are expressed. But the figure is meaningless in a practical sense. The United States will not sell gold (convert) at any price; few nations are willing to sell it to the United States, or to anyone else, at any price. Gold remains an inert component of reserves, a form of national patrimony, all $45 billion officially held.

The reformers have not as yet formulated new views on gold. In the scenario outlined earlier to patch up convertibility, gold would have been used proportionately with other reserves in the settlement of balances; but that scenario is but one suggestion for reform. Another is that officially held gold be exchanged for SDRs, the new reserve unit, but this is not likely to win approval. Other scenarios suggest that the nations or the IMF be allowed to sell some official gold to the private markets, thereby lowering the price in those markets and mopping up some inflationary liquidity into the bargain. The idea of raising the official gold price to $100 or $200 per ounce—to refurbish the value of the American supply and permit pre-1971-style convertibility to continue—is still occasionally put forward, particularly by the French. There is little support for this idea from others, however, and there is active hostility from the United States, in whose view that solution misses the problem, would be inflationary, would undermine the SDR, and be generally retrogressive.

At present, SDRs are stated in terms of gold, at the official gold price, although they are not convertible. It has been suggested that SDRs are acceptable for this reason. But the wide spread between the official gold price and the free market price will jeopardize the entire utility of the SDRs as long as they retain their gold denomination. In the future, with SDRs the system's *numéraire*, it has been suggested that gold would be valued in terms of SDRs rather than dollars. It is difficult to see the practical value of this suggestion.

The future of gold remains murky. For the present it is likely to remain a useless national patrimony, certainly so if convertibility is not restored. More frequent exchange rate moves in the future will prevent the cycles of underconversion and overconversion, if convertibility is restored, and further reduce the reliance on gold. It is certain, however, to be among the hotly debated issues.

## Capital Flows

The question of capital flows is now very central in discussion of future reform of the system. Capital flows have become increasingly important in the international monetary system, both as precipitants of change and in their size. At present they have about as much weight as trade and service payments in the international adjustment process for the industrial nations.

The attempt to dampen capital flows by widening the support price bands in 1971 has been ineffective; direct controls have proliferated in Europe and Japan instead. The intense movement of "hot money" or short-term capital began after the mid-1960s. Both speculation and leads and lags were directed against England prior to 1967. Those who gambled that a currency so patently overvalued must fall, and that the central bank defenses could delay but not prevent that fall, made enormous profits. Those who failed to profit quickly got the message: Don't miss next time. The United States was next time, from 1969 on. A simple hypothesis was a sure winner: The strong currencies must rise and/or the dollar fall; when in doubt move against the dollar. There was no way for the dollar to rise vis-à-vis the strong currencies. Nothing could be lost by moving money from dollars to marks or Swiss francs or guilders—or yen, if possible—and leaving it there, but much could be (and was) gained. Surely these would not decline against the dollar. This hypothesis was true, and the rewards great, into 1972. Significantly, there was no speculation *for* the dollar on private foreign exchange markets. Only the central bankers had their finger in the dike, because that is what they are paid to do, right or wrong. Few sophisticated in foreign exchange believed Smithsonian had solved all. When trouble came in 1973, they were quick to move into the mark. And with the mark pegged, to be moved to a new peg (or the dollar down to a new peg, 10 percent as it turned out), these gains would be sizable and instantaneous—not gradual—when the political decision was made to move the peg, a decision the Americans made in February 1973. Had the mark been floating, its price would have eased up after the first inflows to stop subsequent inflows. The *Economist* estimated that with a floating mark, the first $30 million on May 4, 1971, would have gently raised the price so that the remaining $970 million would find it useless to move in.

It was in this period of intense hot money or lead-lag payments that capital controls were born to support what remained of fixed exchange rates. The idea of permanent controls as part of the reform package appeared then, too. But the time must surely come when some of the speculators will lose. The dollar will, at some point, not be overvalued. Some speculators will go long on the dollar, and the shorts will lose. Parenthetically, this is the time that central bank intervention becomes meaningful—not when it faces overwhelming odds for good historic reasons, but when opinion is split and the intervention can shove the decision one way or the other. A bear squeeze on those who have shorted the dollar consistently and won will end the game that has prevailed from 1969 into 1973. And with the prospect of loss as well as gain, with a two-way risk, "hot money" will move very much less. Hot-money speculative moves will be greater the more rigid and fixed the exchange rate; they are minimized by floating exchange rates and ameliorated in varying degrees by crawling or gliding pegs.

The case for "permanent" short-term capital controls, therefore, is a concomitant of fixed exchange rates, albeit with wider parity bands. It is a reflection of the overvaluation of the dollar. Born in a period that a perspective view would call transitional—a period of lengthy adjustment to the very serious overvaluation of the dollar —the obsession for controls is apt to fade as the dollar floats to a market-set equilibrium value. Some who favor floating rates (or gliding pegs) also want permanent capital controls, which may, in this case, prove an unnecessary adornment.

A more subtle version of the case for controls of short-term capital flows rests on the alleged capacity of financial flows to overcompensate. The trade balance is slow to adjust. Devaluations have taken 18 months to have visible effects, but money flows are very fast, and some hot-money owners are very nervous. Thus, it is argued, even when a national economy is making the required but slow adjustment to a currency change, nervous speculators can upset the procedure. The continued speculation against the dollar in 1973, for example, might have driven the value of the dollar too low; an excessively strong recovery in 1974–1975 will invite inward capital flows to the United States which will again drive the dollar up too much. The effect is similar to that of a Yo-Yo: The trend line should be straight but is instead characterized by waves above and below the trend line. The purpose of controls would be to dampen the amplitude of this modulation around the trend line.

And if those who exercise the controls knew what the correct trend line is, this argument might have great validity. It is more likely that markets themselves will dampen speculation once some kind of rough equilibrium (as opposed to the gross disequilibrium of the latter 1960s and early 1970s) is reestablished. Again, the more flexible the exchange rate, the faster will be the return to, and the more persistent will be, the equilibrium.

## Antireform

The view has grown in the post-Smithsonian period that reform as conventionally perceived and outlined above may no longer be necessary, or that only marginal reforms are needed. Perhaps before the collapse of the system, these reforms might have made sense to keep Bretton Woods afloat. But what is to be reformed now?

The heart of Bretton Woods was convertibility. The dollar was the trusted key and the reserve currency because it was "as good as" (and convertible to) gold. The deputy governor of the Bank of Italy, Dr. Ossola, has been quoted earlier to the effect that a realistic view of the world must conclude that convertibility will not be restored in this decade. Consequently, Ossola argues, currencies must float in value; hopefully, from his viewpoint, the European currencies will float jointly, in a bloc against the dollar. But the operative word is *float*, whether in blocs or individually.

Dr. Ossola is quoted because his view reflects a growing consensus that is otherwise difficult to quote—it has formed no committees, issued no releases, and must be felt rather than heard.

Following his (representative) logic, if convertibility is out, floating must continue. One can also argue that if floating continues, there is no need for convertibility: The problem of convertibility remains academic.

And if floating works, something like 80 percent of the required international monetary reform will have been achieved. Since five major currencies are now floating independently, apart from the European joint-float it would seem academic to ask whether floating can in fact work. It does. To be sure, it has been accompanied by a plethora of short-term capital controls. But these are apt to look less necessary as floating rates overcome the basic disequilibrium evident in the early 1970s, particularly the dollar's overvaluation, which gave rise to capital flows against the dollar—perfectly sensible under the circumstances. The minor and constant adjustments in currency value, implicit in continued floating, do not discomfit nor have they slowed the business of international trade and investment; the creation of working forward-markets in the 1960s has been of great help.

Antireform has been expressed most overtly in the British press. The *Economist* has supported floating rates, pointing out that even the United States plan submitted to G-20 for discussion leading to exchange rate adjustments, to be triggered by changes in reserves, would also trigger speculative capital flows. Stable exchange rates, i.e., flexibility by movement from one peg to another, would exacerbate those flows. An article entitled, "Trying to Keep the System in Order," in the *Financial Times* of April 10, 1973, also argues that more formal reform is not necessary.

Part of the antipathy to reform is that attempted political solutions would be counterproductive if superimposed on the solutions the exchange markets have been making. Part also reflects some doubt as to the capability of the G-20 to come up with anything new. The *Financial Times* article states:

> It is no secret that the United States and some of the EEC governments have expressed dissatisfaction with the progress of G-20 work ... the Deputies (may) have been given an impossible task. ... The G-20 Deputies evidently see themselves as civil servants watching their masters and the course of events ... rather than in a position to try to decide on a new system. ...

Perhaps the most forceful antireform case has come from Professor Harry Johnson in "The Problems of Central Bankers in a World of Floating Rates," *Euromoney*, July 1973.

> ... there is a somewhat less faint hope that if the central bankers keep on acting as they have been acting, we shall never have a fundamental reform of the international monetary system. That will be all to the good because what is described in the platform oratory as fundamental reform is some sort of restoration of the fixed exchange system. So long as European and American central bankers ... remain stalemated over what is ... nominally a technical issue but essentially a political issue, dirty floating will continue—and the world will eventually become used to floating exchange rates, the system that the majority of academics of scientific integrity have always recommended ...

The issues involved in reform are politely disguised as difficult technical issues but clearly recognized as political by the participants, and concern whether the purpose of international monetary reform is to hamstring the United States or to put it on a par with other major countries.

Johnson goes on to support the United States position as "irrefutably logical and consistent." He ascribes the European antipathy to a reform which involves more flexible exchange rates as emanating primarily from the French "as wreckers."

I make no bones about my conviction that it is criminally irresponsible of the French to threaten to wreck the possibility of an orderly international monetary system by playing such games for the despicably narrowly self-interested motives of reaping a profit on French gold holdings and humbling the United States . . .

Because the differences in approach to monetary reform, although couched in technical terms, are in fact deeply political, many felt from the outset that the Group of Twenty had an impossible task. The Group could only reflect various national views which were in conflict. It lacked in its membership an overwhelmingly authoritative figure like Keynes had been at Bretton Woods to whom all nations could defer, even while failing to accept all elements of his plan.

While the authors of this book in general tend to favor the antireform view and floating rates, certain shortcomings in a system based on floating rates have appeared which ultimately should be resolved. The primary problem is the lack of a store of value in the international monetary system. Men throughout the world could once look either to gold or to the dollar as the basic store of value in the world, against which their currency or their goods might be measured. This has ceased to be true with the giant depreciation of the dollar since 1969 against other currencies, and because of the wild gyrations in gold prices during the recent period. It may be true that ultimately, once the pent-up devaluation of the dollar has been completed and it reaches something resembling a stable value against other currencies, it may again become a store of value. Gold is much less likely to resume this role. It is currently speculatively priced, and even normally it can fluctuate by as much as $20 per ounce simply as a result of vagaries in its value in the jewelry and related commercial markets. It would appear desirable, since the world needs a store of value, that SDRs should take on this role, rather than gold or any national currency. The future of SDRs will of course depend upon the ultimate resolution of the monetary system's reform. Elsewhere in these pages the authors have quoted the late Paul Einzig to the effect that the widespread ownership of SDRs among individuals as well as central banks would give to that instrument a market-determined price—a *numéraire* ... against which currencies will fluctuate—which would reflect its true value and enable it to become the store of value that no currency or gold now provides.

# 11.
# Capital Flows:
# Eurodollars

n 1971 the Bretton Woods system ended. The persistent and growing American deficits had undermined the system for two decades, particularly during the five or six years before its demise.

It was not the trade deficits as such that precipitated the end, but rather the vast movements of short-term capital among nations. In 1971 the basic American deficit was just over $9 billion, the highest postwar figure but less than one-third of the total United States deficit of $29.8 billion. It was this great cascade of dollars pouring into the rest of the world and particularly into the strong currency countries—Germany, Switzerland, the Netherlands —that broke the system. Over $10 billion of this is cataloged in Table 12 as short-term capital exiting through accountable channels euphemistically called "errors and omissions," the sources of which are diffuse and not easily accounted. This category had averaged about $1 billion in the previous decade; its elevenfold increase was unprecedented. No effort was made to restrict or control these outflows. The philosophy of "benign neglect" would suggest no such effort and might even condone the outflows if they produced the desired effect—dollar devaluation.

In addition to flows from within the United States, there exist vast supplies of moneys outside their countries of origin called Eurocurrencies or Euromoneys. These can be dispatched from country to country with great speed; they are as mobile as a phone call or telex message. Further, these funds are not subject to any supranational monetary authority, since none exists.

The precise amount of these funds is unknown, but the Bank for International Settlements, acknowledged the best source of information, estimates them to have totaled $56.8 billion in 1969, $75.3 billion in 1970, $97.8 billion in 1971, and some $131.9 billion at the end of 1972, according to the Bank's *Annual Report* for the year ending March, 1973. The great bulk of these Euromoneys are dollars, or Eurodollars. At the end of 1972 some $96.7 billion, or 73.3 percent (p. 161) of the total were dollars, the balance in other currencies. Euromarks, Eurofrancs, and other currencies deposited outside their country of origin comprise the other 26.7 percent of Euromoneys in the world. It has been popularly believed that Eurodollars represent the cumulative sums of past American deficits. But more recently the view has gained that a good part of this supply appears to be the result not of deficits, but of the "bookkeeper's pen," to use Milton Friedman's phrase. As $1 of new deposits can become $5 of bank credit with a 20 percent reserve requirement in the United States, so "prime" deposits can be expanded manyfold in the Eurodollar markets, where there are no reserve or other requirements.

The degree of expansion in the Eurodollar markets is subject to dispute. Fred Klopstock of the New York Federal Reserve argues there is no multiple expansion; private papers circulated by European central bankers put the expansion at roughly seven times the prime deposits. While Friedman's view would seem more accurate, there is no need to attempt to arbitrate the dispute, as the behavior of the Eurodollar market is the same whether multiple expansion takes place or not. The point will have greater relevance if the primary deposits return to the United States in the future and the Eurodollar market shrinks, a prospect considered at the end of this chapter. If the expansionists are right, a small primary deposit withdrawn for return to the United States will lead to shrinkage of some multiple value.

The adjustment ideas implicit or explicit in the Bretton Woods system bear on the movements of real resources. That is, the return to equilibrium was meant to come about through changes in exports, imports, more tourism, aid—i.e., the movements of real goods and services among nations through changes in relative prices. Prices could be affected by internal policies aimed at relative reductions of costs or by currency devaluation, which amounts to the same thing.

But there has now arisen a purely monetary dimension of vast size that also affects the movements of exchange rates. It was neither present at the creation of Bretton Woods nor planned for, and it is without precedent in size. Because the monetary dimension is new and vast—and uncontrolled—it is often frightening. The central banker fears the movements of money as destabilizing to exchange rates. The government treasuries fear that movements can work contrary to their interest rate and their monetary and economic policies. The layman has a vague fear that the system is out of control and could destroy him. Such feelings are exacerbated by disclosures, more precisely estimates, of the whole supply of short-term capital, including but not limited to the Euromoney totals given above, capable of quick movement. The United States Tariff Commission study of early 1973 estimated the world supply of liquid assets at $268 billion in 1971, against which central banks can pose a total of $114 billion of reserves to defend their currencies, on the dubious assumption that they could work together. The reserves of any one nation are of course smaller, at most some $35 billion. Details of this estimate are found in Table 16, and the text accompanying the table itself warns of "purposeful" double-counting and other limitations. Some of the funds for example, are, themselves central bank or government reserves, nearly $18 billion, and these are, of course, offsetting liabilities. The point is not to probe the TC data in any detail but rather to point to their existence and size, and to note that the bulk of the assets are controlled by United States multinational companies ("foreign affiliates of United States nonbanks"), $110 billion, and foreign branches of American banks, another form of multinational business, $61 billion in 1971.

The presence of vast amounts of highly mobile international moneys suggests a number of deceptively simple questions. Although there are a great many sources of liquid funds around,

**Table 16**
Estimated short-term asset and liability positions of principal institutions in International Money Markets, 1969–1971
(billions of U.S. dollars)

| Holder of assets or liabilities | Denominated in dollars | | Denominated in foreign currencies | | Total | |
|---|---|---|---|---|---|---|
| | Assets | Liabilities | Assets | Liabilities | Assets | Liabilities |
| United States banks[a] | | | | | | |
| 1969 | 8.9 | 28.1 | 0.5 | 0.2 | 9.4 | 28.3 |
| 1970 | 10.1 | 21.8 | 0.6 | 0.2 | 10.7 | 28.3 |
| 1971 | 12.1 | 15.8 | 0.9 | 0.2 | 13.0 | 16.0 |
| United States nonbanks | | | | | | |
| 1969 | 3.5 | 1.7 | 0.7 | 0.4 | 4.2 | 2.1 |
| 1970 | 3.6 | 2.2 | 0.6 | 0.5 | 4.2 | 2.7 |
| 1971 | 4.7 | 2.2 | 0.9 | 0.4 | 5.2 | 2.6 |
| Foreign banks[b] | | | | | | |
| 1969[c] | 64.9 | 52.3 | 10.7 | 10.6 | 75.6 | 63.0 |
| 1970 | 43.0 | 31.7 | 5.8 | 5.8 | 48.8 | 37.5 |
| 1971 | 44.3 | 38.3 | 8.4 | 8.2 | 52.7 | 46.5 |
| Foreign governments, central banks, and international organizations[d] | | | | | | |
| 1969 | 4.9 | NA | 0.4 | NA | 5.3 | NA |
| 1970 | 10.0 | NA | 2.8 | NA | 12.8 | NA |
| 1971 | 10.7 | NA | 8.0 | NA | 18.7 | NA |
| Foreign nonbanks[e] | | | | | | |
| 1969 | 7.3 | 6.2 | NA | NA | 7.3 | 6.2 |
| 1970 | 7.6 | 9.4 | NA | NA | 7.6 | 9.4 |
| 1971 | 6.8 | 11.4 | NA | NA | 6.8 | 11.4 |
| Foreign affiliates of U.S. nonbanks[f] | | | | | | |
| 1969 | NA | NA | NA | NA | 59.9 | 34.9 |

Foreign branches of U.S. banks[h]

| | g | g | g | g | g | g |
|---|---|---|---|---|---|---|
| 1969 | 34.6 | 36.1 | 12.7 | 11.3 | 47.3 | 47.4 |
| 1970 | 40.2 | 42.1 | 21.2 | 19.4 | 61.4 | 61.5 |
| 1971 | | | | | | |
| Totals | | | | | | |
| 1969 | 89.5 | 88.3 | 12.3 | 11.2 | 161.7 | 134.5 |
| 1970 | 108.9 | 101.2 | 22.5 | 17.8 | 212.0 | 165.9 |
| 1971 | 118.8 | 109.8 | 39.0 | 28.2 | 267.8 | 201.0 |

[a] Data are total foreign short-term assets and liabilities of U.S. banks as reported to U.S. sources, *less* claims on and liabilities to official monetary institutions.

[b] Basically, these data are those reported to the BIS by banks in eight European countries (Belgium-Luxembourg, France, Germany, Italy, Netherlands, Sweden, Switzerland, and the United Kingdom), plus Canada and Japan. Figures from U.S. sources relating to foreign branches of U.S. banks have been subtracted from these figures and are shown separately in the table for 1970 and 1971. Also, the eight European countries' assets and liabilities vis-à-vis the United States (denominated in dollars) were removed from the totals, and data from U.S. sources on *total* dollar claims and liabilities against foreigners were added.

[c] Includes foreign branches of U.S. banks.

[d] Data cover (1) identified official holdings of Eurodollars, (2) unidentified holdings of Eurocurrencies plus residual sources of reserves—both as estimated by the IMF—plus (3) claims on U.S. banks of nonmonetary official institutions such as the IBRD and IADB. "N.A." = not available.

[e] Available data cover United States, and foreign banks' claims on and liabilities to all foreign nonbanks, including foreign branches/affiliates of U.S. nonbanks. To insure elimination of double counting, since positions of the U.S.-affiliated firms are shown separately, the available data have been reduced by 50 percent—i.e., it is assumed that half of the assets and liabilities reported by U.S. and foreign banks against foreign nonbanks actually are liabilities and assets, respectively, of foreign affiliates of U.S. nonbanks.

[f] Data are estimated current assets and liabilities of nonfinancial affiliates of U.S. firms.

[g] Included under "foreign banks."

[h] Figures are from U.S. sources citing *total* assets and liabilities of branches. Therefore, some long-term items are included.

Sources: *Federal Reserve Bulletin*, September 1972; *U.S. Treasury Bulletin*, September 1972; Bank for International Settlements, *Annual Report*, 1972; U.S. Commerce Department, Office of Foreign Direct Investment, *Foreign Affiliate Financial Survey*, July 1971, and *Foreign Direct Investment Program, Selected Statistics*, July 1971; and data furnished by U.S. Department of Commerce, Bureau of Economic Analysis, Foreign Investment Division.

Eurodollars are among the most important and accessible. Focusing on Eurodollars, the questions are: What are Eurodollars, and how did they arise? Why do they move around? Are their movements destabilizing? Do they threaten sovereign authority, and what can be done about this? And what about the future?

There now exists an extensive literature relating to Euromoney. A monthly magazine of that name examines the market for them. The writings of Machlup and the late Paul Einzig are standard; a recent book by Geoffrey Bell is succinct and authoritative. It is not our purpose here to review that literature but rather to summarize and interpret the significance of Euromoney in the light of the questions posed earlier.

Turning to the first question, a Eurodollar is, most simply, a dollar different from others only because it is deposited in a bank (or otherwise held) outside the United States often but not necessarily owned by a nonresident of the United States. If the same deposit, even when owned by a foreigner, were deposited in the United States, it would be counted an ordinary dollar (although a "foreign claim"). Eurodollar deposits are often assailed as a source of instability, since they can be moved quickly. Yet the fact is that deposits can also be moved quickly out of the United States, or most countries, with equal ease. The outpouring of some $21 billion of "short-term capital" and "errors and omissions" money from the United States in 1971 is illustrative. The focus of anxiety on Eurodollars as a source of mobility seems misplaced; any liquid capital can move fast.

In large measure, the controls on capital instituted by the United States under the Kennedy and Johnson administrations created both the Eurodollar and its long-term cousin, Eurobond markets. The distinction between the two is simply time. A Eurobond is a loan at fixed interest rates for a longer period, normally 10–20 years, while Eurodollars are deposited and loaned for short periods, often at market, i.e., changing interest rates. Like all markets, these money markets must have a demand and a supply side, which explains their existence.

The Interest Equalization Tax in 1963 made it impossible for European companies and municipalities to borrow in the United

States. This exclusion created a demand for a new, "parallel" source of borrowing; the demand, so to speak, shifted out of New York. Brokers and investment bankers were very quick to discover that a supply of money to match this demand already existed in the form of dollar deposits in the hands of non-Americans, often in secret tax havens like Switzerland. At this early date, other foreign owners of dollars, less concerned with secrecy, still held their dollars as deposits or in the form of Treasury bills inside the United States. The rest is simple. The brokers went to the owners of the dollars, who loaned the dollars—in exchange for bonds or other instruments of debt at good interest rates—to European companies or municipalities, that were closed out of the New York market. In embryo form, a parallel market to New York was born. Starting from a volume of only $200-$300 million per year, the Eurobond market grew to 10 or 12 times this volume later.

The second American control gave a real boost to this market. OFDI controls inhibited the amount of capital that American multinational companies could shift out of the United States to invest abroad. So side by side with the lesser-known European companies and the City of Copenhagen and the Kingdom of Holland, there appeared, soliciting loans from the owners of dollars abroad, such names as IBM, Ford, the oil companies—in short, the giant multinationals. Since the owners of money abroad had great faith in these names, they were very quick to lend them money through the now burgeoning parallel market. The American companies were also very quick to adapt themselves to the European techniques. Thus an American company would establish a financial subsidiary in such places as Luxembourg or Curacao, which did not insist that the companies, when paying interest on bonds, deduct any taxes. Furthermore, the companies issued the bonds in the name of "the bearer," a preferred European anonymity. If interest rates were higher than in the United States, the money was at least usable, free of any controls; moreover, when the stock market was good, bonds convertible into shares could be sold to investors at cheaper rates. Early analysts of the Eurobond market, as it came to be known, were astounded by its lack of situs. "It exists," they wrote, "in the air." Since interest payments were net of taxes, the return to the lender was higher than he could obtain in other capital markets. Most of the loans were "denominated", e.g., repayable, in dollars, although later, as confidence waned, other currencies, notably marks, were in demand. The currency of denomination is a pretty fair index of the market's confidence in currencies.

The multinational and other demanders of money also turned to banks for short-term loans in the Eurodollar market. Interest rates consequently rose in the "short end" of the Euromarkets as well, exceeding American or most European national money market rates. The Eurodollar banks solicited deposits as the supply to meet this demand. They could afford to pay depositors interest rates in excess of those obtainable as American or national European deposits. While interest rates on deposits in the United States were subject to ceilings imposed by Regulation Q, Eurobanks were free of any restrictions or ceilings. Furthermore, American banks had to keep reserves. If reserves are, say, 10%, at 6% interest, these reserves cost 6% of interest; Eurodollar banks need hold no reserves, and interest payment was not subject to 30-day delay, as in the United States.

With these developments, depositors (American and foreigner alike) who held their money in New York deposits found it expedient to withdraw their money from New York, redeposit it abroad in London or other centers of the Eurodollar market—often with branches of American banks who were exempt from American law because they were under the regulation of the local government. These deposits yielded better interest than the U.S. market paid. Even when the American rates rose, as in the 1968–1969 crunch, Regulation Q ceilings kept Eurodollar deposits attractive. Ironically the Eurodollar market is said to have been invented by the Russians. This probably apocryphal account has it that the Russians had a certain number of dollars, earned through foreign trade or the sale of gold in their reserves. They were afraid to deposit these in American banks for fear that, thanks to some twist of the cold war, the deposits might be seized and they would be unable to use them when needed for wheat or other import purchases. Consequently, they deposited their dollars in London, which was less prone to such seizures. The banks holding Russian deposits discovered that they could lend them out at attractive rates of interest. Others soon followed, and the Eurodollar market, starting from meager sums in 1955 for reasons noted above, bounded upward to reach totals of $71 billion by 1971 and $86 billion by 1972, gigantic sums by any reckoning. Whether the story of the Russian origin is apocryphal or not matters little. The fact is that whoever started the market has seen his example followed hugely. And the further irony is that it was the very American controls—the IET on bank lending abroad, and OFDI—which were the major inspiration of demand in this market, as they drove borrowers out of the United States, to funds abroad. Other American regulations, notably Q, helped drive lenders—the supply—to Eurodollar markets. And the fixed exchange rate system and the pre-1971 parities that the controls were meant to save were finally destroyed by the cascades of money through the markets. Money is mobile in these markets in several ways. It can be moved from place to place at the drop of a telex. More important, it can be moved from one currency into another by the same process. Thus when the dollar appeared hopelessly weak, it was not difficult for holders of fluid short-term capital to convert dollars to German marks or Swiss francs at the going exchange rate, by the same quick telex procedure.

Which raises the third question posed at the outset: Why do moneys move? What are the motives? The question assumes a more forbidding complexion if posed differently: Whose fault is it that vast sums have moved through the markets, with destabilizing consequences?

First, it should be emphasized that all movements through the Eurodollar markets have not been destabilizing for exchange rates. As that term has come to be used since 1969, it has generally meant movements against the dollar or other weak currencies into the stronger currencies. But, as earlier pointed out, in 1968–1969 during the credit crunch in the United States, large amounts of money were borrowed by American banks through their foreign branches in the Eurodollar markets and brought into the United States. This resulted in one of the two surpluses in recent years for the United States. More recently, there have been very considerable inflows of longer term capital into the United States as the dollar became cheaper and foreigners found it expedient to buy American corporations or other assets. A British tobacco company in 1973 purchased the assets of an American department store chain by borrowing the funds to do so in the Eurodollar market and spending them on the controlling shares of the chain in the United States. The dividends of the department store were reportedly sufficient to pay the interest charges on the Eurodollar loan and to leave some profitable residual as well. The actual cash outlay of the tobacco company was thus virtually zero, in exchange for a very considerable and potentially much greater physical asset plus several million dollars of profits above and beyond interest charges. As foreign companies become increasingly multinational and invest in the United States, the use of devices such as this may be expected to increase.

Two forces make money move in quantity: (1) the search for higher interest rates, and (2) the search for capital gain in the event of a currency revaluation—what for the moment may be termed "speculation." Obviously, interest rates matter. The whole Euromoney system has attracted its supply partly because Eurodollar interest rates have consistently been higher than alternatives. But there are market qualifications on the interest-rate pull on money.

If a government raises the rate of interest to attract money, will money in fact move in? Not necessarily. There exists an almost perfect parallel between the premium or discount on the forward price (i.e., future value) of any country's money and the interest rate which that money commands in the Euromoney markets. Thus, for example, the expectation into January 1973 was that the yen was a very strong currency and the dollar a weak one. The cost of making a loan denominated (i.e., repayable) in yen was very low, some 2 percent, because the general expectation was that the yen which must be repaid in the future would be more expensive than at present. The differential or forward premium on the yen, added to the rate of interest, made that rate of interest about equal to the cost of borrowing and repaying in dollars. The interest rate on yen was low because the forward premium was high. On the other hand, the expectation for the dollar was fairly negative, i.e., it would continue to be fairly weak, and it was therefore selling at a discount. The rate of interest for the dollar was therefore considerably higher. The relation between the United States and the Canadian dollar also affords another example. United States short-term interest rates are higher than Canadian. Nevertheless, not much Canadian money crosses the border in search of these interest rates, as the discount on the American dollar just about equals the interest rate differential.

In this "law of parity" the differential between interest rates is reflected in the difference in discount or premiums in the forward exchange rate.

The working of the law of parity depends, of course, on the extent to which the forward foreign exchange market is well organized. While the forward market for foreign exchanges is said to have more than doubled in size since 1970, it is still held by many to be inadequate. Banks have been criticized for not permitting individuals or smaller businesses to use the forward market on the grounds that their activity constitutes "speculation." The same banks have provided forward accommodations to the larger companies whose forward market activities are regarded as hedging, a legitimate concomitant of trading, rather than speculation. One consequence of the banks' limitation of the use of the forward market has been to limit the effectiveness of the forward market to equilibrate exchange rate movements. Thus, for example, when the dollar is dropping in value, treasurers of large companies are traditionally required to take only hedging positions against the dollar, which further drops its value. But if speculators who think that the dollar has dropped enough attempt to take positions for the dollar, they would find these difficult to negotiate, given the current policies of the large banks. This criticism of the banking business is more true for the United States than in Europe. Still, on the whole, the floating-rate system would function more effectively if the forward markets could be used by all without prejudice as to the size or purpose of a loan.

The second motive is "speculation"—to reap capital gain or to avoid capital loss. In 1971, for example, when the dollar was in trouble, those who held mobile "hot money" could convert it into, say, marks, hoping that if the dollar devalued or the mark revalued, they would stand to earn a gain in the capital value of the money. Thus if $1 million were transferred into marks and the dollar devalues by 10 percent there is an earning of $100,000 when the marks are reconverted into dollars. When, as in February 1973, the dollar devalues 10 percent and the mark in addition revalues 3 percent, the earning is $130,000, which is a fine return for the cost of a telex and a little forethought.

The bald movement of money in this way, in anticipation of devaluation and revaluation, is usually referred to, highly pejoratively, as "speculation." President Nixon in his August 15, 1971, address blamed the "speculators" for much of the trouble of the dollar. Similarly, multinational companies, Arab oil millionaires, and the gnomes of Zurich have at times been accused of engaging in this type of speculation, which is said to be highly destabilizing to the world's monetary system. But speculation and self-defense are opposite sides of the same coin.

There are other motives for moving short-term capital. When, for example, a multinational company moves money from a weak to a strong currency it is, from its own viewpoint, doing so not to speculate but rather to defend itself. In fact there is very little evidence of large movements of money per se by the multinational corporations. Rather there is evidence of what are called "leads and lags" in payments by multinational corporations among their own affiliates. These can be of many varieties. In the simplest form, if an American company must pay $100,000 to the German subsidiary, it will rush to pay that amount before the dollar has been devalued or the mark revalued—a 'lead' payment. This inrush of money and the magnitude of the amounts involved help to precipitate the very devaluation or revaluation which it is feared will happen. A lag payment is the reverse: The German subsidiary will delay paying its dollar obligations until the dollar is devalued, for the simple reason that it can then buy more dollars for its marks and will pay out fewer marks. By the same token, however, this lag prevents the flow of money into dollars when the dollar is weak and in need of support and inflow. Only changes of timing of payments are involved.

In February 1973, just before the dollar devalued by some 10 percent, about $6 billion flowed into German marks. It is estimated that about half this amount represented not speculative inflows but rather "lead and lag" payments by exporters and importers, especially the multinational corporations.

There are of course two views relating to these capital flows. The pejorative view holds them to be "speculative" and destabilizing. A second view holds that they are derivative, i.e., that they are a reaction to erroneous, hence unstable, exchange rates, and not their cause. The basic instability is caused by the trade balance, in short by failure to respond to real resource movements. Put differently, this view holds that some movement of exchange rates may always be in order, but in any event big moves of exchange rates were very much in order in the period from 1969 to 1973. Implicit in this view is the observation that governments have been wedded to maintaining fixed exchange rates in the past, even when change was clearly necessary. Governments would not adjust the rates, in any reasonable time, as the basic balance required. Rather they would finally be forced to do so. Money rushed around the world seeking to profit from, or avoid losses from, exchange rate adjustments. The exchange rates were out of joint: One hypothesis, that the dollar must be devalued, could guide all actions from 1969 to 1973.

Are governments simply blindly stubborn, or is the institutional mechanism to force needed change deficient? We would argue that both are true. Proposals to reform the system to avoid just the huge short-term capital movements that in fact took place in 1971 and 1973 had been put forward from the early 1960s on. At least one book, Rolfe's *Gold and World Power*, could by 1966 catalog a family of soundly conceived plans for greater flexibility of exchange rates designed by academic economists to prevent the kind of explosion that in fact took place. For a long time thereafter, these plans were refined and extended, and have been steadily available. The unwillingness of governments to plan for improved adjustment mechanisms, although forewarned, left the governments no recourse but to be at the mercy of violent adjustment. If "benign neglect" was not the most orderly policy to force change, it was the only policy available when so many Europeans and the Japanese were intent on trying to sustain unrealistic, undervalued currencies and thereby their export surpluses.

As early as August 28, 1971, the London *Economist* could present an alternative scenario to the flight of dollars into marks, had there been flexible instead of fixed exchange rates.

The management of funds will be more stable because people will have no incentive to stampede out of fixed-price dollars at moments of crisis. Under a floating system there just could not be a rush of $1 billion from dollars into Deutsche Marks such as occurred in 35 minutes one Wednesday morning [in May 1971]. The movement of the first $30 million would now push the price of the Deutsche Mark gently up to a level where the holders of the other $970 million would no longer want to buy it.

Whether the movement of money was speculation or protection, whether money physically moved or moved through leads and lags, was less important than the fact that the monetary movements were reflections of the fundamental malaises. Contrary to the pejorative view, the very movements of money were inevitable and forced an overdue equilibrating change in the exchange rates.

By 1971 the resistance to change had created a world in which the fixed pattern of exchange rates was no longer valid. The more astute company treasurer and exporter felt it his duty to protect his money and defend its value by anticipating the coming, inevitable change. Once again the markets succeeded where, and because, governments had failed to respond to market reality.

Those who favor fixity tend to call the movements of money speculation and evil. Those who favor exchange rate flexibility see the movements as inevitable and without premeditated evil, but rather protective and equilibrating. The protective treasurer, even the aggressive speculator, serves a useful, equilibrating function in the market.

Actually, apart from massaging one's emotions, it matters very little whether one calls the movements of short-term money speculative or protective, or whether one favors them or not. They were needed adjustments and were inevitable, if overdue.

The more important fact is that the continuation of three elements of the monetary system had by 1971 become incompatible. These were free short-term capital movements, fixed exchange rates, and economic sovereignty, i.e., the right of each nation to do its own thing regardless of the consequences elsewhere. One or more of the three had to be changed.

And this raises the question of sovereignty. The response of governments to the monetary explosions of 1971–1973 has been mixed. Five major currencies are floating; others still attempt to preserve fixed rates. Nearly all countries have imposed some form of controls on capital movements. The deficit countries, notably the United States, still control the outward movements of capital, although the limits have been relaxed and the United States proposes to abolish all controls before the end of 1974. The surplus nations have imposed controls on the inflow of capital; Germany, for example, imposed the "bardepot." German residents (including corporations) had to deposit in non-interest-bearing accounts in German banks 50%, and later 100%, of money borrowed abroad. This increased the effective interest rate of money borrowed abroad—to double with a 100% bardepot to discourage such borrowing.

Foreigners are forbidden to buy bonds or stocks, and consequently a vast trade in loopholes has appeared. Switzerland from time to time has forced depositors to pay interest to put their money into Switzerland rather than be paid interest on deposits by the banks. Even the two-tier exchange rate system is designed to control the inward flow of money. For example, France has a commercial and a financial franc, as do Italy, Belgium, and several other countries. This device is aimed either at keeping foreign capital out, the initial French motive, or at keeping domestic capital in (the current Italian preoccupation). When the exchange rate is strong, the premium "financial rate" deters entry of foreign capital, but in the best mercantilist fashion, exports are sold at a relative discount at the "commercial rate." The subsidy tends to encourage export growth and therefore the country's trade position. On the other hand, when the export rate is at a premium, the financial rate is at a relative discount and so deters the exit of domestic capital. Many believe, therefore, that the two-tier system tends to be self-defeating. To be sure, since the French imposed the two-tier system the French franc has been strong, and consequently, from the French point of view, it has been a success. But a strengthening of the dollar and consequently a weakening of the European currencies, especially the franc, is apt to have the opposite results.

The establishment of a two-tier system tends to create conflicts of interest between countries in which the ultimate decision rests with the dual-rate country. Thus, for example, if a British business purchased forward French franc cover from a British bank, the transaction would be recognized as commercial by the British authorities, but the French authorities would insist on payment in "financial" francs. Similarly, if a British business borrowed lira from a British bank for a transaction recognized as commercial by the British authorities, while the Italian authorities thought differently and called the repayment money "financial lira," the Italians would win. Britain paradoxically has controls over both the inflow and outflow of money. The Japanese markets are highly controlled to exclude inflows.

The nature of controls is less important than their likely durability. Some analysts foresee capital controls as a permanent feature of a reformed system. And this would be unfortunate, since the operation of an effective international financial market is a necessary adjunct to an integrated economy among the developed nations, the best hope for an optimum use of resources. It seems likely, however, that the fever for controls will fade as the nations finally achieve a better pattern of exchange rates, even if upheaval was required to get there. In one sense, the mechanism of exchange rate flexibility introduced into a reformed system will determine the future of capital controls. If exchange rates can move in small and frequent steps, as needed, there will be little reward for speculation or need for protection via large movements of money. A rational view would therefore suggest reduction of capital controls. But this depends on the nature of a reformed system.

So the reaction to 1971 has been to try to preserve sovereignty by controlling capital movements. But in any event, sovereignty must be reduced at some time in the future. The movements in the Common Market for joint monetary action will require a degree of harmonization in such broad areas as economic and fiscal policy, and even company law.

The nations have so far demonstrated a perverse ability to avoid bowing to the seeming inevitability of some supranational authority, in an age when the national border is no longer a significant economic barrier. In one sense, increasing acceptance among intellectuals for greater exchange rate flexibility acknowledges this nationalist penchant, for a truly integrated system could exist better on a fixed exchange rate, with a single central bank and a single monetary policy, as do the states of the United States. But that day seems far off. Even within the Common Market there is no agreement on the basics of unification, although there have been numerous plans for monetary unification or harmonization, all to date thwarted.

Finally, what of the future of the Eurodollar market? One of the elements in the literature relates to the perspective view of the Euromarket: Will it last? We have ascribed the origins of the market largely to American controls, a most unexpected and in some ways unwelcome secondary consequence of those controls, which amazed the control devisers who had only bothered to think through the first consequences of their controls. By the same token, if those controls are removed, as is now promised for 1974, will the deposits be returned to the United States and the Eurodollar market die or be substantially diminished?

The first observation to make on this question is that all of the controls are unlikely to be lifted. IET and the controls on multinational companies may be lifted, and this will again make New York a major capital market, reducing the importance of the Eurodollar markets. But Regulation Q is less likely to be ended. To be sure, there is no reason it should be retained; the banks would certainly prefer its demise so they could compete for deposits by paying such interest rates as are necessary to do so. In theory, Regulation Q is a populist measure designed to protect the small borrower against high rates. The theory is that if banks are restricted from paying too much interest they will, by the same token, be restricted from charging too much interest for their loans, and thus the small borrower will be protected. If this theory had any merit before international finance became quite so international, it certainly has little now. For the consequence of Regulation Q is simply that deposits owned by nonresidents are withdrawn, particularly from savings banks, and there is a consequent diminution of credit availability to the small borrowers when interest rates abroad are higher. Higher rates may hurt the small borrower; lack of money may kill him. Even with purely domestic funds, Regulation Q forced a shift of money from savings banks to better-yielding instruments, including United States Treasury bills. This "disintermediation" did not help the small borrower either. Mortgage money in 1969, for example, was simply not available or was very expensive. If rates had maximum controls, points were charged to bring the real interest rate up. Yet another well-meant control has backfired because its secondary consequences went beyond the planners' schemes.

Finally, reserve requirements will not be changed. But an enclave banking system of foreign-owned deposits, exempt from reserve requirements, is conceivable, operating on different rules from American-owned deposits in the same banks. Technically, it is possible to do this. It is being done today in Great Britain, and the Bank of England's ability to allow and to guide a parallel banking system based on Eurodollars, without overt controls, has made London the major Eurodollar center of the world. The benefits to London are considerable. It is estimated that over 30,000 jobs and tax income of several hundred millions of pounds per year are the tangible benefits; in addition, London retains its prime financial importance even with a weak, controlled currency. Whether the American banking regulators can be as nimble as Bank of England officials remains to be seen, but the probable answer is no. Some Eurodollar operations, therefore, will doubtless continue outside the United States, but with considerable shrinkage if the first regulations that created it, IET and OFDI, are abolished. Regulation Q's abolition would further shrink the Eurodollar market. The return of these funds to the United States would, of course, have an enormously strengthening effect on the American balance of payments position. Does it matter?

The conventional wisdom holds that the Eurodollar markets outside the United States are the source of much of the money that flows around the world in quest of higher interest rates or exchange rate changes and are therefore "destabilizing." Our view is quite different. The Eurodollar market is important but not central to the problem of money flows. If there were no Eurodollar market, money would still flow. Again the experience of 1971 is relevant. Two-thirds of the $30-odd billion American deficit that year is accounted for by flows from the United States itself. If there were no Eurodollar market, the events of 1971 would still have taken place. And if controls, once lifted, were reimposed, the Eurodollar market is apt to reappear. Not only London but Luxembourg, Nassau and Cayman Islands, Singapore, the New Hebrides, and Beirut are Eurodollar centers now. Somewhere a market as necessary as this one will flourish in the modern world; the love of money will find a way. None of these phenomena are new, of course. There were capital flows in the 1920s, as noted earlier. Modern communications make it easier, and modern size makes it bigger.

The final question that has vexed analysts of the Eurodollar market is the quality of its credit. By 1972 deposits had poured into the Eurodollar market, greatly increasing its supply. Among other things, the Japanese put large amounts into the market to show a lower reserve total in an effort to forestall further rises in the value of the yen. At the same time, much of the demand for Eurodollar loans slackened. This was in part due to the recession in European business, which reduced the demand for loans from that source, and to lower interest rates in the United States, which took many large American companies out of the Eurodollar market as borrowers.

The consequence of this increased supply and reduced demand was that the Eurodollar banks began to make loans to companies and countries that had hitherto been considered unworthy of credit. With great pride "tombstone" announcements appeared in the familiar financial newspapers saying that a group headed by some highly reputable bank had made a $25 or $50 million loan to the government of Greece or to Air Zaire, to the Soviet Union, Hungary, or other states in Eastern Europe. Various private ventures and governmental units in Brazil, Peru, and elsewhere also became "credit worthy."

The lending banks were in fact taking little arbitrage (i.e., interest rate) risk in making these loans. They simply acquired deposits from anybody with dollars, or from other banks with excess dollars or other currencies, for which they paid the going rate of interest, known as the Interbank Rate, or since London is a very important source of this type of business, the London Interbank Rate (Libor). The borrower in turn paid to the bank the Libor rate plus an override percentage. Since the Libor rate changes every six months, the borrowers never knew exactly what rate they would be paying; only the bank's override or service charge was tied. Therefore rate risks were borne by the borrowers and not the bankers.

Concern has arisen because in the intense competition for such loans, the override or service charge fell to a narrow margin. Whereas this charge for nonprime borrowers had been in the vicinity of 1–$\frac{3}{4}$% in 1971, it fell to amounts often unstated, but generally said to be $\frac{1}{2}$–$\frac{3}{4}$% by 1972. In other words, second-quality borrowers were getting prime rates, and this was considered a deterioration of the quality of the loans. Furthermore, whereas IBM as a borrower is unlikely ever to default on a loan, the new borrowers were thought to be much better candidates for default. Presumably the spread or service charge was to be a hedge against loss in the event of default. A smaller spread ceased to be such a hedge. And the banks consequently are running a risk, not in terms of interest rate but in terms of the possibility of default.

The lending banks, however, are adamant that they have examined the quality of credit in each case and that their loans are sound. Many allege that the complaints against the quality of loans arose from competitors who did not wish to give such loans or from more conservative elements in the banking community and amongst the international organizations conducting uninvited surveillance, such as the OECD. They also point out that the loans which originate in London (some 48% of all Euromoney loans and presumably a larger percentage of term loans—three years and over) are under the general surveillance of the Bank of England. And while the Bank of England made no hard-and-fast rules, nor was in any sense restrictive about this business, nevertheless it kept a constant finger on the pulse, insisting on traditionally high standards of performance. These standards are not defined precisely but include adequate rates of bank capital to loans, and generally astute perception.

The fact is that no one will know the extent of defaults until they have happened. Those familiar with the history of lending are not unaware that at one time consumer credit in the United States was considered a very risky business and something beneath the dignity of the banking system, relegated to the gray world of small-loan and automobile-finance companies. However, over the years consumer loans have proved to be just as good as more traditional bank business, and the banks themselves are now large and competitive lenders to the consumer. Standards change. What was considered risky in the past may, in the light of experience, be considered solid today. On the other hand, the round of bank loan defaults in 1931, starting in Austria, had disastrous consequences in many countries later.

That there will be some defaults in the new term-lending to the less developed countries, and to lesser companies, there can be no doubt. But defaults are inherent in the lending business. In the United States the Penn Central failure did not bankrupt the system, nor in England the Rolls Royce default, both considered prime names.

Perhaps the best formulation that can be made for the future of these loans is, again, one derived from the experience with consumer loans in the United States. In a sea of stability there will be islands of default. But they will be small and quite tolerable. Banks are, after all, paid to take risks; they manage to make money even with the defaults to which their business is heir. But under unstable world economic conditions, there will be only islands of stability in a sea of defaults, and that can be disastrous for the banks and the system. The question is, therefore, less whether the banks have made a mistake in going further afield for lending than they have done in the past, but rather whether the leaders of the world's economy—roughly the leaders of the Group of Ten—can create and sustain a stable and growing world in which the less-developed countries can participate by selling the output and products that the new loans are designed to create.

# 12.
# The Political Economy of World Money: Mercantilism Revisited

t has been the hypothesis of this book that the dynamism of the post–World War II Bretton Woods system rested on the growing trade surpluses, particularly of Europe and Japan. These were matched, more or less, by the consistent deficits of the United States (and to a lesser extent, those of the United Kingdom). And these surpluses in turn were the result of undervalued currencies in the growth countries, deliberately depreciated in 1949 by American action. They remained undervalued, and *pari passu* the dollar overvalued, by the political action (or inaction) of all nations until the formal end of gold convertibility, the crisis in 1971.

The basic reform now proposed—officially by the United States—is a continuously functioning adjustment mechanism. Exchange rates would move as needed—up or down—so that any nation's future deficit or surplus would be automatically limited. Equilibrium, a zero balance, is the goal.

This presumably sensible solution would end the persistent and huge American deficits that have brought forth such anguished complaints. But paradoxically, the American plan for symmetry and equilibrium has met with resistance from the same trading partners who have complained in the past about asymmetry and disequilibrium, and now about the "dollar peril." They are reluctant, to put it mildly, to give up their surpluses, but at the same time reluctant to allow a continuation of the disequilibrium that those surpluses reflect: a real dilemma. This apparent contrariness on the part of the leaders of the surplus nations in fact reflects a deep conflict within the system itself. That conflict is between the idea of equilibrium on one hand and mercantilism—the political and economic philosophy which best summarizes the preference for persistent export surpluses and the acquisition of reserves—on the other.

Those familiar with the idea think of mercantilism as a philosophy held long ago by nations that wanted surpluses to gain gold—useful to fight wars, buy off rival monarchs, build a politically powerful nation-state—but a philosophy that became extinct in the seventeenth or eighteenth century, as the British-inspired ideas of free trade became dominant.

Not so. Since roughly the Crusades, mercantilism has run like a red thread through the actions of virtually all nations. In its modern resurrection in Anglo-American thought, mercantilism is espoused by no less a modern than Lord Keynes. A rereading of his "Notes on Mercantilism" in the *General Theory of Employment, Interest and Money* is instructive.

To explore the matter further, a few deceptively simple questions can act as guide. First, what is mercantilism? Second, why do modern states continue to embrace the idea? Are there alternatives? Third, how does it relate to the gold exchange (Bretton Woods) system, and how can it relate to proposed reforms?

At heart, mercantilism is statecraft designed to stimulate exports and thus gain reserves. It is the economic concomitant of nationalism. The mercantilists, Keynes quotes Heckscher,

> killed two birds with one stone. On the one hand the country was rid of an unwelcome surplus of goods, which was believed to result in unemployment, while on the other, the total stock of money in the country was being increased, with the resulting advantage of a fall in the rate of interest.

The early emphasis on a low rate of interest appealed, of course, to Keynes. At heart his system was based on an interest rate always lower than the marginal efficiency of capital (i.e., rate of profitability), as a key inducement for industrialists to invest and thus for an economy to grow. Keynes' advice to governments fits precisely the mercantilist point of view:

> Where there is no question of direct investment under the aegis of public authority, the economic objects with which it is reasonable for the government to be preoccupied are the domestic rate of interest and the balance of foreign trade.

One of the questions never wholly clarified in Keynes' exposition is why, in a modern state, it is necessary to rely on an export surplus to increase "the total stock of money." In earlier times when gold and silver were the only money, circulating as well as reserve, it had to be got from other countries (or from a nation's own mines, a rare resource). But modern governments can control the money supply by deficit spending, the printing press, central bank action, and in other ways.

Another question never wholly answered anywhere has to do with the very rationality of mercantilist ideas. An export surplus means real resources are being sent away in exchange for money. Looking at the other side of the mirror, in the 1950s and 1960s Americans were receiving a "consumer surplus," real goods—Volkswagens, wines, electronic goods, etc.—at cheap prices, in exchange for IOUs, paper money that others piled up as reserves. Similarly, American firms bought productive assets abroad. Even when the United States IOUs were convertible—to gold—the real resource balance was heavily in American favor. Goods and factories were exchanged, so to speak, for a money or gold fetish. Now, these United States deficits are to be ended and confidence in the dollar restored. But this will cost Americans a primary burden of greater real export shipments and a secondary burden of higher import prices. The struggle to become an exporter, a surplus nation, is a struggle to lose the consumer surplus. Real goods must be exported, cheaply priced imports forsaken. Convention and a nation's "self-respect" require this view, and this book follows the convention. Strict rationality might suggest otherwise.

Nevertheless, Keynes embraced the basic tenets of mercantilism, including domestic economic growth via a constant balance of payments surplus. At the same time, he espoused all the devices needed to retain (or regain if lost) the favorable balance: tariffs and quotas (not yet outlawed in 1936) but in moderation, lest they call forth countervailing restrictions that might nullify the benefits. Even the surplus itself should be moderate but persistent: Witness the fate of immoderate Spain when gold and silver from Mexico and Peru poured in during the sixteenth century, creating a rise in the "wage unit" (in modern terminology, inflation), which priced Spain out of competition and led to her collapse. And if for any reason a nation lost its surplus, there was always currency devaluation to set it right.

The object of the exercise is clearly domestic economic growth and employment. It is not, as was Churchill's 1925 policy, to have a "strong" currency that would be used internationally for trade or as reserves and would thus be a source of earnings for the City's bankers; nor is it to restore the value of bonds and other capital assets to the rentier class, at the expense of England's workers and exporters. Keynes' acerbic *The Economic Consequences of Mr. Churchill* had made his dissent from that position perfectly clear.

Nor was Keynes under any illusion about whose benefit mercantilism served: not "the world" or a community of nations, but the home country alone—it was and is the economics of nationalism.

> It should be understood that the advantages claimed are avowedly national advantage and are unlikely to benefit the world as a whole. . . . The mercantilists were under no illusion as to the national character of their policies and their tendency to promote war. It was national advantage and relative strength at which they were admittedly aiming.

A March 9, 1973, dispatch in *The New York Times* about France reads in part:

> At this point, French policy is defensive—to defend the common agricultural policy, defend exports, defend gold stocks which might have to be used if a too strong West German mark requires franc adjustment, and defend the very satisfying national growth rate. . . .

Except for reference to the Common Agricultural Policy, this policy could have been a mercantilist prescription. And for "France" in this dispatch there might be substituted with accuracy any of the surplus countries, including most of Western Europe and Japan. And this has been their policy during the entire post–World War II period.

The competition to export and gain surpluses has been compared to a sailing ship race; undervalued currencies started the surplus nations downwind. Unless currency values were reshuffled, the advantage could hardly be overcome. Political action (or inaction when appropriate) kept the surplus countries currencies downwind, hence in disequilibrium as long as possible (with minor exceptions) until the system broke down in mid-1971.

The post–World War II "wunderwirtschafts"—miracle economies —were indeed little more than export-led booms, based on low labor costs, undervalued currencies, and to be fair, very hard work and technological expertise, which foreign competition sharpened but which the protected home markets—English style—dulled.

The first consequence of the export-led booms for the surplus countries was to gain dollars and gold from the deficit Americans. In addition, increasing numbers of workers were attracted into the export industries—quickly absorbing the unemployed Germans (who in the 1950s threatened that nation's stability) and later several million Greek, Turkish, and other foreign workers as well; similarly in other lands, millions of underemployed Japanese or Italian farmers were thus absorbed. As in the United States in the 1920s, tho now workers enabled German and Japanese production to expand while unit labor costs remained relatively stable at the outset, but rising sharply by the 1960s. Europe's export industries also proved the most profitable, attracting capital, managerial and marketing skills, and other resources. The growth of powerful and profitable exporters in turn created political blocs devoted to exports. Steps to diminish exports, therefore, even when the surplus became excessive, could only be met by resistance from the exporters.

If market signals had early failed to wake industries to export opportunities, government signals were quick to prod them. Subsidies or forgiven taxes (administratively easy in Europe's value-added tax system) or easier credit (in credit-hungry Japan) or combinations of incentives were used. And in France, which lacked some of the "natural" advantages of others, devaluations were freely used to get the relative costs and prices of French goods down to competitive export levels and to get the reserves up and keep them up. Repeatedly the franc devalued. De Gaulle's first act in 1958 was to devalue, hard on the heels of France's 1957 devaluation. A strong France, he argued, required a temporarily weaker franc. The ensuing enhancement of French reserves doubtless strengthened his voice in international councils. After his fall in 1968, Frenchmen—made uneasy by the mini-revolt euphemistically called *les événements* —withdrew their capital to Switzerland and other havens; the French again devalued in 1969 to rebuild reserves and preserve a surplus position. It is doubtful that the French trade position per se merited devaluation. In the Smithsonian negotiation of December 1971, the franc was maneuvered into a "pivotal" position which need not revalue as the mark, the yen, and others did. The two-tier system is designed to keep French export prices (the commercial franc) down, while the financial franc fluctuates.

In virtually all the surplus countries, exports are far more important than in the United States: At $40 billion per year, rising in 1973 toward $60 billion, exports constitute 4 to 5% of a trillion-dollar-plus American GNP. In Europe the comparable figure ranges from 20 to 40%. In Japan where exports represent the offput of huge domestic industries, the figure is closer to 10%. A dollar of lost exports is a loss of 4 to 5 cents in the United States, a dime in Japan, but 20 to 40 cents in Europe. And since the Europeans and Japanese also import a far greater percentage of their food, oil, machinery, and other goods than do the Americans, they are more dependent on those exports to maintain their living standard. Yet for the United States to increase its exports from 4 to 5% of GNP, as it did in the early 1970s, an additional $20 billion of goods must be absorbed by the rest of the world.

And these relationships also explain the unwillingness of surplus countries to revalue upward. They lose surpluses, employment, maybe even gold in doing so. Their industries become less profitable as the relative price of their goods rises in the importing nations. A VW squareback, a bargain at $2,200, is comparable to a Chevrolet wagon and more expensive than a Vega or Pinto wagon when it costs $3,200 in the United States market. VW's alternatives are to sell fewer cars in the United States and lay off its workers, or reduce its quality standards (to its future jeopardy), or reduce its profits to keep its prices down and production and employment up.

"Let me make it clear," *Newsweek* quotes VW President Leiding at the July 1972 shareholders' meeting, "if it weren't for a currency crisis ... the annual report we're offering here would have been perfectly respectable."

Since these nations are such unrelenting surplus seekers, why have they revalued at all since 1971? Because they have been forced to by the flood of incoming dollars, which threaten to increase their money supply and create inflationary pressures, worse, in their view, than the hated revaluation. Indeed, as spelled out in Part III, the rate of growth of reserves compared to rate of growth of the money supply—or put differently, the seepage from gained reserves to money supply—is the key criterion to watch as a tip-off to revaluation. If large enough, as in Germany in 1969, in 1971, and again in 1973, it cannot be resisted.

When Germany revalues, it serves the international system's needs well. It permits the United States (and the United Kingdom) to gain some surpluses, employ more workers, enhance corporate profits from exports, and to get downwind in the battle. But Germany's (or Japan's, or France's) export industries and unions, well organized, are quick to put pressure on the government not to ruin them and throw the workers into unemployment, or face the voting consequences. The rules of the game say "surplus"—and the rules extend deep into the economic fabric. They are not easily changed.

Even when government policy was not overtly mercantilist, i.e., when governments have permitted their exchange rates to rise, there is still a tendency on the part of exporting corporations to behave in ways which are mercantilist in the sense that the continued effect is to accrue large export surpluses. Recent developments in Germany illustrate the point. German companies have continued to push exports, even at the expense of profits, so that the effect of exchange rate changes has been minimal. A recent speech by the chief economist of the Dresdner Bank, Dr. Kurt Richebächer, underscores the point:

> ... in 1971, with capacity still well employed, both profitability and the self-financing ratios (of export industries) dropped to their lowest point in more than 10 years. At 5 percent gross and 2.4 percent net the average

return on turnover by industrial joint stock companies was extremely bad compared internationally, and this return was paralleled by the steady fall of an initially low equity ratio.

Richebächer excoriates Germany policy of absorbing profits to offset rising exchange rates as "harmful, or worse still: suicidal."

> There is of course a certain tradition to attach more importance to turnover than to profit. ... Export profits are hit instead of the volume of exports. Since the deflationary effect of revaluations entirely depends on how quickly they affect the volume of exports and imports, a measure of this kind—if it aims at dampening down demand and prices—is wide of the mark.

Digging deeper, Richebächer points out that since 1967, on a dollar basis, taking into account inflation as well as revaluation of the mark, the unit wage cost of German industry increased by more than 70%, compared with some 20% in the United States and France and 50 to 60% in Japan.

> A disastrous result from the German point of view. Yet we are about to see a new spate of German exports.

German prices and marketing strategy are geared to the retention of exports.

> They would not dream of giving up ... market positions won with considerable effort and at great expense simply because there has been a shift in prices which may be temporary at that. And they would be even more inclined to adopt this attitude if sales at home dropped sharply as they have done for some two years in the Federal Republic. Existing production and marketing facilities bear high overheads whether they work or not. Faced with the choice of maintaining a certain volume of sales at lower prices and utilising existing capacity or to cut back sales and production, most companies plump for the former as by far the easier way. Underlying this strategy is the consideration that in the last analysis every export order that helps to cover the overheads over and above its regular costs affects profits less than a complete stoppage of production. And most important of all, the valuable pool of skilled labor is preserved in this way. Lower earnings from exports are made up if at all possible by way of higher prices at home.

From this German experience Dr. Richebächer concludes that

> Revaluations and devaluations are not the precision instrument to control the movements of trade that they are cracked up to be. They are exceedingly slow to take effect ... at the same time we have turned the exchange markets into a madhouse.

Richebächer's view would seem to suffer from lack of a time dimension. There is a limit to the capacity of companies to absorb losses and keep exports high with revaluations: Eventually the revaluations will do the job. And the job, incidentally, would be done more rapidly if the German banks, which are very considerable shareholders in the larger German corporations, insisted that the rate of return on those shares should not be permitted to fall to the historically low levels Richebächer has cited.

It is true that Germany may be more insulated from the revaluation effect than other economies, since so much of the German export is in machinery and capital goods, which are relatively price inelastic and for which the consumer has difficulty quickly finding alternative sources. Richebächer's comment relating to falling profits would doubtless first affect consumer goods exporters, e.g., automobiles. Yet eventually the revaluation effect must spread throughout the economy.

While the surplus nations marched ahead to the beat of a mercantilist drummer, the deficit countries found it necessary to replot their course from increasingly weak bargaining positions. The major deficit country—the money machine of the post–World War II world—was, of course, the United States. A lesser one was the United Kingdom. While the experiences of the United Kingdom are of great historic importance, they are well documented and can be disposed of briefly. In 1949 the United Kingdom devalued against the dollar along with others from a $4.00 to a $2.80 pound, some 30 percent. But unlike the others, the result was not an export-led boom. Britain never got downwind. It suffered continued deficits despite numerous schemes, plans, and even prayers to export more successfully. Any number of explanations have been offered for the British failure to join the surplus club, ranging from intransigent unions to the lack of commercial expertise, and a variety of other structural and historic factors. And all are partly true. But the most persistent fault seems to have been poor economic management by a succession of governments. The money supply was never adequately controlled; business could therefore sell its output in swollen domestic markets, ignoring exports and the accompanying technological sharpening from competition. Labor's response to inflation was of course to press for higher wages, which management could always recoup in inflated home markets. At the same time, the myth that devaluation is a sin trapped British officials and politicians. As late as 1964–1967, Labour party leaders, behaving like MacDonalds and Snowdens, or like pre-Keynesian Tories, doggedly fought devaluation. They argued alternatively that as fading world-banker, the pound must be "responsible," or that prices really do not matter, and thus forced Britain to suffer huge losses of employment, output, and growth by maintaining a clearly overvalued $2.80 pound. In addition, the nation lost some $5 billion of reserves—owned and borrowed—buying back surplus pounds on the foreign exchange markets in an effort to protect the unprotectable pound. These losses had to be made up by exports, real resources produced with hard work, as additional payment. To be sure, these policies precede Labour, as Samuel Brittan's *Treasury Under the Tories* made clear. Their continuation under Labour is hard to understand or justify.

The United States saw the pound as the front line of defense for the overvalued dollar, and to its dubious credit urged the British to hang on, organizing vast loans of reserves for the purpose. To no avail. In 1967 the pound was forced to devalue, and for no particularly good reason, $2.40 was selected as the next peg price. It is not unrelated that in 1938 the British standard of living was second only to the American. By 1971 it had fallen behind every Common Market country except Italy, and behind Canada, Australia, New Zealand, and Scandinavia as well, thanks in large measure to these policies.

But as the trauma was greatest in Britain, so too has been the change in attitude. For Britain under Prime Minister Heath is now the strongest advocate of a floating exchange rate policy. "Floating is fun," proclaimed the *Economist;* that remarkable journal's long-time campaign to convert the British government (and the world) to floating rates must rank as one of the more successful conversions, to its great credit. With the exchange rate freed, full attention can be paid to domestic problems, including growth, for so long forgone under a fixed rate regime. Even the attitude toward the "sterling area" has changed. Fear of causing reserve losses to countries holding sterling as reserves had long been cited as a prime inhibition to devaluation or a floating rate. Under the Basel Agreement of 1968, the British had agreed to reimburse holders of sterling for reserve losses if the pound should fall below an undisclosed figure, thought to be $2.38. When, for example, in November 1972 the pound had gone below this figure, the Bank of England made virtually no attempt (or at best marginal attempts) to support it—it was cheaper simply to reimburse sterling holders. The final irony is that the City of London's banks are more profitable and successful with a floating rate than under the fixed rates.

In the United States too there has been a sharp change of course, which serves to explain one of the most important but least understood policies of modern history, "benign neglect," to which earlier pages have been devoted.

The ultimate objective of this policy is reform of the monetary system which will provide, *inter alia*, for the United States as well as for other countries, greater exchange rate flexibility. This too has been slow in coming because the Europeans and Japanese realize that this reform means the end of the mercantilist-surplus game; this is the central barrier—no small one—to reform, American style. It means that each year of surplus must bear the seeds of its own destruction, as it must inevitably be followed by deficits to let the other fellow—including the United States—have his year of surplus. The net result over a period of years is a zero-sum game. All nations will balance out, i.e., achieve an equilibrium of zero surplus or deficit, over time. And that is a far cry from the mercantilist-surplus game of the 1940s, 1950s, and 1960s that was so beneficial to growth, if unstable. Unless, of course, a new money machine can be found or created, which, like the inflow of new gold in the years before 1914, or the U.S. deficits to 1971, can change the game from a zero-sum to an everybody-plus game, a question to which the last pages of this chapter will turn.

This, then, attempts to explain what the economics of mercantilism is, why the mercantilist-surplus nations have been reluctant to abandon this position until forced to by the American benign-neglect strategy. The second question posed—why modern nations continue to embrace it—is implicit. They fear a loss of exports, hence of output, hence of employment, which could lead to the collapse of governments unable to observe the mid-twentieth century's first commandment—thou shalt suffer no significant unemployment.

In summary then, there was in the postwar world an unrelenting drive toward export-led booms in Europe and Japan, for some elemental and deep reasons. Surpluses are time-honored evidences of success. The American-inspired depreciations of 1949 were designed to stimulate export-led booms, and succeeded. A whole structure of export industries and their political adherents depend on them, so that they cannot be restructured very rapidly, if at all. Further, no country wants to be without "adequate" reserves, partly because fixed exchange rates require a cushion to protect currencies if they must make a transition to new levels. And if those reserves are largely in gold, primordial gratifications are served as well. As the dollar weakened in the 1960s, the surplus nations' preference for gold assumed a far saner dimension; dollar devaluation would (and did) mean a windfall profit to the gold reserve. At the moment this profit, and indeed the entire gold asset, is frozen; virtually no gold is being bought or sold among governments. But that may change. There are also other objections to the abandonment of a surplus position, more political than economic in their thrust. First, there is reluctance to turn to deficit spending as an alternative to exports, to maintain full employment and economic growth. Second, there are political objections to what the United States might do with its surplus (or overcome deficit). These may be examined in turn.

Countries prefer exports to the modern alternative, deficit spending, which Keynes had called "direct investment under the aegis of public authority." Exports are profitable and technologically sharpening; social expenditures are less so. Exports require neither battles with Congresses for appropriations, nor adjudication of priorities among competing groups; social expenditures do. The whole idea of social expenditures to replace export-led booms requires a break with economic tradition and raises formidable questions regarding economic incentives, the feasibility of public-authority planning in an age that has grown thoroughly disenchanted with bureaucratic ineffectiveness and that has witnessed the hideous excesses to which centrally directed economies can lead, even when they are successful in their own terms. Few countries can make such a transition without an enormous wrench.

Even Keynes was ambivalent about the prospects for the "aegis of public authority." At one point he wrote, from the relative innocence of a 1936 perspective, that

> the policy of an autonomous rate of interest, unimpeded by international preoccupations, and of a national investment programme directed to an optimum level of domestic employment ... is twice blessed in the sense that it helps ourselves and our neighbours at the same time.

But further on, in the same book, he shies away from the power implicit in central planning or economic direction:

> ... dangerous human proclivities can be canalized into comparatively harmless channels by the existence of opportunities for money-making and private wealth, which, if they cannot be satisfied in this way, may find their outlet in cruelty, the reckless pursuit of personal power and authority, and other forms of self-aggrandisement. It is better that a man should tyrannise over his bank balance than his fellow citizen ....

Nevertheless, if the new monetary arrangements force nations to find a substitute for surpluses, more central direction of economies seems likely. The first government priority is to keep full employment by whatever economic means required. Nor is it inconceivable that departures from the type of democracy now dominant in all the developed world may be part of the price, unless a way can be found to reconvert the present system back to a surplus-for-all game.

The country that may well be forced to be the first to undertake public-authority spending as an offset to lost exports is Japan. The bulk of the American trade deficit by the 1970s was with Japan. Part of the European resistance to American devaluation was the argument that the United States needed surpluses vis-à-vis Europe to overcome its huge deficit to Japan. The problem, as the Europeans saw it, was bilateral, between the United States and Japan alone. The

American reply was twofold: that European restrictions on Japan in effect forced the United States to import the bulk (about a third) of Japan's exports, or run the risk of seeing Japan slip out of the geopolitical network of the free world, perhaps driven to seek less desirable trade channels and political affiliations; and secondly, given the American need to see the free world as a whole, the United States must look to its overall balance of payments position, in effect earning even larger surpluses in Europe. The geopolitical heart of the argument is difficult for Europeans. On the economic side, they would like the United States alone to cope with maintaining a strong economic and defensive front against the East. But they also rely on American troops, the nuclear umbrella, military research and development, and so have not, with the possible exception of France, been too negative about the U.S. geopolitical view. Part of the resolution of the Japanese problem lies in trade negotiations to open European markets a bit more and to force the Japanese to offset their export proclivities with imports—which they are now doing although not without some profound political trauma, so far withstood by the democratic Sato-Tanaka-type governments. Another part of the solution lies within Japan, where a shift of economic resources to social improvements—housing, pollution control, sewage systems, and the like, all lacking and neglected in the rush to economic and commercial development—are to be undertaken.

Second, there exist, especially in Europe, other political objections to a system designed to restore the U.S. surplus. Some of these objections have their roots in political postures, although the argument is couched, as in the case of Japan, in the rhetoric of economic orthodoxy. The term "political economy" may have grown old-fashioned, but its reality is very current. This complex network of relationships rested on the Atlantic Alliance, most recently formulated in a formal sense by the Kennedy administration. The Alliance has worn thin as Europe has grown strong and the Americans buried their energies in Asia and sought bilateral détente with China and the USSR. President Nixon has designated 1973 the "year of Europe." The administration has made initial proposals to "cement the relationship," which have not been well accepted. How the Atlantic relationships will be patched, if at all, is a matter for negotiation.

Some of the major elements are noted below. They are relevant here because the new attack on Europe's mercantilism is designed, *inter alia*, to permit the United States to bear the cost of these responsibilities without incurring deficits, i.e., through trade-surplus earnings.

The military and AID programs of the United States must also be paid for by exports, if they are not curtailed. And devaluation to permit this type of expenditure produces mixed reactions in Europe. NATO and American troops in Europe evoke strong official yeas in Germany, England, and elsewhere, but nays from minorities there and from official France. Within the United States there also exists strong antipathy to keeping troops abroad, as shown by the Mansfield Amendment in the Senate and the consistent criticism by the Joint Economic Committee. This item has consistently cost some $2–$3 billion per year, about the size of U.S. deficits until the 1970s when this number paled. The problem will continue, even with U.S. surpluses. Its resolution will have to take the form of unilateral U.S. troop reductions, or contributions by Europe and Japan to offset the cost of U.S. protection (preferably leading to a "zero foreign exchange cost"), or some arrangement with the Russians for mutual reduction of forces in Europe, whereby a new and less costly balance is struck as NATO and the Warsaw Pact parties withdraw troops together.

American AID to bolster friendly, if sometimes unpleasant re-gimes, appears to many Europeans hardly the type of thing for which they should sacrifice exports. As for Vietnam, the major source of the dollar's downfall, or anything resembling it in the future, the Euro-pean verbal response has been mixed; but, since no European nation has shown the slightest inclination to help, it must be judged in fact antipathetic. Swedish and French sources were quick to note that in the peace of March 1973, South Vietnam won a settlement slightly worse than it had under the Geneva Agreement 19 years earlier.

The multinational corporations constitute yet another area of political-economic resistance to American surpluses. Europeans are quick to note that the proposed U.S. surplus is also designed to cover long-term capital outflows from the United States. The promised end of the Interest Equalization Tax and the Office of Foreign Direct Investment restrictions in 1974 might, they fear, swell the present total of U.S. outflows for portfolio or for direct (plant and equipment through multinational companies) investment. This will allow American multinational companies to continue to expand into Europe, buying up the most advanced and desirable firms, in the past with deficit money ("our own money") borrowed in Eurodollar or Eurobond markets, or, in future, with "cheap" exports.

This antipathy has been particularly sharp in France, although it has abated there for the present, as the French have tried to move the situs of antipathy to the EEC commission in Brussels, to blanket the whole of the Common Market. The French argue that the Americans are pushed to foreign acquisitions by ambitious international divisions of companies and are insensitive to their rate of return on foreign investment. In 1963 the French tried to reduce U.S. investment by screening applicants for their usefulness to the French economy, notably their capacity to bring advanced technology. The campaign ended when companies excluded from France found easy entry to other Common Market countries, notably Belgium, thus bringing the companies inside the EEC wall. French companies are relatively easy prey for foreign take-over. In part this reflects French secrecy, so that even the shareholders do not know how much is being earned and can thus be induced to sell fairly cheaply. In part, too, French nationalism plays a role. Few other developed countries have in the past shared the overt French antipathy to American multinationals. Europeans invest vast sums in the shares or Eurobonds of the Americans, testifying to their confidence in these companies and their management. Nevertheless, it is probably true that antipathy to American investment has spread in Europe recently. The Japanese miracle took place without, or with few, U.S. multinationals; Europeans and particularly developing nations are increasingly impressed with it.

Multinational corporate investment spurted into Europe, particularly in manufacturing, after the Common Market began in 1958. A now vast academic literature has made clear some reasons, some costs, and some benefits, which need not be reviewed here. But the fact is that a Common Market tariff wall forced American companies to get behind it for defensive motives by internationalizing production. The alternative for the American multinationals was to face the loss of those expanding markets to competitive producers. Lower wage costs and undervalued currencies gave the companies a chance to combine factors of production most efficiently by producing abroad, an offensive motive. And, by and large, this investment was welcomed, especially at the outset, for good mercantilist reasons; it stimulated employment, helped gain surpluses through capital infusion, and above all brought with it the most advanced technology, reducing the "technological gap" with which the U.S. started the post–World War II era, a gap that worried the Europeans enormously and that some congressmen had counted on to keep the United States in perpetual surplus. From a world, i.e., nonnational point of view, the movement was highly salutary as it integrated the world economy, at least in the developed world. As in the United States two or three decades earlier, integration meant a tendency toward equalization of wages, interest rates, and technology, in effect wiping out "backward areas" and making for a more even economic landscape.

The European objections to American Investment abroad—more specifically to *le défi américain*, the American challenge through the multinational company—may now well be out of date. Time and events have overcome most of the initial motivations to the internationalization of production, or at least to the rapid spread of the American multinational company. It is less welcome since the Europeans have now acquired the new American technology and certainly want no more capital inputs at present. The overvaluation of the dollar (or, the other side of the same coin, the undervaluation of European currencies) has been ended or reduced by devaluations and revaluations, so that the Americans have less motive to go abroad to seek optimum use of the factors of production. For example, machinists' wages in Germany are now substantially the same as in the United States, fringe benefits included. American companies certainly will not pack up and come home, but the rate of expansion has run out of steam for natural and good economic reason.

At the same time, the next wave of multinational corporate activity is apt to be into the less-developed world, where cheaper wage costs, less concern about pollution, and the like beckon. But it will be different. Western European and Japanese-based corporations will be among the leading investors, as well as Americans. North Europe's policy of importing labor to produce and export from the home country has created social problems that make it more willing to move its industries south, to the labor supply. Japan's now high wage costs (exacerbated by revaluations) will make for even greater movement of its industry to the Asian fringe or to other developing regions. And industry from both areas is finding it increasingly attractive to establish production units within the United States itself; direct foreign investment with book value of some $13 billion in 1971 was nearly double the 1962 figure. *Le défi* has become, and will be, more international than American.

In the developing world, 100-percent-owned multinational subsidiaries are much less likely to prevail than joint ventures, local share participations, or even various forms of technology—transfer without ownership, such as "fade-out" or licensing arrangements. Legislation in many developing areas, themselves impressed with the "Japanese model," is forcing that. And in Communist Europe this must be the pattern. Communist Europe, indeed, is one of the most promising areas for the new multinationalization because, as the *Economist* phrased it in a March 17, 1973, article entitled "Eurodollars, Multinationals, Goodbye?":

> In communist Europe . . . the inefficiency of a non-market economy means that a well-educated and non-trade-unionized labour force is being used at far below its potential manufacturing productivity.

One point remains to be defended in this exposition of European reluctance to countenance U.S. devaluation, until forced to do so. What alternatives did the Europeans propose? Some have been alluded to as being not very constructive.

There is no single European "remedy," just as there is no single European voice; Europeans have tried without success for some agreement, even on defensive measures. For example, most have imposed some form of short-term capital control, although in form it varies from place to place: France, Belgium, and now Italy use a two-tier system. The United Kingdom floats. Germany restricts inflows of capital, less successfully than Japan, which controls most things.

In the face of the "dollar peril," as it came to be known, several attempts to forge a joint European float (versus the dollar) have been made, without success. The strong pressure on the mark has driven that currency up, not only against the dollar but in terms of cross rates, i.e., the mark versus the franc, the pound, and others with which it trades.

If there was so little unity on the dollar peril, there was not likely to be more on reform of the system. Most Europeans have agreed that the United States should "discipline" itself. In practice this would mean applying the "classical medicine" of recession, or of higher interest rates, or of an incomes policy to inhibit the level of inflation and/or economic growth and employment. It is in part to meet this view that the Nixon administration imposed price controls in 1971, although purely internal motives were also important. But as a policy matter, no nation is going to impose serious unemployment, of the dimension required, on its people to correct a foreign payment problem. The spirit if not the letter of Bretton Woods does indeed place the burden of adjustment on a deficit nation to do just this; but that spirit conflicts with full-employment legislation and policies, and in an age when no government could stand real unemployment, the "classical medicine" must effectively be ruled out as a serious prescription.

Some in Europe, notably in France, have proposed raising the gold price to permit the United States to revalue its hoard and continue to play Bretton Woods style convertibility. The gold solution and its rejection by the United States (and others) has been discussed earlier.

The net result for Europe is a quandary. Europe and Japan are understandably unhappy with the present situation but at heart reluctant to give up undervalued currencies and surpluses, the roots of the present malaise. Their past preference for fixed exchange rates reflects the same mercantilist desire. Rates were to remain fixed at undervalued levels. As the tables turned, i.e., as the dollar moved down, strong European preference for flexibility, i.e., the joint float versus the dollar, has appeared. But even this attempt at a unified European response has been so far unsuccessful and will come, if at all, slowly. Nor has the initiative for a new vision to replace the old emerged from Europe. At the same time, the American initiatives leave much to be desired in Europe's view.

We have argued that mercantilist beliefs are at the heart of the problem. Is a solution possible, in which equilibrium and surpluses could live side by side?

## A New Money Machine?

The object of floating or more flexible exchange rates is to permit the United States to earn surpluses too. The money machine of the U.S. deficit, which sustained economic growth and surplus for all others from 1950 to 1971, is now dead. Thus, as in the past, surpluses must be scored off one's neighbor and be only short-lived.

Can the world live with this system? Must it? It is hardly conducive to harmony or growth. It very much resembles the bad old days, of which Keynes wrote:

> Never in history was there a method devised of such efficacy for setting each country's advantage at variance with its neighbour's as the inter-national gold (or formerly silver) standard. For it made domestic prosperity directly dependent on a competitive pursuit of markets. ...

But as Keynes was aware, a money machine can mitigate the competitive drive:

> When by a happy accident the new supplies of gold and silver were comparatively abundant the struggle might be somewhat abated.

Historically, we have seen this "happy accident" twice in the last century. The supplies of gold from South Africa provided a money machine that made for growth and surpluses (albeit with inflation) in the years before 1914. The United States deficits and the consequent running down of its gold stock from 1950 to 1971 served the same purpose.

An analogy may be borrowed from astronomy: Fred Hoyle has offered the hypothesis that the universe expands because somewhere, for some unknown reason, there is a constant injection of hydrogen gas into the firmament. Similarly all nations have had, and can have, economic growth with surpluses so long as new money/gold, analogous to the hydrogen, blows in. When it stops, the analogy suggests, so does the expansion.

Can the Special Drawing Rights (SDRs) be the new money machine? Can this "paper gold" become the new expansionary force enabling us, including the United States, all to be mercantilists and earn surpluses, not off each other but off the new supply? Can we run another non-zero-sum game?

The volume of SDRs to be issued is based on general agreement of the IMF members. Thus SDRs have the advantage of being in place, operative, and managed in volume. While the original idea was to issue only the amount needed to expand liquidity with the needs of world trade, that amount can obviously be changed as the managers so agree from time to time.

To date SDRs have been highly acceptable to both strong and weak currency nations, perhaps because their price is linked to gold, although there is no gold backing for them. If they continue to be regarded as "good as gold" and issued by the money managers to deliberately expand the supply of liquidity, the non-zero-sum game system can work: all nations can be in surplus. But if their quality is questioned as their quantity increases, if they are regarded as paper rather than being as good as gold (as now) and SDRs are not accepted, as was the case with the dollar, their use and issue will diminish, and the money machine will break down.

The difficulty of predicting their future acceptability is that there is absolutely nothing familiar about the whole procedure. Most nations still regard gold the center of the system, although for all practical purposes, it is a useless resource. Some believe that governments can "always" sell it in private markets for currencies. In fact it would not take a great sale to reduce its price in those markets drastically, an adjustment which a stronger U.S. dollar may well perform in any event. Moreover, gold earns no interest and is rarely used now in trade settlements. Historically, the shift from metallic gold to paper gold (SDRs) parallels the extension of paper money throughout the world. In the U.S., Federal Reserve notes replace gold (or a variety of private bank paper) earlier this century. A ten-dollar bill as such has no redemption value—one Doubting Thomas who sent one to the U.S. Treasury to be "redeemed" was sent two fives in exchange—yet it is used with confidence. Whether SDRs, which do earn some interest—currently 1-½ percent—will continue to be used with the same confidence remains to be seen.

There are numerous plans to mop up or "refund" the "overhang" of dollars in foreign hands—i.e., those dollars nations or private holders feel are in excess of their reserve or working balance needs, and which now find use as Eurodollar deposits. One refunding plan would convert excess dollars for SDRs. The IMF would issue SDRs in exchange for dollars; the dollars would be recycled to the United States, which would in exchange pay to the IMF long-term (or perpetual "consol") Treasury bonds, on which the United States would pay a yet unspecified interest rate. Most of this interest would in turn be passed through to the holders of the SDRs (formerly dollar holders). This would, of course, vastly increase the importance and magnitude of SDRs in the system. Some fear such a deluge of SDRs would destroy their yet meager creditability; they propose a special IMF note issue instead.

On the other hand, the late Paul Einzig, writing in the January/February 1973 *International Currency Review*, suggested that to limit SDRs to official government holdings is a dangerous mistake. They should be available for private holdings, used as collateral for bank loans, etc.—in short become a kind of single international money. Einzig was not very optimistic about any future scenario involving SDRs, but he sees their general extension as the least bad scenario:

> Admittedly, such an extension of the use of SDRs would also increase the risk of exacerbating inflation. But unfortunately, it seems more than likely that, even if the use of SDRs is confined to transactions between central banks, grossly excessive amounts will be issued to satisfy greedy governments. ... It is in the interest of all of us to defer the breakdown of the system by extending the *use* of SDRs ... by gaining time, we at least stand a chance that pressure for economic growth and permissive wage escalation might subside.

Fluctuations in the free, private market of the price of SDRs would also provide some indication of the degree of confidence in SDRs and thus provide warning signals to prevent their overissue by the money managers.

Whether used privately or only officially, and whether regarded with as much confidence as gold or not, SDRs still offer the best hope for a base for a future monetary system without economic warfare. When the idea was first introduced by the United States Treasury in 1966–1967 and accepted by other nations in 1968–1969, this ultimate use may not have been envisioned. But if it works, the world will be deeply in debt to those Treasury officials who persevered until the plan became reality, at a time when more liquidity was the last thing needed by the world.

# Keeping
# Afloat

# 13.
# How Business Can Live With the System

hile the details of the new system that will replace Bretton Woods have yet to be worked out—and are indeed the subject of great controversy—it is already evident that it will involve a much greater degree of exchange rate flexibility than prevailed under the gold standard, the gold exchange standard, or Bretton Woods.

The tragic losses of income that the United States, and more particularly the United Kingdom, suffered in the 1960s while attempting to maintain fixed parities have proved a salutary lesson. Flexible rates are here to stay, and business must learn to live with them.

In this world of floating rates, the foreign exchange manager is central. His operations are of key importance to company profits—one wrong decision could completely wipe out the profits on overseas operations. If he errs, the forecasts of the finance director, production planners, and the rest may be reduced to nonsense by a storm of adverse fluctuations in foreign exchange rates. How can a company minimize foreign exchange losses under these conditions?

First it is necessary to consider the measurement of gains or losses from foreign exchange fluctuations. The details of foreign exchange accounting are best left to professional accountants. Here we present only enough of the general principles to provide a general background for considering what should be done to avoid foreign exchange losses. For this purpose Table 17 shows a highly simplified balance sheet of a subsidiary foreign operation of a U.S. company. All of the figures are in the currency of the country in which the subsidiary operates. Table 17 also shows the calculation from the balance sheet of the so-called exposed position, i.e., the amount stated in local currencies that is susceptible to gains or losses from devaluation or revaluation. Put in another way, where a company is in an exposed position, it will gain or lose from either devaluations or revaluations.

There are two kinds of exposed positions: long positions and short positions.

In long positions, a company is holding the foreign currency either in cash or in some form of future claim on the foreign currency. Thus a company loses from devaluation because, translated into dollars, its foreign currency is worth less. On the other hand, if there is a revaluation, the company gains because its holdings of foreign currency, translated into dollars, are worth more.

In short positions, a company is in some form of overall debtor position where, in the future, it has to pay out the foreign currency to someone else. Under these conditions, the exposure is just the opposite from long positions. In a short position, the company gains if there is a devaluation because it can pay off its debts with depreciated money. On the other hand, if there is a revaluation, a company will lose because it will have to pay off its debts at a higher exchange rate.

The rules on exposed positions thus work this way: If the exposed position is "long" and there is a devaluation, the company loses an amount equal to the long position multiplied by the percentage devaluation. For example, if a company was long by 10 million guilders and the guilder devalued 20 percent, the loss would be equal to 2 million guilders.

Where the exposed position is long and there is a revaluation, the company gains an amount equal to the long position multiplied by the percentage revaluation.

**Table 17**

Example of the calculation of exposed positions (all items in units of a foreign currency, in thousands)

| | Amount | Not counted in exposed position | Counted as exposed position in traditional accounting | Counted as exposed position in monetary-physical accounting |
|---|---|---|---|---|
| *Assets* | | | | |
| Cash | 15 | | 15 | 15 |
| Receivables | 15 | | 15 | 15 |
| Other short-term financial assets | 10 | | 10 | 10 |
| Inventory | 25 | | 25 | 0 |
| Fixed assets | 50 | 50 | 0 | 0 |
| *Liabilities* | | | | |
| Accounts payable | 15 | | −15 | −15 |
| Long-term debt | 70 | | 0 | −70 |
| Net worth | 30 | 30 | 0 | 0 |
| Exposed position | | | 50 | −45 |

With the exposed position short, the company will gain from a devaluation because the short position, which is a minus number, is multiplied by the percentage devaluation which also has a minus sign. For example, if the exposed position is 5 million guilders short and a devaluation is 10 percent, the gain on the short guilder position would be 500,000 guilders.

If the exposed position is short and there is a revaluation, the company will take a loss equal to the short position multiplied by the percentage revaluation.

The calculation of long or short positions is a first step in estimating possible gains or losses that could result from exchange rate changes. This calculation is, however, complicated by the possibility of using different methods of accounting, i.e., different balance sheet items are considered either long or short. In the traditional method, short-term assets and liabilities are considered exposed, but long-term assets or liabilities are not. In the more recently developed "monetary–physical" system, monetary items in the balance sheet are considered exposed, but physical items (inventories and fixed capital) are not.

Table 17 shows which items in the balance sheet are included in exposed positions in each of the two systems. Long items are shown with plus signs and short items with minus signs. If the overall sum of the balance sheet items is positive, the position is long. If the overall sum of the balance sheet items is negative, the position is short.

In both systems cash, receivables, and other short-term financial assets (treasury bills, commercial paper, etc.) are considered exposed positions. All these items will have less (more) dollar value if there is a devaluation (revaluation). In traditional accounting, inventory was considered an exposed position because it was assumed that inventory would be sold for the foreign currency which, if it had been devalued or revalued, would thus be worth less or more dollars. In the monetary–physical system, however, inventory is not considered an exposed position. It is reasoned that a devaluation results from inflation in a country, so that the price of the inventory would be raised to offset devaluation losses. There are objections to this viewpoint since devaluations sometimes result from a drop in a country's exports or a rise in its imports for reasons other than domestic inflation. It is even more difficult to see how the monetary–

physical approach can be applied to revaluations since this would seem to imply that, in the typical cases of revaluations, prices in the country would fall enough to offset the currency revaluation. Some companies consider inventory exposed for devaluations but not for revaluations.

Fixed assets are not considered exposed in either the traditional or monetary–physical systems. It is assumed that losses from devaluation or gains from revaluations are offset by price changes in the stream of future goods or services produced by the fixed asset. Moreover, it is assumed that, in spite of inflation or currency changes, the depreciation of the fixed asset will not require adjustment. These assumptions are patently weak, most of their support coming from the obvious difficulty of developing a manageable alternative system.

Accounts payable are considered exposed in both systems. If there is a devaluation, short-term debts can be paid off with depreciated currency, while the opposite holds if there is a revaluation.

Long-term debt is considered an exposed item in the monetary–physical type of accounting. It is argued that the long-term debt should be written down (up) with a devaluation (revaluation) since it will be cheaper (more expensive) to pay off. In traditional accounting, however, overall long-term debt is not considered an exposed position in the year of revaluation or devaluation. Only when the debt is paid off—and therefore considered part of current expenses of the year or years of repayment—will the repayment(s) be considered as exposed.

Finally, the net worth item is not part of the exposed position in either system. However, if there is a devaluation or revaluation, this item is adjusted to reflect gains and losses on assets and liabilities, so that the balance sheet is kept in balance.

Items in a company balance sheet can sometimes be changed in order to avoid exposed positions—this is known as "changing the natural position." For example, when a devaluation threatens, it may be possible to reduce the cash and other short-term assets of a subsidiary without much damage to the business's liquidity requirements.

Receivables can be cut back when there is a devaluation

risk—though this method may alienate too many customers accustomed to pay on a deferred basis as, for example, in the sales of consumer durables on credit. The danger here is that losses of sales might offset the advantage gained in a reduced long position.

If traditional accounting methods are followed and inventories considered a long position, it may be possible to cut these back. But this can, as in the case of receivables, have unfortunate side effects. Reduced production and sales effectiveness resulting from inventory cutbacks could prove more costly than the gains from a lower exposed position.

Short-term borrowing is a standard method of reducing exposed positions, especially in countries where there is no forward market for the currency. But, here again, the after-tax interest costs of borrowing may be greater than expected losses from devaluation.

After all workable changes have been made in the natural position, a company may nevertheless find itself dangerously exposed, in long positions in currencies vulnerable to devaluation or in short positions in currencies vulnerable to revaluations. Under these conditions the prudent foreign exchange manager of a company will assess the value of using forward currency markets to reduce the vulnerable exposed position.

While the spot foreign exchange market is a market in actual currencies, the forward foreign exchange market is a market in contracts. Forward foreign exchange contracts provide that the seller of the contract will deliver a specific amount of foreign exchange at a specific exchange rate at a specific date ahead. Once a contract is made, the foreign exchange must be delivered at the exchange rate and on the date specified in the contract, regardless of what spot rate actually prevails. Thus forward foreign exchange contracts provide a means of protecting exposed positions. If a revaluation is feared, the company treasurer can "cover" his exposed short position by buying a contract for foreign exchange forward at a lower rate than the expected revaluation.

If a devaluation is feared, he does the opposite—protecting his long position by making a contract to sell the currency forward at a rate that he believes will be above the spot rate in the future.

Banks and individuals who make contracts are, in effect, providing insurance against currencies revaluing or devaluing. They do not, of course, do this without being paid. Like insurance companies, they make a charge for providing this insurance. When the market indicates that there is a risk of revaluation, forward contracts are sold at a premium over spot exchange rates. On the other hand, if the market indicators point to a devaluation, forward contracts are sold at a discount from spot exchange rates. Competition among buyers and sellers of forward foreign exchange contracts determines premiums and discounts. Spot and major forward exchange rates are quoted daily in the press. On the 90-day pound sterling, for example, the discount on October 10, 1972, was 1.40 cents ($2.4192 spot, $2.4052 forward). On the other hand, on the 90-day mark the premium was 0.2225 cents. Often these premiums and discounts are stated as percentages. On sterling, for example, the discount was 0.58%: .0140 ÷ 2.4192 = 0.58%. On the mark, the premium was 0.71% (.314775 forward, .312550 spot): .002225 ÷ .312550 = 0.71%.

It is sometimes convenient to annualize premiums and discounts to make them comparable to per annum rates of interest. The number of months of the contract is divided into 12 (months of the year) and the resulting quotient multiplied by the percentage discount or premium. In the examples given above:

$12/3$ + 0.58% = 2.32% annualized discount for sterling
$12/3$ + 0.71% = 2.84% annualized premium for marks.

Although exposed positions can, in principle, be avoided either by changing the natural position or by using the forward market, it is usually a mistake for a company to attempt to protect itself from every conceivable currency loss. We have already noted that changing the natural position may be counterproductive if it weakens the company liquidity position, loses customers who want to pay on a deferred basis, or upsets production planning via cutting inventories. Likewise the forward currency market may involve greater costs than are justified by the risks of exposed positions.

Implicit in a company decision to cover or not to cover an exposed position is a forecast of that currency's vulnerability to either devaluation or revaluation. Forecasting the exchange rate outlook is considered in detail in the next chapter. It should be emphasized, however, that what is important is not so much that the company treasurer have a precise forecast of where each currency is going to go, over so many months ahead, but that risk of devaluation or revaluations is known. Sometimes this risk may be relatively small, but the cost of a forward exchange transaction may also be small, so that it is worth while to go ahead. This is roughly comparable to the choice of whether or not to buy burglary insurance. People who buy insurance are not forecasting burglaries but rather the *chance* of burglaries. They must decide whether the insurance premium is worth it relative to the probability of burglary and what the burglar might get away with.

A company's adviser on foreign currency policy acts as a kind of insurance broker. Besides evaluating risks in foreign exchange exposure, he has the equally serious responsibility of recommending whether or not foreign exchange cover will be worth its cost. Sometimes the costs of cover may be greater than a reasonable expectation of losses from a currency change. For example, in the summer of 1970 there was perhaps a 25% probability that the Italian lira would be devalued by 10%. But this would not have justified a "cover" operation of selling lira forward at the then prevailing discount of 6.0% on one-year contracts: 25% of 10%, or 2½%—the expectation of loss from devaluation—was less than 6%. Likewise, through most of the 1960s, Mexican pesos sold forward at discounts often as high as 4.0%. In retrospect, it seems clear that the probabilities of a Mexican peso devaluation were not great enough to justify paying such high "insurance."

But there have been numerous cases when there was strong justification for paying the costs of protection against currency losses. On September 16, 1968, French francs could have been sold forward for one year at a 1.72% discount. This cost was a reasonable insurance rate against the August 1969 devaluation of the French franc by 11.1%. More recently, on April 7, 1972, forward sterling sold at a 0.02% discount. Since then it was allowed to float and depreciated about 10%, between April 7 and November 7.

An evaluation of currency risks is usually put in probability form with a rough statement of the chances of future devaluations or revaluations. A simple example is shown in Table 18. The simple rules of thumb on whether or not to cover are as follows:

Cover against devaluation or revaluation when the most likely currency change multiplied by the probability of the currency change happening is greater than the percentage cost of cover.

Do not cover against devaluation or revaluation if the most likely percentage currency change multiplied by the probability of the currency change happening is less than the percentage cost of cover.

To illustrate this admittedly very crude principle, Table 19 gives some examples of when to cover and when not to cover. To put these ideas together, consider the case of the ABC Company. It is short, i.e., it owes, $5 million in Dutch guilders. The company's analysis of the world currency outlook suggests that within one year ahead the most likely development, if any, is a 20% revaluation of the guilder and this has a 25% chance of happening. The expectation —sometimes called actuarial outlook—is thus for a $250,000 loss, calculated as follows:

**Table 18**

Currency risk statement April 1971

*Countries with a 25%–50% probability of revaluation within the next 12 months*

Germany (deutschmark)
Japan (yen)
Switzerland (franc)
Netherlands (guilder)
Belgium (franc)

*Countries with a 25%–50% probability of devaluation within the next 12 months*

United Kingdom (pound)
Sweden (krona)
Norway (krone)
Denmark (krone)

*Countries with a low probability (less than 25%) of currency change within the next 12 months*

Italy (lira)
France (franc)
Spain (peseta)

$$\underset{\text{(short position)}}{\$5 \text{ million}} \quad X \quad \underset{\substack{\text{(most likely} \\ \text{revaluation} \\ \text{amount)}}}{20\%} \quad X \quad \underset{\substack{\text{(chance of} \\ \text{most likely} \\ \text{reval. amount)}}}{25\%} \quad = \$250{,}000$$

The company figures that, on average, it will be better off if it can find a way to spend less than $250,000 as insurance. But if the insurance costs more than $250,000, it simply is not worth it compared with the risks involved.

The forward currency market provides insurance against currency losses. However, before it considers going into the foreign exchange market, the company considers whether there may be a cheaper way of protecting itself against foreign exchange losses. It looks at its balance sheet. Suppose the balance sheet shows that of the $5 million short position, $2 million is in accounts payable. The foreign currency manager proposes to pay off these accounts. However, the head office is caught in a cash bind and can supply only $1 million for this purpose. Thus the exposed position is reduced to $4 million. The company also has accounts receivable amounting to $2 million long. Why not make the long position longer by slowing up the collection of accounts receivable? However, the company's debtors also foresee the possibility of revaluation, and some of them are anxious to repay their debts. (Where revaluation threatens, creditors try to pay their debts early—an example of a "lead.") Nevertheless, the ABC Company does somehow succeed in deferring payment of $500,000 worth of accounts receivable. Its exposed position is reduced to $3.5 million. Assume in this case that the company follows traditional accounting methods. By building up inventories, the company can further reduce its short position. The foreign exchange manager calls the production manager and asks him whether it is possible to build up inventories by $1 million. The production manager is agreeable, but the sales manager says such a policy will be "crazy" because of the danger that styles might change; although the company could gain on its balance sheet, its profit and loss position would be damaged by a buildup of unsalable merchandise. Finally a compromise is worked out where inventories are built up by $500,000 in products that are believed to have a steady market.

**Table 19**

Some examples of crude decisions on whether or not to cover a foreign exchange position

| (1) Forecast devaluation or revaluation | (2) Probability of devaluation or revaluation | (3) Mathematical expectation of devaluation or revaluation (1) × (2) | (4) Percentage cost of cover against currency change | (5) Cover if (3) exceeds (4); do not cover if (4) exceeds (3) |
|---|---|---|---|---|
| 10% | 50% | 5% | 7% | Do not cover |
| 10% | 25% | 2½% | 1% | Cover |
| 5% | 50% | 2½% | 5% | Do not cover |
| 10% | 50% | 5% | 2% | Cover |
| 10% | 75% | 7½% | 10% | Do not cover |
| 20% | 25% | 5% | 2% | Cover |
| 15% | 66-2/3% | 10% | 5% | Cover |

At this stage, by squeezing the natural position as much as possible, the company gets its exposed short position down to $3.0 million. The expected loss comes to:

$$\underset{\text{(short position)}}{\$3 \text{ million}} \quad \times \quad \underset{\substack{\text{(most likely} \\ \text{reval. amount)}}}{20\%} \quad \times \quad \underset{\substack{\text{(chance of} \\ \text{most likely} \\ \text{reval. amount)}}}{25\%} \quad = \$150,000$$

Now the company considers the forward exchange market. One-year forward guilders are selling at a 2.5% premium. This means that the company can make a contract in which to buy one year ahead $3 million in guilders at a cost of $75,000 calculated as follows:

$$\$3 \text{ million} \times 2.5\% = \$75,000$$

The cost of the forward contract at $75,000 is less than the expected loss of $150,000, so that the rule of thumb is to buy the contract. This means that if the guilder revalues by 20%, the company can exercise its contract and buy $3,600,000 worth of guilders ($3 million plus the 20% revaluation) for $3,075,000 ($3 million plus the premium of $75,000). Thus the $75,000 cost of the premium would save a potential loss of $600,000 from devaluation. On the other hand, if there is no guilder revaluation, the company would, under its forward contract, be obliged to pay $3,075,000 for $3,000,000 in guilders. This can, however, be considered a cost of doing business that is probably less ulcer-producing than an uncovered long position with a loss of $600,000.

The reasoning here is essentially actuarial. Up to a certain point, changing the natural position is like building defenses against fire, burglary, or other disasters. Beyond a certain point, however, the cost of these defenses in fireproofing, burglar-alarm systems, etc. becomes more expensive than insurance. In foreign exchange management, the insurance rate is the forward premium or discount. As in any risk situation, under simplified assumptions, the cost of the insurance should not be more than the most likely event multiplied by the chance of its happening.

The rules of foreign exchange management outlined here are, of course, very much simplified. For one thing, complicated and controversial tax considerations have not been taken into account. A more sophisticated evaluation may take into account not just one probability of devaluation or revaluation in a particular period, but the alternative probabilities of devaluation and/or revaluation by varying amounts in different periods ahead. The expected amount of devaluation or revaluation in all periods ahead is the sum of the devaluation or revaluation in each period, multiplied by the probability of it happening. Based on this evaluation, plus an analysis of its own financial position abroad, a company can devise a strategy for optimal insurance against currency risks. For multinational corporations operating large numbers of subsidiaries abroad in multiproduct, multicurrency businesses, management strategy with respect to currency risks may be complicated and, according to some experts, requires the use of computers and operations research techniques.

But it should be emphasized that regardless of financial and operations research sophistication, success in foreign exchange managements depends primarily on an adequate forecast of foreign exchange rate risks.

Otherwise, unless the forecast is a reasonable one, the most sophisticated financial planning models will not improve on bad inputs. The "jijo" rule—junk in, junk out—applies here too: Sophisticated methodologies may be a positive harm if they mask basic input errors. The danger in computer systems is that they require complex forecasts when the success of simple forecasting is dubious enough.

The key question thus still remains: What is the likelihood of devaluation or revaluation? What economic forces provide the necessary conditions to provide the climate for a change in the exchange rate? What political forces provide the sufficient condition to take the de/revaluation action? To answer these questions, continued surveillance, judgment, and perhaps an intuitive sense are still required. An analysis of these forces is presented in the next two chapters.

# 14.
# Forecasting Foreign Exchange Rates

orecasting the foreign exchange rate outlook is a hazardous and complex business. There are many variables in the equation and few certainties. This onerous responsibility devolves ultimately upon the company treasurer. It is he who winds up in the doghouse if the forecasts prove wrong.

In producing a forecast, the company treasurer can make use of various types of analysis—their effectiveness is generally directly linked to the amount of research time involved.

There are, of course, crude lead indicators of the exchange rate outlook, which give a rough guide. But these indicators, while useful, do not generally provide enough lead time for a company to react and protect itself, at minimum cost, from the effects of currency changes.

Balance of payments analysis (discussed below) while more lengthy, tedious, and costly in research time, is likely to give an earlier advance warning of currency rate changes.

But the overriding factor in this equation is the political problem, which cannot be ignored if the forecast is to make any pretense at being accurate.

The behavior of the political animal is difficult to predict, even when closely observed. Economic fundamentals may clearly indicate that a currency ought to be devalued. But in this situation, no two governments, ministers, or central banks will react in the same way. This is the only point that is wholly predictable.

Governments facing elections or having narrow majorities may postpone currency changes. Governments with substantial majorities or with long tenures of office ahead of them may see that the currency change is a necessary albeit unpopular measure and may decide to "get it over with." To come up with a reasonable currency forecast, it is often necessary to put oneself in the politician's place and attempt to foresee how he would react to expected economic conditions.

Focusing on the economic fundamentals—political factors are discussed in the next chapter—lead indicators of devaluation vulnerability are quite different from those of revaluation vulnerability. In the typical case, a country devalues because it is losing reserves and there is a threat of losing all of its gold and foreign exchange reserves if this loss continues. A revaluation is called for when its reserve inflow becomes excessive. This inflow can become intolerable when it (1) raises the money supply to an inflationary extent, or (2) leads to retaliation from countries that are losing reserves.

Reserve levels are, of course, relative. Losses that might seem small to a large developed country could prove overwhelming to the small struggling economy. It is necessary, therefore, to develop ratios indicating devaluation or revaluation vulnerability, without regard to absolute amounts of gains or losses of reserves. With devaluation vulnerability, a rough and ready lead indicator is the ratio of exchange reserves to the latest reported level of imports (usually annualized). Exchange reserves are a country's central bank holdings of gold and foreign currencies—and to be technically correct, include IMF gold tranche positions and Special Drawing Rights (SDR).

To smooth out random variations, imports are often taken as an average of the past three months. The reserves/imports figure can be multiplied by 12 to show the number of months of the current level of imports that could be financed with the current level of exchange reserves. Table 20 provides an example of the calculation of these ratios for major countries.

Countries with reserves sufficient to pay for only a few months' imports are, all other things being the same, more vulnerable to devaluation. But this is a crude indicator. In addition to imports, countries have reserve outflows for services, foreign aid, and capital movements, as discussed further on in this chapter. Nevertheless there is some tendency for reserve/import ratios to tie in with the foreign exchange market's assessment of devaluation vulnerability. As indicated in Table 20, the United Kingdom and Denmark, which have had weak currencies in recent years, show low reserve/import ratios. (The Swedish krona is now a strong currency, mainly because it under-went a brutal deflation to reduce imports during 1971.)

We have less past experience on which to justify the use of a lead indicator for revaluation vulnerability. From the upward float of the German mark and Dutch guilder, and the revaluation of the Swiss franc in May 1971, it is clear that anti-inflation policy was a key element in the decisions to revalue. These countries had a large inflow of dollars that was converted into their national currencies. Excessive national currency creation was so inflationary that these countries adopted revaluation or a "float" to prevent further massive inflows.

The extent of an inflationary change produced by a currency inflow can sometimes be appraised by taking the ratio of the change in a country's reserves in a particular quarter (i.e., the amount of foreign currency taken in by a country's central bank) compared with the money supply at the beginning of the same quarter. For comparability, both amounts should be converted into the same currency. Calculations of this ratio for late 1970 are shown in Table 21.

Although the relationship is not a perfect one, there is a considerable amount of evidence that as a country's money supply increases, its money income increases, and if resources are fully used, rising money incomes will raise prices. Central banks become seriously concerned about inflation, especially when they are in a boom phase in the business cycle, if there is a large inflow of foreign currency that is converted into a national currency. This is the logic behind the use of the ratio of the currency inflow to the money supply as a crude indicator of revaluation vulnerability. It is clear, however,

**Table 20**

Indicators of devaluation vulnerability, April 1971

| Country | (1) Gold and foreign exchange reserves and latest month available ($ millions) | (2) Average of latest three months C.I.F.[a] imports ($ millions) | (3) Ratio of reserves to imports[b] | (9) Months of import cover[c] |
|---|---|---|---|---|
| Switzerland | $ 3,810 Mar. | $ 542 Dec.–Feb. | 58.6% | 7.0 |
| Germany | 15,519 Mar. | 2,583 Dec.–Feb. | 50.1 | 6.0 |
| Spain | 2,009 Feb. | 387 Dec.–Feb. | 43.3 | 5.2 |
| Italy | 5,880 Feb. | 1,252 Dec.–Feb. | 39.1 | 4.7 |
| France | 5,490 Mar. | 1,559 Dec.–Feb. | 28.6 | 3.4 |
| Japan | 5,458 Mar. | 1,637 Nov.–Jan. | 27.8 | 3.3 |
| Belgium | 3,113 Feb. | 1,033 Oct.–Dec. | 25.1 | 3.0 |
| Netherlands | 3,528 Feb. | 1,230 Oct.–Dec. | 23.9 | 2.9 |
| Norway | 743 Feb. | 341 Nov.–Jan. | 18.1 | 2.2 |
| United Kingdom | 3,317 Mar. | 1,951 Jan.–Mar. | 14.2 | 1.7 |
| Denmark | 596 Mar. | 404 Oct.–Dec. | 12.3 | 1.5 |
| Sweden | 850 Feb. | 617 Nov.–Jan. | 11.5 | 1.4 |

[a]C.I.F. = cost, insurance, and freight.
[b]Column (1) divided by 12 times Column (2).
[c]Column (3) multiplied twelve times.

**Table 21**

Reserves and money supplies, major countries and areas ($ millions)

| | (1) | (2) | (3) | (4) | (5) | (6) |
|---|---|---|---|---|---|---|
| | Reserves | | | | | |
| | End of third quarter, 1970 ($ millions) | End of fourth quarter, 1970 ($ millions) | Increase/ (decrease) in reserves third-fourth quarter, 1970 ($ millions) | Money supply end of Sept. 1970 (seasonally adjusted) ($ millions) | Change in reserves as a % of money supply, end of September, 1970 | |
| | | | | | Actual | Annualized[a] |
| United States | $15,527 | $14,487 | $(1,040) | $199,700 | (0.5)% | (2.1)% |
| United Kingdom | 2,666 | 2,827 | 161 | 40,068 | 0.4 | 1.6 |
| France | 4,743 | 4,960 | 217 | 38,201 | 0.6 | 2.2 |
| Belgium | 2,790 | 2,847 | 57 | 8,002 | 0.7 | 2.8 |
| Canada | 4,553 | 4,679 | 126 | 13,070 | 1.0 | 4.1 |
| Japan | 3,996 | 4,839 | 843 | 52,386 | 1.6 | 6.4 |
| Italy | 4,519 | 5,299 | 780 | 43,878 | 1.8 | 7.1 |
| Denmark | 392 | 484 | 92 | 3,747 | 2.5 | 9.8 |
| Austria | 1,672 | 1,757 | 85 | 2,720 | 3.1 | 12.5 |
| Sweden | 671 | 762 | 91 | 2,785 | 3.3 | 13.0 |
| Netherlands | 2,989 | 3,234 | 245 | 7,055 | 3.5 | 13.9 |
| Norway | 710 | 807 | 97 | 2,179 | 4.5 | 17.8 |
| Switzerland | 4,080 | 4,701 | 621 | 9,497 | 6.5 | 26.1 |
| Germany | 11,301 | 13,610 | 2,309 | 25,984 | 8.9 | 35.5 |
| Total—13 developed countries excluding U.S. | 45,082 | 50,806 | 5,724 | 249,572 | 2.3 | 9.2 |

[a]Actual multiplied four times.

that this lead indicator does not always work. Governments—as is now true of France, Germany, Belgium, the Netherlands, Switzerland, and Japan—can use exchange controls to prevent the reserve inflow. And even if reserves do enter a country, their effect on the money supply may be "sterilized" or offset by such methods as raising reserve requirements for the banks, selling bonds to the banks or the public, and raising taxes. Nevertheless, a high reserve inflow/money supply ratio is still a useful indicator of revaluation vulnerability. Table 21 shows high reserve change/money supply ratios for the Netherlands, Switzerland, and Germany, countries that floated upward or revalued in May 1971. On the other hand, this ratio is not infallible. It clearly did not work for Norway, which was not revaluation vulnerable, partially because of its ties to the weaker currencies in Denmark and Sweden.

## Balance of Payments Analysis

The lead indicators previously discussed are by no means sure predictors of devaluations or revaluations. They are often distorted by deliberate government action to conceal devaluation or revaluation vulnerabilities. Governments threatened with devaluations can temporarily raise their reserve levels by short-term borrowing and thus artificially push up the reserve/import ratio. Governments threatened with revaluations can put reserves into long-term assets (usually of a year plus one day maturity so that they are not counted as reserves) that are, however, highly liquid, thereby lowering the reserve inflow/money supply ratio. Another distortion practiced by countries prone to revaluation is to keep foreign exchange at arms length in private banks rather than in central banks.

Moreover, the reserve/import ratio and the reserve inflow/money supply ratios may not give early enough signals of currency changes. By the time the outlook for a currency shows up in its imports, reserves, and money supply, this may already be fully discounted on foreign exchange markets. The costs of covering foreign exchange risks are then prohibitively expensive. The real art is to forecast the factors that in turn lead to depletion or excessive buildups of reserves.

The main sources and uses of reserves—i.e., inflows and out-flows of foreign exchange—can be summarized in a balance of payments analysis. This balance of payments analysis gives us a handle with which to forecast changes in reserves, which in turn affect exchange rates. But balance of payments analysis has the disadvantage of being a more costly and time-consuming method for determining currency vulnerability.

An analogy exists with an individual's spending; this includes purchases of consumable goods and services, gifts and other one-way payments, and purchases of assets such as stocks, bonds, or property. Similarly, items in a country's balance of payments are classified among (1) the current account for goods and services, (2) the transfer payments account, mainly for foreign aid and remittances by immigrants, and (3) the capital account, which includes international asset transactions like investment and international lending. Forecasting each of these items in the balance of payments is, in principle, similar to other types of forecasting. Exports and imports and other current account items are a special case of sales forecasting. Foreign aid forecasting is a matter of foreseeing government policy. As in domestic economies, international capital will tend to be pulled where its rate of return is highest. Nevertheless, forecasting on an international level is probably more difficult than on a national level. In part this arises from greater complexity of the data, and because governments play a greater role via manipulating controls and restrictions on trade and capital movements. Sound political judgment is a first prerequisite for accurate international forecasting.

In the discussion that follows, the U.S. balance of payments will be used as the basic example because it is likely to be the most familiar. However, special problems in analyses of balances of payments of other countries will also be considered.

Balance of payments data are difficult because both conceptually and statistically the items are interlaced and are thus easily confused with one another. Perhaps the best approach is to disentangle the data step by step.

Table 22 shows a simplified U.S. balance of payments for 1971, to which the following comments relate.

First, the balance of merchandise trade—exports minus imports

## Table 22

U.S. balance of payments, 1971 (in billions of dollars)

| | Receipts | Payments | Balance |
|---|---|---|---|
| 1. Merchandise trade (goods) | 42.8 | 45.5 | - 2.7 |
| 2. Services | 23.3 | 19.9 | 3.4 |
|    Military | 1.9 | 4.8 | −2.9 |
|    Investment income | 12.9 | 4.9 | 8.0 |
|    Travel | 2.5 | 4.3 | −1.8 |
|    Other | 6.0 | 5.9 | 0.1 |
| 3. Balance on goods and services | 66.1 | 65.4 | 0.7 |
|    Remittances, pensions and other transfers | — | 1.5 | −1.5 |
|    U.S. government grants, excluding military | — | 2.0 | −2.0 |
| 4. Balance on current account | 66.1 | 68.9 | −2.8 |
|    Long-term government capital | 2.1 | 4.5 | −2.4 |
|    Long-term private capital | 2.3 | 6.5 | −4.2 |
|    Direct investment | −0.1 | 4.8 | −4.9 |
|    Portfolio investment | 2.3 | 0.9 | 1.4 |
|    Bank and other loans | 0.1 | 0.8 | −0.7 |
| 5. Balance on current account and long-term capital (basic balance) | 70.5 | 79.9 | − 9.4 |
|    Nonliquid short-term capital (net) | - | 2.4 | − 2.4 |
|    SDR allocations | 0.7 | – | 0.7 |
|    Net errors and omissions | — | 10.9 | −10.9 |
| 6. Net liquidity balance | 71.2 | 93.2 | −22.0 |
|    Decline in private liquid dollar assets abroad | | | −7.8 |
| 7. Balance of payments, official settlements basis, including SDRs | | | −29.8 |

Note: Figures may not add up because of rounding.

Source: U.S. Department of Commerce, *Survey of Current Business*, June 1972, Tables 1 and 2.

—(at $2.7 billion deficit) is for most countries the most important item in the balance of payments. Second, the services account (at $3.4 billion surplus) covers nonmerchandise current account transactions, royalty payments, and receipts and payments of investment income. This service account item is of particular current interest, as it is the sum of some very diverse international money movements, which are worth a further word. The big plus is income remitted by multinational corporations by way of dividends or interest or royalty payments; in 1971 this totaled about $9.5 billion of the $12.9 tabulated as investment income and was a major element of American balance of payments strength. This income is reduced, however, by net outflows in the other elements noted in the service account. Note also that the $9.5 billion inflow from American multinational investment abroad is much higher than the outflows for new direct investment (plant and equipment), some $4.8 billion, which is tabulated under Item 4 of Table 22, as "long-term private capital."

So, third, the balance on goods and services (at 0.7 billion surplus) comprises the sum of elements 1 and 2 above, i.e., the merchandise and service accounts.

Fourth, the balance on current account (at $2.8 billion deficit) is obtained by subtracting "remittances, pensions and other transfers" and "U.S. government grants, excluding military" from Item 3, the balance on goods and services. Remittances (at $1.5 billion outflow) are by immigrants in the United States and philanthropic organizations. Government payments to pension recipients abroad are also included in this item. The "government grants" item (at a $2.0 billion outflow) is government foreign aid, excluding military aid.

Fifth, the "balance on current account and long-term capital," often called the "basic balance," is the sum of the current account balance (Item 4) and net long-term capital account item, defined to include assets maturing or presumably to be held over one year. Most long-term government capital (at $2.4 billion deficit) arises from U.S. government lending to foreigners (mostly governments) net of repayment. The net $4.2 billion outflow on private capital transactions arises from international payments to acquire or sell long-term assets abroad. This element includes the outflow of funds by U.S.

multinationals for plant and equipment abroad, which is called direct investment (at $4.8 billion outflow). It also includes portfolio—stocks or bonds—investment (at $1.4 billion net inflow); and bank and other loans (at $0.7 billion net outflow). In the case of direct investment, the investor has direct control over the management of his funds. He either has a controlling interest in a firm abroad or extends a branch of the American parent company abroad, as for example in building a new plant. In portfolio investment, on the other hand, funds are used to buy stocks or bonds in a foreign company but do not result in control of the foreign business. The "bank and other loans item" comprises loans by banks and other financial institutions.

Sixth, the "net liquidity balance" (at $22.0 billion deficit) is formed by adding short-term capital (at $2.4 billion outflow), SDR allocations (at $0.7 billion), and"errors and omissions" (at $10.9 billion outflow) to the basic balance. SDR allocations are a type of "paper gold" issued by the IMF, which, subject to minor restrictions, IMF members have agreed to accept in settlement of international obligations. Short-term capital typically consists of holdings by individuals of savings accounts, Treasury bills, commercial paper and other short-term assets, i.e., maturing in a year or less. Demand deposits and currency are liquid assets, cashable immediately, and are therefore excluded from this category.

Special attention is devoted to the "basic balance" in any balance of payments analysis because it is believed to reflect more fundamental elements than the "net liquidity" and "official settlements" balances (items 6 and 7 of Table 22). These latter balances are more affected by short-term capital movements, which respond to rumors or speculative movements, than is the basic balance.

Estimates of most items in the balance of payments are not exact, and there is thus no strict equality of debits and credits as would occur in bookkeeping. For this reason an "errors and omissions" item (at $10.9 billion) is put into the balance of payments. "Errors and omissions" is the difference between total net payments, as already discussed, and total means of payment—by gold, foreign currency flows, SDRs, and changes in foreign private and official liquid short-term indebtedness of the United States.

While the net liquidity balance shows the outflow of gold, foreign exchange, and SDRs from the United States, plus the buildup of net liquid short-term claims on the United States, not all of this outflow and/or the buildup of claims against the United States necessarily ends up in private banks or other private holdings. Adding the increase or decrease in private liquid dollar assets abroad to the liquidity balance results in the "balance of payments, official settlements basis" (at $29.8 billion outflow). In effect this item shows the net inflow into foreign central banks of foreign exchange, i.e., dollars and/or claims on the United States, or sometimes gold. This definition of the balance of payments, while it is strongly affected by flight capital and other transitory currency movements, is perhaps most important for indicating forces pushing the exchange rate of the dollar up or down. It is, however, notoriously difficult to explain because it comprises not only the dollar outflow from the United States but also the movements of dollar holdings scattered all over the world—of which Eurodollar deposits are of great importance —from private holdings into central banks.

Having considered the broad picture of balance of payments components, we turn to methods of forecasting the major components.

## The Trade Balance of Developed Countries

The trade balance arises from the difference between exports and imports. Forecasting these items is similar to forecasting a company's sales volume, although the number of export and import products of a country is greater than the number of products sold by a company. In both cases there is significant econometric evidence that the volume of imports rises with real income, or to use the jargon, there is a positive income elasticity of demand for imports. There is also a somewhat less general tendency for exports to rise and imports to fall when a country's price level declines, i.e., there is price elasticity as well. The opposite tends to hold when the price level rises.

A study by Houthakker and Magee shows that a significant proportion of changes in exports and imports can be explained by incomes and prices. Exports and imports are also influenced by strikes and capacity utilization rates (meaning that more or less capacity is available for export or to compete with imports). These and other complicating factors are taken into account in studies of trade patterns of major countries by the Organization for Economic Cooperation and Development (OECD) in Paris and by the U.S. Department of Commerce.

These statistical approaches tended, however, to underestimate U.S. imports in 1971. This was partly because the estimates of imports failed to take into account imports into the United States in anticipation of revaluation of currencies abroad, and also neglected the effect on U.S. imports of recessions abroad. Countries in recession were under unusually strong pressure to push exports into the U.S. markets.

These difficulties in past forecasting methods illustrate that implicit in any statistical estimate of trade movements is the assumption that history will repeat itself—that past relationships will hold in the future. Even the most carefully estimated statistical relationship will go wrong if there is a change in structure, as there was, for example, when the United Kingdom joined the Common Market, Japan liberalized its trade, or if the automobile trade agreement between the United States and Canada were altered. The effects of structural changes can be evaluated to a certain extent by surveys in which exporters and importers are asked their opinions on the probable outlook. The National Foreign Trade Council has carried out such surveys for the United States.

The analysis in the OECD, Department of Commerce, and Houthakker–Magee studies attempted to give a basis for projecting overall imports and exports from and to each country. A more ambitious approach is to attempt to project a breakdown of exports and imports according to classifications by commodities and/or destinations. For example, U.S. exports might be projected to each country receiving U.S. exports. The U.S. Department of Commerce produces quarterly data on the share of the United States in total imports of each major country. Using these data projections for total imports in each country, the U.S. share and finally the amount of each country's imports originating in the United States can be determined. This level of detailed analysis, while a useful part of a basic research project, seems impractical for business use since most firms have limited resources for international economic research. Moreover, there is little evidence that such detailed procedures are much of an improvement over the more aggregative methods. And of course, for many countries detailed export and import data are not available until too late to be useful for exchange rate forecasting.

There is, however, a strong argument for excluding from total export and import data certain products for which the demand has a special structure. The OECD analysis excludes "car trade between the United States and Canada, German imports of weapons, Canadian exports to Communist countries, and U.K. imports of aircraft from the United States." U.S. Department of Commerce projections of U.S. exports and imports exclude U.S. agricultural exports, civilian aircraft exports, and auto trade with Canada. If these special elements are excluded, forecasting can be based on the remaining items, which react more readily to market forces.

The problem of projecting exports and imports is not completely solved even if an equation is found relating these items to such other variables as national incomes, prices, capacity utilization rates, etc. Forecasting imports and exports then becomes a problem one step removed in forecasting national income or the other variables on which exports and imports depend. Most businesses are not equipped to attempt forecasts of this complexity. There are, however, a number of organizations that do make such forecasts. It is up to the business economist to choose the forecasts that seem most logical and most suited to his purposes. Forecasts of major economic variables abroad are made by various public and private groups, e.g., the OECD (Paris), the National Institute for Economic and Social Research (London), Business International (New York), the UN Economic Commission for Europe (Geneva), and Eurofinance (Paris). OECD forecasts are probably backed up by more staff work than are others. However, the OECD may be under some political pressure to issue forecasts with a somewhat optimistic slant.

## The Trade Balance of Less-Developed Countries

For the developed countries, imports tend to be correlated to incomes and relative prices. In less-developed countries, however, imports depend not so much on incomes as on available foreign exchange reserves. Requirements for imports are typically insatiable and are held in check by controls that are tightened or relaxed in accordance with the supply of foreign exchange.

Foreign exchange in the less-developed countries is either earned from exports or arises from inflows of capital for new investment. The OECD studies found that imports in less-developed countries tie in with exports of the previous year, capital inflows, and the level of reserves.

Another way of projecting imports of less-developed countries is to project all other balance of payments items except imports and thus estimate how much will be available for spending on imports. This method has the disadvantage that it requires forecasting each balance of payments item separately—an ambitious project in view of the lack of adequate data and forecasting methods.

It is clear, however, that projecting imports of less-developed countries usually requires projecting exports. A breakdown of a less-developed country's main export commodities is necessary to produce any meaningful figure. These are usually few in number and mainly primary products. Both volume and prices of primary product exports are very volatile, except in oligopolistic industries like petroleum and aluminum. Fortunately, a considerable amount of research has been done on projecting prices of primary products. Background material for agricultural products can be obtained from the U.S. Department of Agriculture and the Economic and Social Department of the UN's Food and Agricultural Organization (Rome); for primary metals from the Clearinghouse for Federal Scientific and Technical Information at the United States Bureau of Standards, and from the United States Bureau of Mines.

## Service Items in the Current Account Balance

The current account balance, as shown in Table 22, includes—in addition to exports and imports—travel, remittances, foreign aid grants, investment income, and a wide range of miscellaneous items. Not all of these items are important.

To project military expenditures, one has to take a view on a country's military policy. For the United States there is now a consensus that since the Vietnam War, United States military expenditures abroad will tend to decline. A substantial volume of military expenditure is, however, the "pipeline" between appropriations and expenditures. Thus there may be a lag before reduced appropriations show up in reduced expenditures. Foreign contributions to United States defense expenditures (at $1.9 billion) are shown in the receipts side of the military item in Table 22. Projections of this item are also a political judgment on how successful the United States will be in urging other countries to contribute more to its overseas defense efforts. In the future, significant reductions in United States military expenditures abroad are probable. In Europe, negotiations with the Soviets for mutually balanced force reductions could speed this process.

Investment income (shown in Table 22 at $8.0 billion surplus net) depends on amounts of U.S. assets and liabilities abroad and the rates of remittances on these investments. A detailed analysis of these data is presented in the latter part of each year in the Department of Commerce *Survey of Current Business*. Holdings of U.S. government securities abroad are a significant factor in determining the outflow from the United States of remittance payments. Much of the 1971 outflow from the United States was invested in Treasury bills, resulting in a greater interest payment burden on that country.

Remittances on private capital are more difficult to forecast. Rates of return on these investments vary, and part of these returns is reinvested without being remitted to the United States. Some clues to the outlook can be gained from data on productivity, wages, prices, and other indicators affecting profit margins. There is, however, a lack of reliable data on profits abroad. While such data are published for United States companies by the United States Department of Commerce, a careful analysis is difficult because of lack of uniformity of accounting standards.

Travel is an important debit item in the balance of payments of developed countries, particularly the United States ($4.3 billion in 1971) and Germany. Conversely, the balance of payments of Switzerland, Italy, Spain, Portugal, Mexico, Greece, and the Caribbean benefits significantly from travel. In general, countries with higher incomes tend to spend more in travel to attractive countries of lower incomes and price levels, Switzerland being an exception.

Private remittances, pensions, and other transfers (at $1.5 billion deficit), including United States government pensions, are mainly social security payments going abroad and funds sent home, usually to relatives, by immigrants to the United States. Private remittances are an important part of balance of payments income in Italy, Spain, Ireland, Greece, and Portugal. But in Germany and Switzerland, they are an important debit item. Immigrant remittances have tended to rise steadily since the early 1950s, except in recession years when the numbers of immigrants into Western Europe were curtailed. In the future, Western European nations are apt to restrict further immigration and to move plant, i.e., invest directly in developing countries, instead. This balance of payments item also includes donations abroad by philanthropic organizations—an important item in Israel's balance of payments.

## Government Items in the Balance of Payments

Apart from military expenditures, the government account includes government capital: loans (at $2.4 billion deficit) and grants, i.e., gifts abroad (at $2.0 billion deficit).

There are, of course, loans among developed countries, including the loans of the 1960s to the United Kingdom to support sterling, the loans to France after the mini-revolution of 1968, and the purchase of Roosa bonds by other developed countries from the United States in order to support the dollar. But a large proportion of international lending is from developed to less-developed countries.

Loans to less-developed countries are usually long-term and low-interest and are generally grouped with government grants under the heading of "foreign aid." As in the case of military expenditures, there is a lag between appropriations and expenditures. Only the latter appears in actual balance of payments results. Moneys in the "pipeline" may be spent even though appropriations are cut off. Moreover some types of aid, including Export-Import Bank loans and farm product disposal programs, including Public Law 480, are funded several years ahead.

After World War II, the United States was the biggest donor for foreign aid but its donations have since declined, both in absolute amounts and in the proportion of total aid given. As a percentage of GNP, United States aid dropped from 0.57% in 1964 to 0.31% in 1970. For all major aid-giving countries, the drop was from 0.49% to 0.34%.

The outlook for United States foreign aid is highly uncertain. It may be that the United States will be influenced by its declining percentage contribution to foreign aid and feel obliged to raise its contributions; Vietnam would probably be the biggest beneficiary here. But there is also strong conviction in certain United States government circles that, on a more realistic basis, the United States already contributes its fair share and that a large part of the foreign aid given by European countries is so closely "tied" that it is not really foreign aid. There is considerable United States criticism of arrangements where foreign aid is spent for high-salaried administrators of the former colonial power (as in the case of France) or where there are strict requirements that foreign aid grants be spent entirely in the donor country.

## Long-Term Private Capital

Long-term private capital comprises direct investment (at $4.9 billion net outflow), portfolio investment (at $1.4 billion net inflow), and other lending (at $1.7 billion outflow).

### DIRECT INVESTMENT

As noted above, data on direct investment, including outflows, book values, and earnings are published in the latter part of each year in the *Survey of Currency Business*. These data are, however, only on an annual basis (except for outflows shown quarterly in the *SCB*). United States investment in Europe began on a large scale in 1958 simultaneously with nonresident convertibility of European currencies, with the formation of the Common Market, and with the overvaluation of the dollar. There is thus only a limited amount of data for forecasting purposes. Since 1965 and mandatorily since 1968, outflows of United States investment have been restricted by the Office of Foreign Direct Investment. Nevertheless, direct investment has increased from $3.0 billion in 1968 to $4.8 billion in

1971, indicating that these regulations have been applied rather liberally. In general, companies unable to get OFDI approval of investments abroad have borrowed abroad. Much of this borrowing has, no doubt, been financed by short-term outflows from the United States. It seems likely, therefore, that OFDI regulations have unwittingly undermined the United States balance of payments. This anomaly is no doubt one reason why the Nixon administration is, in principle, against OFDI controls and has pledged to remove them in 1974. A likely future scenario would be a reduction of American direct investment abroad. Eroding profit margins in Europe and increasing restrictions in the developing countries both act to slow down investment abroad. With a more realistic exchange rate of the dollar since devaluations, investment in the United States can be expected to have a greater comparative advantage.

Foreign direct investment in the United States (at about $100 million outflow in 1971 compared to $1 billion inflow in 1970) tends to be sensitive to earnings of United States business and also to the outlook for the dollar. Neither was favorable in 1971, accounting for the outflow rather than the usual inflow. But in the future, the opposite may be expected.

PORTFOLIO INVESTMENT

Portfolio investment in the United States tends to react to gyrations in the United States stock market.

Stock market indexes compared to foreign purchases of U.S. securities

| Average of quarter | Prices on N.Y. Stock Exchange— composite index (end-1965 = 50) | Net foreign purchases of U. S. securities other than Treasury issues (millions of dollars) |
|---|---|---|
| 1967 — I | 47.61 | $ 133 |
| 1968 — IV | 59.36 | 1,312 |
| 1970 — III | 42.84 | 720 |
| 1972 — I | 58.53 | 1,067 |

Source: New York Stock Exchange and *Treasury Bulletin.*

When the market moved up 11.75 points from the first quarter of 1967 to the fourth quarter of 1968, net foreign purchases rose almost tenfold, from $133 million to $1.3 billion. The market tumble to 42.84 by the third quarter of 1970 was accompanied by a drop in net foreign purchases to $720 million. the subsequent market recovery by the first quarter of 1972 to 58.53 brought the figure back up to $1.067 billion.

Movements into foreign stock markets are also price sensitive. In some major markets, notably France and Italy, lack of complete or accurate information is an obstacle to security purchases, and many foreign stock markets are thin and without controls comparable to the United States Securities and Exchange Commission (SEC) regulations. The fear of security price manipulation is an obvious deterrent to portfolio investment. International capital movements in bonds are determined by much the same principles as long-term bank lending, discussed below.

If the dollar can be stabilized, a rising trend in purchases of United States securities from abroad appears likely. This seems reasonable in view of greater savings, attempts to find hedges against inflation, and better organization of the United States capital market as compared with markets in most other countries.

Purchases by United States citizens of securities from abroad (except for Canada) are restricted by the 1968 Interest Equalization Act, which puts special taxes on such purchases. The IET is scheduled to end in 1974, but for reasons cited above, the portfolio investment outflow from the United States is likely to be much smaller than foreign purchases of United States securities.

## Long-Term Bank and Other Lending

Along with the phasing out of the OFDI restrictions and the IET, the Federal Reserve Board in 1974 is expected to remove "voluntary" restrictions on bank lending. When bank lending is not subject to controls, there is a clear tendency for international lending to move in the direction of higher interest rates adjusted for expected risks. The caveat about expected risks is important. A bank or other lender will not ordinarily lend to a firm of a lower credit standing without charging additional interest over the going market rate. Likewise, in international lending higher interest rates are usually charged to countries considered to have a greater risk (usually political) of loan default. Against this background (all other considerations remaining unchanged) there will tend to be a movement of long-term lending capital toward countries with higher interest rates, e.g., Denmark in 1971–1972, and countries with lower political risk, e.g., Brazil in 1965–1972. The opposite is of course true for countries of declining interest rates or increasing risks of default.

## Short-Term Capital

Capital flight and interest arbitrage are the factors responsible for short-term capital movements. These movements are usually away from weak currencies expected to devalue and/or into strong currencies expected to revalue. Devaluation fears produced a flight from the British pound in 1967 and, conversely, the scramble to get into the mark in 1971 and 1973, and periodically into the yen. Forecasting flight capital thus depends basically on forecasting when a country's balance of payments will become so weak or so strong that a devaluation or revaluation becomes unavoidable. It follows therefore that forecasting flight capital depends on forecasting all the other elements in a balance of payments. Clearly, the manager of a company's international accounts should attempt to anticipate devaluation or revaluation before flight capital becomes a deluge. At this stage, forward discounts or premiums are likely to become so expensive that covering foreign exchange risks may not be worth the cost.

In the simplest case, interest arbitrage moves short-term money because interest rates in one country are higher than in another. This type of capital movement becomes more complicated, however, when lenders want to avoid the risks of devaluation and borrowers to avoid the risks of revaluation. These risks can, as already discussed, be hedged by buying currency forward to avoid risks to lenders. Investors who want to avoid exchange rate risks will put more short-term money into a country when the short-term interest rate plus the premium (or minus the discount) of the forward contract is greater than interest rates elsewhere. This is what happened in Germany in early 1971.

For example, if the rate of interest on a three-month Treasury bill is 5% and three-month forward contracts sell at a 1% discount, the hedged rate will be 4%. If this is greater than comparable interest rates of equal maturity abroad, short-term capital will tend to enter the country; if it is less, capital will tend to leave. Table 23 shows an example of the calculation of United Kingdom hedged interest rates during March–May 1971 on three-month sterling. Eurodollar rates are taken as representing interest rates outside the United Kingdom. This table indicates that except for a brief period around March 12, 1971, Eurodollar short-term investments were, on a hedged basis, preferable to sterling investments.

A country in balance of payments difficulty will sometimes adopt higher interest rates in order to pull in short-term capital, superficially strengthening the balance of payments. Such a policy, often followed by the United Kingdom in the 1960s, may boomerang, however, if the rise in short-term rates is recognized in the money markets as a desperate move to protect the currency. The forward discount on the currency declines widens as a consequence and leaves covered interest differentials relatively unchanged. Governments may, as the United Kingdom did shortly before the 1967 devaluation, then attempt to prevent a higher forward discount by selling forward contracts. This has its drawbacks, too; if devaluation becomes unavoidable, the government will be caught holding large amounts of obligations to buy the currency forward at the predevaluation rate, which is in fact what happened to the United Kingdom—to its considerable loss.

## Special Drawing Rights

SDR allocations (at about $700 million in the United States 1971 balance of payments) were first issued by the IMF in 1970, when it was widely believed that the world faced a general liquidity shortage. The massive 1971 United States balance of payments deficit has brought widespread agreement that the world faces an excess of international liquidity. Discussions of SDRs now focus more on how they might gradually replace the dollar in international reserves. The

Table 23

Comparison of investment yields: pound sterling securities versus Eurodollar investments, March–June 1971

| Date | Current yields on 90-day Eurodollar investments | Current yields on 90-day Pound Sterling investments (prime hire purchase paper) | Cost of 90-day hedge (expressed on a % per annum basis) | Net yield on Pound Sterling investments after cost of 90-day hedge | Net yield on Pound Sterling investments after cost of 90-day hedge over (under) Eurodollar investments |
|---|---|---|---|---|---|
| 3/5/71 | 5.00% | 8.13% | (3.70)% | 4.43% | (0.57)% |
| 3/12/71 | 5.06 | 8.50 | (3.43) | 5.07 | 0.01 |
| 3/19/71 | 5.06 | 8.13 | (3.21) | 4.92 | (0.14) |
| 3/26/71 | 5.31 | 8.13 | (2.94) | 5.19 | (0.12) |
| 4/2/71 | 5.63 | 7.25 | (2.39) | 4.86 | (0.77) |
| 4/8/71 | 6.37 | 7.25 | (2.58) | 4.67 | (1.70) |
| 4/16/71 | 5.75 | 7.25 | (2.75) | 4.50 | (1.25) |
| 4/23/71 | 6.00 | 7.13 | (2.36) | 4.77 | (1.23) |
| 4/30/71 | 6.25 | 6.50 | (2.10) | 4.40 | (1.85) |
| 5/7/71 | 7.25 | 6.63 | (1.31) | 5.32 | (1.93) |
| 5/14/71 | 6.87 | 6.50 | (1.17) | 5.33 | (1.54) |
| 5/21/71 | 6.56 | 6.88 | (1.17) | 5.71 | (0.85) |
| 5/28/71 | 7.88 | 7.25 | (0.93) | 6.32 | (1.56) |
| 6/4/71 | 7.00 | 7.00 | (1.17) | 5.83 | (1.17) |

Source: Morgan Guaranty Bank, New York

SDR outlook is complicated, however, by strong pressure from less-developed countries, which want additional SDR allocations as a form of foreign aid.

## Errors and Omissions

The errors and omissions item is put into the balance of payments to account for the discrepancy between total reported receipts and total reported payments. Four factors contribute to this discrepancy.

1. Errors in reporting exports and imports—duty-free goods in many cases are often given very careless valuations. Customs reports for one period may be delayed and included in a later period. In some countries, smuggling is a significant factor in the errors and omissions item.
2. Estimates of current account items, other than exports and imports, are notoriously inaccurate. Except where there are very strict exchange controls, it is almost impossible to estimate tourist expenditure abroad with any degree of accuracy. Tourist expenditure figures are often, in fact, part of flight capital.
3. Exports and imports are recorded when they are received in a country. Payments are often delayed, especially when devaluation threatens, or speeded up, when there is a possibility of revaluation. This so-called leads and lags effect can assume major importance. For example, if imports and exports are each $20 billion, a 10% slowdown in exports and a 10% speedup in imports can swing the balance of payments a surprising $4 billion.
4. Finally the errors and omissions figures include large amounts of unreported short-term capital. This goes unrecorded because of inadequate reporting by banks and government agencies, or for tax evasion purposes.

Types (3) and (4) of errors and omissions became significant in 1971 when there was pervasive distrust of the dollar. In the few months preceding the December 1971 devaluation of the dollar, there was an unrecorded, or errors and omissions, outflow estimated at as much as $10 billion. This accounts for a major part of the unprecedented deficit of 1971. This movement helped force a devaluation that had in any case become inevitable, and was probably long overdue. Much the same picture unfolded in Britain in 1967. The precise source of the United States outflow is unknown because there is no detailed reporting of this type of capital. But flight capital moved by wealthy individuals—both Americans and foreigners alike—and leads and lags payments by multinational corporations and exporters/importers seem to account for the bulk of the $10 billion.

## The Liquidity and Official Settlements Balances

The "liquidity" balance of payments shows the net outflow or inflow of liquid funds from the United States into either private holdings or central banks. The "official settlements" balance shows the outflow into central banks from the United States and also from private holdings of dollars abroad. It does not include the outflow of United States dollars into private holdings abroad. The difference between the liquidity balance and the official settlements balance is, therefore, equal to the change in private liquid dollar assets held abroad by individuals and by private, but not central, banks. In 1971, for example, the liquidity balance of payments was $22.0 billion deficit, and the official settlements balance was $29.8 billion deficit—a $7.8 billion decline in private liquid dollar assets abroad.

The official settlements balance is more difficult to estimate. In principle it involves an analysis of the balance sheets of holders of dollars in each country to determine whether they are likely to put their funds into Eurodollars or exchange them for national currencies. The problem is further complicated because central banks often put dollars into Eurodollar deposits, which may earn higher interest rates.

Where to deposit dollars is a problem for the central banks. If they deposit in the Eurodollar markets, the quantity of Eurodollars expands by some multiple of the deposits, creating an ever larger market outside any national control. On the other hand, if they put the dollars in the United States, presumably investing in Treasury paper, this tends to lower United States interest rates. Money is then drawn from the United States to foreign deposits in search of better interest rates; thus the dollars boomerang back to the Eurodollar market. Until there is a basic improvement in the United States balance of payments, capital controls by Europe and Japan will continue to be used as a device against dollar inflows. It has been recommended at a Bank for International Settlements meeting of central bankers that they avoid Eurodollar deposits. This recommendation appears not to have been followed; the TC study cited earlier shows a rising volume of central bank money in Eurodollars.

# 15.
# The Politics
# of Exchange
# Rate Forecasting

 o far account has been taken of the purely economic conditions that can lead to a currency devaluation or revaluation. But these are necessary, not sufficient, for an exchange rate adjustment. The sufficient condition, like the second blade of the shears, is a political determination to adjust the exchange rate.

Except for the special case of a "clean float," where only market forces determine exchange rates, governments and central banks have widely different responses to foreign exchange disequilibria. Some governments, of which France and Canada are perhaps the best examples, react quickly when a devaluation or revaluation is required. But, at least through the 1960s, other countries, like the United States and the United Kingdom, have adopted almost every possible stratagem to avoid currency changes even though economic analysis indicated that changes were inevitable. The fact that both the United States and the United Kingdom now defend floating as fervently as they once defended fixed rates and overvalued currencies only underscores the importance of the political climate to exchange rate decision-making.

The political aspects of currency adjustment thus become critical to success in currency management. U.S. dollar disequilibrium was clear in the early 1960s. But for a company to have sold the dollar short for the whole period up to August 1971 would have been a needless expense. On the other hand, the disequilibrium of the Canadian dollar in 1970 was by no means self-evident when Ottawa, in a generally unexpected move, allowed its currency to float upward. A similar surprise currency change came in August 1969 with the devaluation of the French franc.

The currency manager has—in addition to the quantitative problem of determining when there are likely to be foreign exchange disequilibria—the difficult qualitative problem of determining which countries will attempt to delay currency adjustments and which countries will jump the gun and adjust exchange rates before this is required. There are many conditions that lead countries to procrastinate in making currency adjustments and many also that lead to currency adjustments which could be postponed. It is not difficult to see why governments should anticipate devaluation or revaluation pressures and act accordingly, before such action is forced upon them. By so doing they escape the side effects of currency changes. If they foresee devaluation pressures, by a timely devaluation they avoid the losses of reserves that follow general anticipation of devaluation. On the other hand, if they expect revaluation pressure, they can avoid being swamped by inflows of speculative capital.

In view of the benefits of changing an exchange rate before a full-fledged exchange crisis develops, it is hard to see why countries have often adopted a "defense of the Alamo" attitude toward currency changes and postponed them to the bitter end, often by deflationary policies that were disastrous for incomes, profits, and employment. Reasons for these delays arise from both external and internal politics.

The United States and the United Kingdom in the 1960s were the archetypes of exchange rate defense for essentially external reasons. In both of these countries, the resistance to devaluation was a consequence of a view of themselves as bankers for, and policemen of, the free world. As bankers, the opposition to devaluation was threefold. First, there was the fear of financial chaos if their exchange rates were changed. Second, there was the fear that they would not be able to supply capital to the world if their currencies were identified as "weak." Third, there was the more understandable concern that central banks trusting the United States or the United Kingdom by holding dollars or sterling would lose from devaluations. Their dollar holdings would be worth less. To be sure, dollar devaluation implied an increase of the gold price, so that gold holdings would rise as dollar values fell. But this only added fuel to the antidevaluation fire. The "wrong" people—Russians, South Africans, gold hoarders—would be rewarded. Those who had "co-operated" by holding dollars would be hurt.

Events have belied the first fear. There has been no chaos; international trade and investment did not suffer even in the 1971 and 1973 crises. The second fear can be turned around; borrowers prefer to borrow weak currencies because of the possibility of repayment at depreciated exchange rates. The third fear was real but, looking ahead, it will cease to be real as SDRs are substituted for dollars or sterling as reserve assets. Moreover—as has been done in swap agreements between U.S. and European central banks and in the Basel Agreement of 1968 between the United Kingdom and sterling area countries—monetary authorities holding devaluation-prone currencies can be guaranteed against devaluation losses.

Perhaps the world-policeman argument for fixed exchange rates was even more important than the banking argument. As self-appointed guardians of the free world, the United Kingdom and especially the United States resisted devaluation because they wanted at any time to be able to finance the police actions or foreign aid disbursements that might be required by cold war strategy. These activities were too important to be constrained by the niceties of international accounting. In this view it was essential that the dollar and the pound be accepted throughout the free world in any amount paid out. As one U.S. diplomat put it, "You can't be a world power with a shoddy currency." Devaluations became emotionally identified with military defeats.

Both the banking and policing motivations for currency stability are losing credibility. World banking, while it may come up against problems of loan quality, has emerged stronger than ever from the currency changes since 1967. The rapprochement of the United

States with China and the Soviet bloc, and the general consensus in the United States not to have any more Vietnams, have reduced the significance of the policeman argument for a steady dollar. It is striking, however, that in both the United States and the United Kingdom, in both major parties and among all major interest groups, steady exchange rates had majority support even though this policy, since it failed to constrain cheap imports, was antilabor. U.S. trade unions, backing the Hartke–Burke Bill for draconian controls on imports, would have done better to have backed a cheap dollar in the 1960s. But at that stage in the cold war, the dollar, as perhaps the prime cold war weapon, was too much a part of the flag. Trade unions opposed devaluations even though such action was clearly in their own interests. They did not want the public-relations stigma of "destroying the dollar" (or sterling) for their own self-interest. Only in rarified academic circles was dollar devaluation actively espoused.

Thus in the 1960s U.S. and U.K. policies toward their currencies were not determined by the usual methods of public policy formation—by politicians balancing rival claims of rival interest groups. Ideology dominated international financial policy, and the ideology sprang mainly from illusions of exaggerated power. In the 1960s it was almost impossible to discuss the value of the dollar without also talking about the United States defending the free world.

In the future, it seems unlikely that visions of themselves as world bankers and world policemen will enable many countries to obtain almost total support from all interest groups for holding exchange rates. On the other hand, governments, and particularly central bankers, unwilling to dissipate their own powers, are unlikely to go to the opposite extreme and let their exchange rates fluctuate without any official intervention. It is more likely that governments will treat exchange rate policies either as (1) a balancing act between domestic interest groups, or (2) a technical problem to be delegated to some branch of the bureaucracy. This is already evident in currency adjustments that have taken place since August 1971. Thus the forecaster of exchange rates should attempt to simulate the conflicting pressures that are likely to descend upon presidents, prime ministers, finance ministers, and central bankers when the economics indicate that a currency should change its value.

In general, and to the extent that "rational" self-interest is expressed, revaluation will be opposed by export industries; at higher costs of their products in foreign currencies, their sales abroad or their profits—or both—must suffer. On the other hand, export industries will not oppose devaluation since their prices in foreign currencies will decline and sales can be expected to rise; nor will those industries suffering from "cheap" foreign competition oppose devaluation. For example, the automobile, steel, and textile industries in the United States have all been vastly helped by dollar devaluation.

But industries highly dependent on imports take the opposite political stance. They will disapprove the higher costs of imports arising from devaluation and approve the lower costs of imports arising from revaluations.

The position of trade unions in most countries has been, paradoxically, negative toward both devaluations and revaluations. Devaluations are opposed on the ground that the cost of living will rise as prices of imports rise. Revaluation is opposed because it may take away jobs in export industries. The tendency of devaluations to give overall protection to home industry against imports has not generally been appreciated by most unions. When faced with foreign competition, they usually advocate tariffs or import controls relating to the industries in which imports appear to have caused unemployment. However, the position of unions may change in years ahead, as union leaders become more sophisticated about world money. It may become evident that if devaluations are not adopted, the major alternatives are tariffs, import controls, and deflation. The first two invite retaliation from abroad. Deflationary policies result in unemployment, which may mean a loss in the real income of labor much greater than that caused by the cost-of-living rise following devaluation.

If exports are of approximately the same magnitude as imports, it might be supposed that the political pressures from export-affected industries and import-affected industries would be about equal. But such a conclusion would be unrealistic because, for all kinds of institutional reasons, the two groups may not have equal representation. Sometimes a particular faction may simply have less representation in a government because of a country's method of choosing its government or because the faction was the loser in an election. The Australian dollar was revalued not long after the 1972 defeat of the Conservative-Country party coalition in which the Country party—representing the interest of agricultural exports—had opposed revaluation. Germany in 1972 resisted floating the mark upward partly because the Free Democrats, strongly influenced by large exporting companies, opposed the move. The Free Democrats held the balance of power between the Socialists and Christian Democrats. In Japan revaluation was resisted in the Liberal Democratic party mainly because the political influence of the exporting industries is very strong.

There are, of course, no hard-and-fast rules on which areas of the political spectrum will be prodevaluation and antidevaluation. But, in general, it is remarkable that both the far right and far left stand opposed to currency changes. The far rightist (excluding conservatives of the Chicago school who favor floating exchange rates) is likely to be more emotionally attached to ideas of the country as a world banker and world power. The far leftist, with his penchant for planning, wants a predictable future; otherwise the Plan can go haywire. A moving exchange rate is yet another unpredictable—one more danger threatening the Plan and increasing the possibility that it may have to be scrapped and done all over again. This penchant for planned predictability helps explain the preference in some less-developed countries for fixed exchange rates.

As with most sensitive political decisions, devaluations or revaluations are unlikely to take place before elections. In almost all cases, governments will avoid alienating key pressure groups until after the ballots have been cast. After elections, promises to the contrary notwithstanding, they will be more likely to make the necessary currency change, perhaps with the excuse that it was "forced upon us."

Having indicated some of the political forces tending to freeze or thaw exchange rate structures, it is important to recognize situations in which exchange rate policy may be an area where politicians have, at least for all practical purposes, abdicated authority. Sometimes, in a country with a multiparty system and multiple factions within each party, politicians will arrive at an early consensus that exchange rate policy—and perhaps monetary policy as well—is too hot and too technical to be in the political arena. (Perhaps the classic case of this kind was Italy under Carli as governor of the central bank, particularly before 1969.) Politicians of almost all persuasions may feel that the chaos of a public brawl on the subject is likely to cost them more than anything they and the interest groups they represent could gain from attempting to influence the country's monetary policy. The opposite, of course, has applied in France where there is a tradition, dating back to Louis XIV at least, that monetary and foreign exchange policies are an integral part of national and especially international politics.

Exchange rate forecasting thus requires, in addition to a weighing of the influences of the pressure groups for or against devaluations, some sensitivity to where, among government authorities, decisions are likely to be made. Are politicians yielding authority to the bureaucracy or the central bank? Or is a strong political leader reaffirming his control over monetary policy and international finance?

Looking ahead, there is one other political element of great importance in assessing the outlook for a currency. This is a judgment of the strength or weakness of international agreements to stabilize exchange rates or at least limit the extent of fluctuations. The Common Market, for example, has had a procession of schemes to fix rates among themselves, to protect the Common Agricultural Policy in the short run, and to make for unity in the long. The Werner Plan provides for the gradual unification of Common Market currencies. At present the Common Market countries, except the United Kingdom and Italy, which temporarily dropped out of the arrangement are holding their commercial exchange rates within 2.25% of each other (though "financial" exchange rates are floating in France, Belgium, and Italy). This is the so-called joint float. Under the Werner Plan this band will be gradually narrowed until there will be fixed exchange rates between Common Market currencies, although en masse they will remain free to fluctuate against currencies outside the Common Market.

In its fixing of exchange rates, the Werner Plan thus has clear similarities to the pre-1971 IMF agreement. As with IMF, the Werner Plan was to provide for contributions to a fund to support Common Market currencies that would otherwise weaken. The difficulties of the IMF are also the difficulties of the Werner Plan. For exchange rates to remain stable without outside support requires coordination of rates of growth in each country. Coordination of economic growth requires coordination of economic policies in member countries. Coordination of economic policies means loss of sovereignty unless by coincidence fiscal-monetary policies are in 'harmony. Such a coincidence seems unlikely, though not totally impossible, because most countries have similar aims to control inflation and reduce unemployment. However, the aim of controlling unemployment is not fully compatible with the aim of controlling inflation. Most countries swing back and forth between excesses of one or the other. Synchronizing these swings seems unlikely unless these countries are willing to surrender a great amount of authority to a European finance ministry and/or a European central bank. If fiscal-monetary policies are not synchronized, the Werner Plan could nevertheless endure by the financially stronger countries supporting the exchange rates of the weaker ones. Such support might be consistent with the "regional policy" positions, i.e., aid for the more backward parts of the Common Market—notably Ireland and Southern Italy. On the other hand, such regional aid might be politically objectionable to givers and ultimately to receivers.

In summary, political analysis in exchange rate forecasting will first of all appraise the historical role of the exchange rate. Is its fixity one of the trappings of empire, as in the United Kingdom of 1879–1914? Or is it a flexible political weapon, as in France under de Gaulle? Or is it a purely technical economic instrument, as in Italy—at least until 1969? Aside from the traditional currency roles, another key question is, Who is the decision maker? The prime minister? The ministry of finance? The legislature? The central banks? And in each of these entities, are decisions made at the top, or are the top people Merovingian types while actual decisions are really made by the mandarins of the civil service? Finally if the centers of power can be identified as to personages, ideologies, and traditions, the final step is an appraisal of how they are likely to react to pressures from other countries (e.g., creditors or signatories to an agreement to fix exchange rates, which is perhaps regretted) and from pressure groups in their own countries. What is the political clout for exchange rate policy of, for example, exporters, importers, fixed-income recipients, trade unions, low-income groups, and organized consumers?

It is axiomatic that politics is the art of compromise, hence "messy" to the mathematical mind, and assayable but never predictable. Yet political conditions are the second blade of the shears in determining exchange rate moves. It is true, if less than comfortable, to conclude that continued surveillance and sensitivity to power relations not readily apparent is a sine qua non for understanding in this area.

# Appendix

# By the Numbers: The Econometric Approach to Balance of Payments Forecasting

In the chapter on exchange rate forecasting, we listed most of the key variables affecting major components of the balance of payments. But we did not discuss *how* these variables are combined to make a forecast. This is the econometric problem.

Consider, for example, the case of forecasting imports. Suppose that imports, on the basis of past experience, are equal to 4% of a country's gross national product. Then it is relatively easy to calculate the outlook for imports from expected gross national product. Forecast imports would be 4% of forecast gross national product. But forecasting becomes more complicated when one thing depends, not on one other thing but on several other things. Imports, as discussed earlier in this book, depend not only on gross national product but also on relative prices, capacity utilization rates, strikes, and other variables. Under these conditions it is necessary to set up a formula—usually called a regression equation—showing the relative importance of each variable.

Almost always in modern forecasting, regression equations are done by a computer. We will not consider how the computer gets the regression equation. That is a problem for professional statisticians and computer specialists. But it should be emphasized that there is no necessity to understand advanced statistics or electronic data processing in order to make effective practical use of regression equations. To eat cake one does not have to be a baker. This point has become widely recognized; econometrics is now too important to be left to a few specialists. Also, econometric analysis is much less expensive than it was a dozen or so years ago, before the advent of readily accessible computers, when many man-hours of hard calculation were required to work out a regression equation. Now the same calculations can be done in seconds—and much more cheaply—on a modern computer. The use (but not necessarily the theory) of regression equations has become standard practice, not only for statisticians but also for company planners, financial managers, and economists.

In the usual case, to find a regression equation, we put into the computer—by way of punch cards, magnetic tape, or a teletype, data for the past history of the variable we are trying to forecast and of the variables on which it is believed to depend. This is often called the "specification." The computer responds with a printed formula showing a possible past relationship between the item to be predicted and the other variables. As an example of computer output. consider the following regression equation that was developed by Evelyn Parrish and Anthony DiLullo in the May 1972 *Survey of Current Business*. Based on 16 years of quarterly data, 1955–1970, the equation analyzes fluctuations in U.S. imports (adjusted for seasonal variation and to exclude auto imports from Canada, the effects of strikes, and a few other special situations):

$$M = -7558.73 + 23.65 \text{ PCE}$$
$$(11.63) \quad (32.50)$$

$$+ \ 11.02 \text{ CBI} + 6.45 \text{ CPSQ}$$
$$(3.33) \quad (5.50)$$

$$+ \ 57.88 \text{ Pus} - 8.85 \text{ Pf} - 58.86 \text{ T}$$
$$(8.91) \quad (1.44) \quad (22.25)$$

$$\bar{R}^2 = .999 \quad \text{S.E.} = 75$$
$$\text{D.W.} = 1.76$$

In the above equation, the algebraic symbols are defined as follows:

M: adjusted U.S. imports in millions of dollars.

PCE: U.S. personal consumption expenditures, in billions of dollars, seasonally adjusted annual rates from the U.S. national income accounts.

CBI: Change in U.S. business inventories, in billions of dollars, seasonally adjusted annual rates from the U.S. national income accounts.

CPSQ: U.S. capacity utilization indicator. The makeup of this variable is somewhat technical and is explained in the Parrish-DiLullo article. (Plus signs for this variable indicate production above normal. Minus signs indicate production below normal.)

Pus: U.S. wholesale price index of manufactured goods, 1963 = 100.

Pf: Weighted average of foreign wholesale price indexes of manufactured goods in Canada, Japan, United Kingdom, Germany, France, Italy, the Netherlands, and Belgium, with adjustments for exchange rate changes.

T: Time. This means that for this variable, the first quarter of 1955 at the beginning of the series is designated as 1, the second quarter as 2, the third quarter as 3, etc., all the way through to the fourth quarter of 1970 being designated as 64.

Table 24 shows values for adjusted U.S. imports and each of the variables in the regression equation for each quarter, 1955–1970. These are the data that are punched on cards or otherwise put into the computer to result in the regression equation. In effect, the regression equation says that the best way to "explain" U.S. imports, 1955–1970, is to take each variable, multiply it by its so-called regression coefficient, and then add up all the resulting products. In regression equations, the regression coefficient is shown in front of each variable. The regression coefficient for PCE is 23.65, for CBI is 11.02, etc. In most regression equations, there is also a "constant," usually put at the beginning of the equation. In this case it is -7,559. The constant, in effect, says that for every quarter, due to factors not fully explained, imports have turned out to be 7,559 million dollars lower than indicated by the other variables in the regression equation. When all of the variables for each quarter are multiplied by their regression coefficients and then added to the constant, we have what the computer has indicated will be the closest approximation of the value of imports. This will not be exactly equal to imports; but, as shown, multiplying the values of each of the variables by its regression coefficient, along with the constant, results in calculated imports close to the actual value.

As Table 25 shows, actual and calculated results are not far apart in a successful regression. In this case, calculated adjusted imports were never more than 4.7% different from actual adjusted imports.

To see how the regression equation works, take as an example calculated U.S. adjusted imports for the first quarter, 1959 (shown in Table 26).

**Table 24**

Variables in the regression equation to explain U.S. imports, 1955–1970

| | M | PCE | CBI | CPSQ | Pus | Pf | T |
|---|---|---|---|---|---|---|---|
| **1955** | | | | | | | |
| I | 2718 | 247.7 | 4.6 | 2.02 | 91.0 | 90.4 | 1 |
| II | 2802 | 252.7 | 6.1 | 2.04 | 91.2 | 90.3 | 2 |
| III | 2919 | 256.8 | 6.0 | 0.04 | 92.0 | 90.5 | 3 |
| IV | 3088 | 260.4 | 7.1 | 3.76 | 93.0 | 90.9 | 4 |
| **1956** | | | | | | | |
| I | 3174 | 262.0 | 6.0 | 8.29 | 93.8 | 91.9 | 5 |
| II | 3184 | 264.4 | 4.3 | 11.49 | 95.1 | 92.7 | 6 |
| III | 3315 | 267.5 | 4.1 | 5.95 | 95.8 | 93.2 | 7 |
| IV | 3130 | 272.8 | 4.3 | 2.59 | 96.9 | 94.3 | 8 |
| **1957** | | | | | | | |
| I | 3292 | 277.2 | 2.1 | 0.21 | 97.9 | 95.2 | 9 |
| II | 3297 | 279.3 | 2.3 | 0.74 | 98.2 | 95.4 | 10 |
| III | 3355 | 283.8 | 3.2 | 0.18 | 98.8 | 95.7 | 11 |
| IV | 3287 | 285.4 | 2.2 | −0.13 | 98.9 | 95.9 | 12 |
| **1958** | | | | | | | |
| I | 3141 | 284.5 | 5.4 | −4.37 | 99.3 | 94.9 | 13 |
| II | 3171 | 287.4 | 5.1 | 29.05 | 99.4 | 94.3 | 14 |
| III | 3203 | 292.2 | 0.1 | −39.06 | 99.5 | 94.1 | 15 |
| IV | 3418 | 296.2 | 4.1 | −20.25 | 99.7 | 94.0 | 16 |
| **1959** | | | | | | | |
| I | 3597 | 304.0 | 3.9 | −9.67 | 100.1 | 93.8 | 17 |
| II | 3833 | 309.8 | 8.0[b] | −5.11 | 100.5 | 93.0 | 18 |
| III | 3837 | 314.8 | 7.4[b] | −3.69 | 100.4 | 92.9 | 19 |
| IV | 3766 | 316.3 | 6.0[b] | −4.62 | 100.2 | 93.5 | 20 |
| **1960** | | | | | | | |
| I | 3768 | 321.1 | 9.4[b] | −5.62 | 100.5 | 93.9 | 21 |
| II | 3810 | 326.3 | 3.9 | −6.81 | 100.5 | 94.1 | 22 |
| III | 3643 | 325.9 | 3.1 | −15.05 | 100.8 | 94.4 | 23 |
| IV | 3432 | 327.7 | −2.4 | −28.68 | 100.1 | 94.9 | 24 |
| **1961** | | | | | | | |
| I | 3388 | 328.4 | −3.5 | −40.37 | 100.7 | 95.4 | 25 |
| II | 3481 | 332.3 | 2.1 | −27.36 | 100.0 | 96.2 | 26 |
| III | 3752 | 336.7 | 3.8 | −19.40 | 99.8 | 96.7 | 27 |
| IV | 3890 | 343.1 | 5.5 | −11.11 | 99.9 | 97.3 | 28 |

| | M | PCE | CBI | CPSQ | Pus | Pf | T |
|---|---|---|---|---|---|---|---|
| **1962** | | | | | | | |
| I | 3957 | 348.3 | 6.7 | −7.38 | 100.2 | 97.7 | 29 |
| II | 4072 | 351.7 | 6.1 | −4.23 | 100.1 | 97.7 | 30 |
| III | 4062 | 357.2 | 5.2 | −3.43 | 100.3 | 98.1 | 31 |
| IV | 4118 | 363.0 | 6.4 | −3.22 | 100.1 | 98.7 | 32 |
| **1963** | | | | | | | |
| I | 4081 | 368.2 | 4.7 | −4.63 | 99.8 | 99.5 | 33 |
| II | 4183 | 372.0 | 4.8 | −4.80 | 99.8 | 99.7 | 34 |
| III | 4357 | 378.3 | 6.0 | −2.43 | 100.2 | 100.0 | 35 |
| IV | 4371 | 381.5 | 8.1 | −1.38 | 100.3 | 100.7 | 36 |
| **1964** | | | | | | | |
| I | 4388 | 391.7 | 4.8 | −0.28 | 100.5 | 101.3 | 37 |
| II | 4568 | 397.6 | 6.1 | −0.03 | 100.2 | 101.7 | 38 |
| III | 4707 | 406.6 | 4.8 | −0.02 | 100.5 | 102.0 | 39 |
| IV | 4817 | 408.9 | 7.7 | −0.09 | 100.8 | 102.7 | 40 |
| **1965** | | | | | | | |
| I | 4895 | 419.8 | 10.9 | 0.81 | 101.2 | 103.4 | 41 |
| II | 5138 | 427.9 | 8.9 | 2.25 | 101.9 | 104.0 | 42 |
| III | 5431 | 436.3 | 9.1 | 6.25 | 102.6 | 104.5 | 43 |
| IV | 5623 | 447.4 | 9.7 | 14.44 | 103.1 | 105.3 | 44 |
| **1966** | | | | | | | |
| I | 5864 | 457.8 | 11.3 | 23.04 | 104.0 | 106.5 | 45 |
| II | 6010 | 461.9 | 16.2 | 22.28 | 104.8 | 107.0 | 46 |
| III | 6366 | 471.2 | 11.9 | 20.61 | 105.7 | 107.0 | 47 |
| IV | 6382 | 474.5 | 10.0 | 22.56 | 105.6 | 107.2 | 48 |
| **1967** | | | | | | | |
| I | 6365 | 480.7 | 9.6 | 12.39 | 105.8 | 107.5 | 49 |
| II | 6366 | 489.6 | 4.5 | 10.89 | 105.8 | 107.2 | 50 |
| III | 6632 | 495.5 | 8.7 | 11.56 | 106.3 | 107.7 | 51 |
| IV | 6686 | 502.5 | 10.0 | 9.61 | 106.7 | 108.1 | 52 |
| **1968** | | | | | | | |
| I | 7052 | 519.3 | 2.9 | 11.83 | 108.0 | 107.5 | 53 |
| II | 7356 | 529.0 | 9.6 | 18.32 | 108.6 | 106.4 | 54 |
| III | 7690 | 544.0 | 7.7 | 18.32 | 109.1 | 106.7 | 55 |
| IV | 7793 | 552.5 | 8.1 | 16.13 | 109.6 | 107.9 | 56 |
| **1969** | | | | | | | |
| I | 7980 | 564.3 | 6.6 | 12.96 | 111.0 | 109.5 | 57 |
| II | 8234 | 575.8 | 6.8 | 8.94 | 112.1 | 110.8 | 58 |
| III | 8438 | 584.1 | 10.4 | 8.94 | 113.0 | 111.8 | 59 |
| IV | 8533 | 594.2 | 5.7 | 1.35 | 114.2 | 113.4 | 60 |
| **1970** | | | | | | | |
| I | 8987 | 604.0 | 0.4 | −0.27 | 115.7 | 115.8 | 61 |
| II | 9034 | 613.8 | 2.1 | 1.69 | 116.4 | 117.0 | 62 |
| III | 9135 | 620.9 | 7.0[a] | 3.10 | 117.3 | 118.1 | 63 |
| IV | 9471 | 631.2[a] | 6.3[a] | −7.29 | 117.9 | 119.7 | 64 |

[a] Adjusted for effects of auto industry strike.
[b] Adjusted for effects of steel strike.

At this juncture it should be emphasized that while a computer can find a regression equation, it cannot tell the forecaster what variables to put into the equation. Variables not carefully chosen can result in meaningless regression equations. The signs—whether plus or minus—of the regression coefficients should be examined to make sure that they are reasonable. For example, a minus regression sign for personal consumption expenditure would indicate that as its spending increased, the public would spend less for imports. Such a result seems contrary to ordinary behavior and would usually be rejected.

## Table 25

Actual values of adjusted U.S.
imports and values calculated
from regression, 1955–1970 (millions of dollars)

| | Actual | Calculated | Difference Amount | Difference Percent |
|---|---|---|---|---|
| **1955** | | | | |
| I | $2718 | $2746 | $28 | 1.03% |
| II | 2802 | 2835 | 33 | 1.18 |
| III | 2919 | 2929 | 10 | -0.34 |
| IV | 3088 | 3046 | 42 | 1.36 |
| **1956** | | | | |
| I | 3174 | 3080 | 94 | 2.96 |
| II | 3184 | 3148 | 36 | 1.13 |
| III | 3315 | 3160 | 155 | 4.68 |
| IV | 3130 | 3261 | -131 | -4.19 |
| **1957** | | | | |
| I | 3292 | 3317 | 25 | -0.76 |
| II | 3297 | 3329 | -32 | -0.97 |
| III | 3355 | 3415 | 60 | -1.79 |
| IV | 3287 | 3337 | -50 | -1.52 |
| **1958** | | | | |
| I | 3141 | 3226 | -85 | -2.71 |
| II | 3171 | 3091 | 80 | 2.52 |
| III | 3203 | 3146 | 57 | 1.78 |
| IV | 3418 | 3359 | 59 | 1.73 |
| **1959** | | | | |
| I | 3597 | 3575 | 22 | 0.61 |
| II | 3833 | 3759 | 74 | 1.93 |
| III | 3837 | 3816 | 21 | 0.55 |
| IV | 3766 | 3754 | 12 | 0.32 |
| **1960** | | | | |
| I | 3768 | 3854 | 86 | 2.28 |
| II | 3810 | 3848 | 38 | 1,00 |
| III | 3643 | 3732 | 89 | 2.44 |
| IV | 3432 | 3540 | 108 | 3.15 |

| | Actual | Calculated | Difference Amount | Percent |
|---|---|---|---|---|
| **1961** | | | | |
| I | $3388 | $3423 | $ 35 | 1.03% |
| II | 3481 | 3555 | 74 | 2.13 |
| III | 3752 | 3654 | 98 | 2.61 |
| IV | 3890 | 3819 | 71 | 1.83 |
| **1962** | | | | |
| I | 3957 | 3934 | 23 | 0.58 |
| II | 4072 | 3964 | 108 | 2.65 |
| III | 4062 | 4038 | 24 | 0.59 |
| IV | 4118 | 4114 | 4 | 0.10 |
| **1963** | | | | |
| I | 4081 | 4126 | -45 | 1.10 |
| II | 4183 | 4155 | 28 | 0.67 |
| III | 4357 | 4295 | 62 | 1.42 |
| IV | 4371 | 4341 | 30 | 0.69 |
| **1964** | | | | |
| I | 4388 | 4500 | -112 | 2.55 |
| II | 4568 | 4576 | -8 | -0.18 |
| III | 4707 | 4731 | -24 | -0.51 |
| IV | 4817 | 4769 | 48 | 1.00 |
| **1965** | | | | |
| I | 4895 | 5026 | 131 | -2.68 |
| II | 5138 | 5181 | -43 | -0.84 |
| III | 5431 | 5385 | 46 | 0.85 |
| IV | 5623 | 5670 | -47 | -0.84 |
| **1966** | | | | |
| I | 5864 | 5972 | -108 | -1.84 |
| II | 6010 | 6101 | - 91 | -1.51 |
| III | 6366 | 6256 | 110 | 1.73 |
| IV | 6382 | 6368 | 14 | 0.22 |

| | Actual | Calculated | Difference Amount | Percent |
|---|---|---|---|---|
| **1967** | | | | |
| I | $6365 | $6286 | $ 79 | 1.24% |
| II | 6366 | 6374 | -8 | -0.13 |
| III | 6632 | 6530 | 102 | 1.54 |
| IV | 6686 | 6658 | 28 | 0.42 |
| **1968** | | | | |
| I | 7052 | 7013 | 39 | 0.55 |
| II | 7356 | 7344 | 12 | 0.16 |
| III | 7690 | 7645 | 45 | 0.59 |
| IV | 7793 | 7790 | 3 | 0.04 |
| **1969** | | | | |
| I | 7980 | 8046 | 66 | -0.83 |
| II | 8234 | 8288 | 54 | -0.66 |
| III | 8438 | 8508 | 70 | -0.83 |
| IV | 8533 | 8643 | 110 | -1.29 |
| **1970** | | | | |
| I | 8987 | 8813 | 174 | 1.94 |
| II | 9034 | 9025 | 9 | 0.10 |
| III | 9135 | 9221 | 86 | -0.94 |
| IV | 9471 | 9392 | 79 | 0.83 |

**Table 26**

Regression equation calculation of adjusted U.S. imports,
first quarter, 1959

| Variable | Value of variable from Table 24 | Regression coefficient | Value of variable multiplied by regression coefficient |
|---|---|---|---|
| Constant | — | — | −7,558.73 |
| PCE | 304.0 | 23.65 | 7,189.60 |
| CBI | 3.9 | 11.02 | 42.98 |
| CPSQ | −9.67 | 6.45 | − 62.37 |
| Pus | 100.1 | 57.88 | 5,793.79 |
| Pf | 93.8 | −8.85 | − 830.13 |
| T | 17.0 | −58.86 | −1,000.62 |
| | Total = Calculated adjusted imports: | | 3,574.5 |
| | Actual adjusted imports | | 3,597.0 |
| | Amount of difference | | 22.5 |
| | Percent difference | | 0.6% |

In the regression equation used as an example here, all the signs of regression coefficients are reasonable. There is a plus sign before PCE. The plus sign before CBI—change in business inventories—is likewise logical. As the economy builds up inventories, it will increase its imports. We would also expect a plus sign in front of CPSQ, the capacity utilization indicator. At higher levels of capacity use, there will be supply shortages that can be filled from imports. As Pus, the U.S. wholesale price index, rises, the United States will tend to buy more foreign goods, all other things being equal. This variable also has a positive regression coefficient. On the other hand, Pf, the weighted average of prices of foreign manufactures, should have a minus sign because, if prices abroad rise, the effect will be to discourage exports to the United States.

The variable T could have either a plus or minus regression coefficient. In this particular case the variable indicates that on average, in every quarter of the period, U.S. imports (aside from the effects of the other variables) decline $58.86 million from each previous quarter. While this "time trend" is statistically meaningful reasons for it are not well understood. In principle it is better to use specific variables rather than vaguely defined time trends in regression equations. But this ideal is not always possible.

Even if the signs of the variables in a regression equation are reasonable, the equation may be quite useless. The variables in the regression equation may simply not be closely enough related to the variable that we are trying to forecast. In such cases, the computer will nevertheless turn out a regression equation, but values calculated from the regression equation may be widely different from actual values. In such cases Table 25, instead of showing mostly differences of less than 4%, could show differences as high as 50%.

Fortunately, modern computers not only show regression equations and actual versus calculated values. The usual computer print-out of regression results also shows certain well-established indicators of the *quality* of a regression. These indicators were shown in our illustrative regression on page 246.

$\bar{R}^2$ is perhaps the oldest and best-known indicator of regression quality. Technically called the coefficient of determination, in actual practice it is usually spoken of as "R squared." (There is a technical difference between $\bar{R}^2$ and "R squared" that we will omit here; as a rule $\bar{R}^2$ is the more useful indicator.) $\bar{R}^2$ indicates the proportion of variation in the variable on the left side of the regression equation —the variable to be forecast—that is "explained" by the regression equation. Put another way, it is the ratio of variation "explained" by the regression equation to total variation. Thus it cannot be more than 100%. Usually, serviceable regression equations will have an $\bar{R}^2$ of over 75%.

**Table 27**

Forecast versus actual adjusted U.S. imports, 1971 (millions of dollars)

| 1971 | Actual | Forecast | Actual Greater Than Forecast | |
|------|--------|----------|--------|------------------|
| | | | Amount | Percent of Actual |
| I | $ 9,720 | $ 9,550 | $170 | 1.7 |
| II | 10,404 | 9,973 | 431 | 4.1 |
| III | 10,468 | 10,154 | 314 | 3.0 |
| IV | 10,732 | 10,309 | 423 | 3.9 |

S.E., called the standard error of estimate, is a type of average —actually the square root of the average of squares of differences between actual and calculated values from the regression equation. $\overline{R}^2$ was stated as a percentage but S.E. is stated as an actual amount—in our case it is $75 million. On average, about 68% of the observed values in a regression will be within one standard error more or less than the calculated value. For example, in the fourth quarter of 1969, the calculated value of imports was $8,643 million. It seems evident that if this same situation were repeated, imports would not be the same every time. Random influences would result in variation, but in 68% of all cases this variation would be within $8,643 million ± $75 million. On average, statistical theory indicates within two standard errors that the chance of variation is about 95%. Thus, if the regression could be repeated with only random variation, it would fall within $8,643 million ± 150 for 95% of the time.

So far we have considered measures of the quality of the whole regression. Now we will look at the measure of the quality of each regression coefficient. These are the so-called $t$ values, which are usually put in parentheses under each regression coefficient and under the constant. For example, the $t$ value for PCE is 32.50; for CBI, 3.33; etc.

$t$ values are shown under each regression coefficient. When a $t$ value is large, it indicates that in most periods the variable made a significant contribution to explaining the regression, and thus played an important role in the correspondence between actual and calculated variables. On the other hand, when $t$ is small, it means that the regression coefficient applies only "on average"; in any particular year it will have the effect of making the calculated value too large or too small compared with the actual value. Thus variables with low $t$ values are usually unreliable in a regression equation. As a rule, regression coefficients with a $t$ value greater than 3 are highly reliable, while coefficients with a $t$ value less than 1 are unreliable. Whether to use regression equations with $t$ values between 1 and 3 is a matter of practical judgment, for which it is not easy to give a categorical answer.

In the regression equation that we are using as an illustration, $t$ values are higher than 3 and thus highly significant for all variables except Pf, for which $t = 1.44$. In this particular case, it was decided to keep Pf in the equation even though $t$ for this variable is somewhat low. In cases where a $t$ value is rejected as too small, the usual practice is to drop the variable and run the regression equation over again, including only variables with higher $t$ values. By a series of experiments, the forecaster works toward a regression equation with significant (high $t$) regression coefficients, $\bar{R}^2$ near to unity, and low S.E.s.

Finally, it is important to look at the D.W.—the Durbin–Watson statistic. This is a more technical concept. Stated crudely, the D.W. measures the extent that variables in the equation are entangled together between time periods. When the D.W. has unacceptable values, $\bar{R}^2$ and S.E.—as calculated for the regression equation—are overstated for $\bar{R}^2$ and understated for S.E., so that the quality of the regression is not as good as it appears to be. Acceptable values of D.W., indicating that there is no serious mismeasurement of $\bar{R}^2$ and S.E., depend on the number of variables in the regression and the number of periods observed for each variable. In many cases, however, a nonacceptable value of D.W. will be less than 1.

If D.W. is less than 1, or otherwise can be shown to be unacceptable as a general rule, a regression cannot be used even though $\bar{R}^2$ and the $t$ values may all look good. Often an unacceptable D.W. indicates that a significant variable has been left out of the regression and in effect cries out to find a variable that was not originally included in the equation. In other cases, however, more complicated methods may be required to correct for a bad D.W. The important thing to stress here is that we should not go ahead and use a regression equation for forecasting if the D.W. is unacceptable. As a rough rule of thumb, low $t$ values often indicate that a variable is not worth including in the regression equation. Bad D.W.s often mean that a significant variable has been left out.

Finally, it needs to be stressed that even if a regression equation has "good-looking" $\bar{R}^2$, S.E., $t$ values, and D.W., it can fail as a predictive device because regression is nothing more than a formalized way of working from the idea that history repeats itself. If something happens to bring a new, previously unexperienced factor into the situation, the regression equation ceases to be useful. This is what happened to the regression equation that we have examined. It worked quite well from 1955 to 1970, as can be seen in Table 25, but in 1971 forecasts from the regression broke down. Imports were higher than the results that would have been predicted from the regression equation. This disappointing outcome is shown in Table 27. In the last three quarters of 1971, actual imports averaged 3.7% above values calculated from the regression equation. This is a much higher degree of error than in the period of the regression, 1955–1970, when the average percentage error was 1.33% (disregarding signs of errors).

Probably the equation was not sensitive enough to cope with the more extreme swings produced by the 1971 recession in Europe and Japan. This perhaps freed resources for exports to the United States, an effect not considered in the regression equation.

The moral here is that regression equations and other econometric methods are useful tools, but no more than that. Even where they seem to forecast accurately, results should be continuously subjected to searching cross-examination in terms of commonsense ideas. Dogmatic, uncritical riding of a regression equation, even if it has worked well in the past, is a sure road to disaster.

# Bibliography

Despite its length, this Bibliography makes no pretense at completeness. It represents a collection of books and articles and other relevant background material which the authors have used and recommend for further reading.

## Part I, Chapters 2–4

Bloomfield, Leonard. *Monetary Policy under the International Gold Standard.* New York: Federal Reserve Bank of New York, 1959.

Clapham, Sir John. *The Bank of England.* Cambridge: Cambridge University Press, 1944.

Clarke, Stephen V. O. *Central Bank Cooperation 1924–31.* New York: Federal Reserve Bank of New York, 1967.

Dulles, Eleanor L. *The French Franc, 1914–1928.* London: Macmillan, 1929.

Ellis, Howard S., and Metzler, Lloyd, eds. *Readings in the Theory of International Trade.* Philadelphia: Blakiston, 1949.

Friedman, M., and Schwartz, Anna J. *Monetary History of the United States, 1867–1960.* Princeton, N.J.: Princeton University Press, 1963.

Gordon, Margaret S. *Barriers to World Trade*. New York: Macmillan, 1941.

Helfferich, Karl. *Money*. Garden City, N.Y.: Adelphi, 1927.

Kemp, Tom. *The French Economy, 1913–1939*. London: Longman, 1972.

League of Nations. *Industrialization and World* Trade. Geneva: League of Nations, 1945.

Lewis, W. Arthur. *Economic Survey 1919–1931*. London: Allen & Unwin, 1949.

————. *Economic Problems of Today*. London: Longmans Green, 1940.

Marcus, Edward, and Marcus, Mildred Rendl. "As Exchange Medium, Gold a Johnny Come-Lately," *The Money Manager*, October 30, 1972.

Nurkse, Ragnar. *International Currency Experience*. Geneva: League of Nations, 1944.

Schlesinger, Arthur M. *The Age of Roosevelt, Volume II: The Coming of the New Deal*. Boston: Houghton Mifflin, 1957.

United States Federal Reserve System. *Banking and Monetary Statistics*. 1943.

## Part II, Chapters 5–8

Bach, Christopher L. "United States Balance of Payments Problems and Policies in 1971," Federal Reserve Bank of St. Louis *Review*, April 1972, pp. 8–15.

Bank for International Settlements. *Annual Report for Year Ended 31 March, 1972*.

Cooper, R. N., ed. *The Economics of Interdependence*. New York: McGraw-Hill, 1968.

————. *International Finance*. Harmondsworth, England: Penguin, 1969.

Friedman, M. "The Case for Flexible Exchange Rates." In *Essays in Positive Economics*. Chicago: University of Chicago Press, 1953.

Halberstam, D. *The Best and the Brightest*. New York: Random House, 1972.

Hawkins, R., and Rolfe, S. *The Plans for Reform*. Bulletin No. 36. New York: New York University Institute of Finance, 1966.

Hein, J. "A New International Money," *The Conference Board Record*, December 1967.

Hirsch, F. *Money International*. Harmondsworth, England: Penguin, 1969.

————. *The Pound Sterling: A Polemic*. London: Gollancz, 1965.

Horie, S. *The International Monetary Fund*. New York: St. Martin's Press, 1964.

International Monetary Fund. *International Financial Statistics*. Various issues.

Keynes, J. M. *Proposals for an International Clearing Union*. Cmd. 6473. London: HMSO, 1943.

Lutz, F. "The Keynes and White Proposals." In *Essays in International Finance, No. 1*. Princeton, N.J.: International Finance Section, 1943.

MacDougall, D. *The Dollar Shortage*. London: Macmillan, 1957.

Machlup, F. *International Payments, Debts and Gold*. New York: Scribners, 1964.

Machlup, F., Gutowski, F., and Lutz, F., eds. *International Monetary Problems*. Washington: American Enterprise Institute, 1972.

Rolfe, S. *Gold and World Power*. New York: Harper & Row, 1966; London: Macmillan, 1966.

Rueff, J. "The West Is Risking a Credit Collapse," *Fortune*, July 1961.

Rueff, J., and Hirsch, F. *The Role and the Rule of Gold: An Argument*. Princeton, N.J. International Finance Section, 1965.

Salant, W., et al. *The United States Balance of Payments in 1968*. Washington D.C.: Brookings Institution, 1963.

Samuelson, P. "Historical Notes on Trade Problems," *Review of Economics and Statistics*, May 1964.

Triffin, R. *Gold and the Dollar Crisis*. New Haven, Conn.: Yale University Press, 1961.

—————. *The Evolution of the Monetary System: Historical Reappraisal and Future Perspective*. Studies in International Finance, No. 12. Princeton, N.J.: International Finance Section, 1964.

—————. *The World Money Maze*. New Haven, Conn.: Yale University Press, 1966.

United States Congress, Joint Economic Committee, *Factors Affecting the United States Balance of Payments*. 1962 and 1964.

United States Department of Commerce. *Survey of Current Business*. Various issues.

## Part II, Chapters 9–11

*Banker* (London). Various issues.

Bell, G. *Les Marches d'Eurodevises*. Paris: Presses Universitaires de France, 1973. (Revised edition to be published in English by Macmillan, London, 1973.)

Cooper, R. N. *The Future of the Dollar*. A paper prepared for the Conference on International Monetary Problems, Ditchley Park, January 3–6, 1973.

*Economic Report of the President for 1973*. Washington, D.C.: Government Printing Office, 1973. (The Supplement to Chapter 5 includes an explanation of the plan for monetary reform presented by United States Treasury Secretary Schultz to the 1972 IMF meeting.)

*The Economist.* (London). Various issues.

Einzig, P. *The Euro-Dollar System: Practice and Theory of International Interest Rates.* London: Macmillan, 1967.

————. *Foreign Exchange Crises: An Essay in Economic Pathology.* London: Macmillan, 1968.

————. *Leads and Lags: The Main Cause of Revaluation.* London: Macmillan, 1968.

*Euromoney* (London). Various issues.

Fowler, H., chairman, and Rolfe, S., rapporteur, et al. *To Modernize the International Monetary System.* Washington, D.C.: Atlantic Council of the United States, 1972.

Friedman, M. "The Euro-Dollar Market: Some First Principles," *Morgan Guaranty Survey*, October, 1969.

Geiger, T. "The Issues in International Monetary Reform," *Looking Ahead*, National Planning Association Monthly Bulletin, February 1973.

Grubel, H. *Forward Exchange, Speculation, and the International Flow of Capital.* Stanford, Calif.: Stanford University Press, 1966.

*Journal of International Economics*, volume II, no. 4 (September 1972).

Kafka, A. *The IMF: A Second Coming.* Princeton, N.J.: International Finance Section, 1972.

Klopstock, F. "Eurodollars in the Liquidity and Reserve Management of United States Banks," "Federal Reserve Bank of New York *Monthly Review*, July 1968.

————. "Money Creation in the Eurodollar Market—A Note on Professor Friedman's Views," Federal Reserve Bank of New York *Monthly Review*, January 1970.

BIBLIOGRAPHY
262

Machlup, Fritz. "The Magicians and Their Rabbits," *Morgan Guaranty Survey*, May 1971.

Manser, W. A. P. *The Finanacial Role of Multinational Enterprises.* Paris: International Chamber of Commerce, 1973.

Robbins, S., and Stobaugh, R. B. *Money in the Multinational Enterprise: A Study of Financial Policy.* Forthcoming, 1973.

Rolfe, S. *Capital Markets in Atlantic Economic Relationships.* Paris: Atlantic Institute, 1967.

————. *The International Corporation.* Paris: International Chamber of Commerce, 1969.

Richebächer, K. "Internationale Liquiditat und der Eurodollarmarket," speech, Freiburg, December 7, 1970.

Samuelson, P. "International Trade for a Rich Country," *The Morgan Guaranty Survey*, July 1972.

Schweitzer, Pierre-Paul. "National Sovereignty and International Monetary Cooperation," address to the American Philosophical Society, April 19, 1973.

United States Senate, Committee on Finance. *Implications of Multinational Firms for World Trade and Investment and for United States Trade and Labor.* Prepared by the United States Tariff Commission. Washington, D.C.: Government Printing Office, 1973.

## Part III, Chapters 13–15

Bank for International Settlements (Basle). *Annual Report.*

Branson, William H., and Hill, Raymond D., Jr. "Capital Movements among Major OECD Countries: Some Preliminary Results," *Journal of Finance*, Papers and Proceedings of the American Finance Association, May 1970.

Commerzbank (Dusseldorf). *Foreign Exchange Market Report* (weekly).

Duprez, C., and Kirschen, E. S., eds. *Megistos, A World Income and Trade Model for 1975.* North Holland Publishing Company, 1970.

*Financial Times* (London). Columns by Samuel Brittan and C. Gordon Tether (Lombard).

Food and Agricultural Organization (Rome). *Yearbook of Agricultural Statistics,* and numerous special studies.

Houthakker, H. S., and Magee, Stephen P. "Income and Price Elasticities in World Trade," *Review of Economics and Statistics,* May 1969.

Hudson, Michael. *A Financial Payments-Flow Analysis of United States International Transactions: 1960–1968.* Bulletins Nos. 61–63. New York: New York University Institute of Finance, 1970.

International Monetary Fund. *Balance of Payments Concepts and Definitions, 1969.*

———. *Balance of Payments Manual,* 1961.

———. *Balance of Payments Yearbook* (annual).

———. *Directions of Trade* (monthly).

———. *International Financial Statistics* (monthly).

Journal of Commerce (New York). *World Money Front* (daily review of foreign exchange developments).

Kruger, Anne O. "Balance of Payments Theory," *Journal of Economic Literature,* March 1969.

Lietaer, B. *Financial Management of Foreign Exchange.* Cambridge, Mass.: MIT Press, 1971.

Morgan Guaranty Trust Company. *World Financial Markets* (monthly).

National Foreign Trade Council. Annual press release on results of their survey of trade expectations.

————. *Breve* (Europe) and *Noticias* (Latin America): digests of leading press articles.

National Institute for Economic and Social Research (London). *National Institute Economic Review.*

Organization for Economic Cooperation and Development (Paris). Annual economic surveys of member countries.

————. Annual reports of the Development Assistance Committee.

————. *Economic Outlook.*

————. *Main Economic Indicators.*

————. "OECD Trade Model: 1970 Version" (by Frans Meyer-zu-Schlochtern and Akira Yajima), OECD *Occasional Studies*, December 1970.

Reimann, Guenter, ed. *International Reports* (weekly). (Includes up-to-date data for interest arbitrage analysis.)

Rundt, S. J. *Rundt's Weekly Intelligence* (New York). (Includes weekly forward rate quotations.)

United Nations. *Annual Report of the Economic Commission for Europe.*

————. *Monthly Bulletin of Statistics.*

————. *Yearbook of International Trade Statistics.*

United States Bureau of Standards. Reports of the Clearinghouse for Federal Scientific and Technical Information.

United States Department of Agriculture. *Annual Foreign Crop Forecast.*

United States Department of Commerce. *Overseas Business Reports, Survey of Current Business*, especially the June 1971 issue explaining the new form and concepts in United States balance of payments accounting.

Wasserman, Max J., Andreas, Prindl, and Townsend, Charles C., Jr. *International Money Management.* New York: American Management Association, 1972.

*Weekly Bond Buyer* (New York). Foreign Exchange and Money Market columns.

Weston, J. Fred, and Sorge, Bart W. *International Managerial Finance.* Homewood, Ill.: Richard D. Irwin, 1972.

# Index

## Catalog

If you are interested in a list of fine Paperback
books, covering a wide range of subjects
and interests, send your name and address,
requesting your free catalog, to:

McGraw-Hill Paperbacks
1221 Avenue of Americas
New York, N.Y. 10020